THE HISTORY OF THE 62nd (WEST RIDING) DIVISION
1914—1919

MILITARY HISTORIES BY THE SAME AUTHOR

The History of the
2nd DIVISION, 1914-1918

The
WEST YORKSHIRE REGIMENT
IN THE WAR,
1914-1918

The History of the
SOMERSET LIGHT INFANTRY
1914-1918
[*In Preparation.*]

The History of the
MIDDLESEX REGIMENT,
1914-1919
[*in Preparation.*]

The History of the
EAST YORKSHIRE REGIMENT
1914-1918
[*In Preparation.*]

The History of the
30th (HOW.) BATTERY, R.F.A.
1914-1918
[*In Preparation.*]

LIEUT.-GENERAL SIR ROBERT D. WHIGHAM, K.C.B., K.C.M.G., D.S.O., who commanded the 62nd (W.R.) Division from 28th August, 1918, to the Demobilization of the Division in 1919.

Frontispiece, Vol. II.

THE HISTORY OF THE 62nd (WEST RIDING) DIVISION 1914—1919

★

By
EVERARD WYRALL

Author of " *Europe in Arms—A Concise History of the Great War* " :
" *The History of the 2nd Division, 1914—1918* " :
" *The West Yorkshire Regiment in
the War, 1914—1918,*"
Etc., Etc.

VOLUME II

WITH 13 PHOTOGRAPHIC ILLUSTRATIONS
AND 11 COLOURED BATTLE PLANS.

JOHN LANE THE BODLEY HEAD LIMITED
VIGO STREET, LONDON, W.

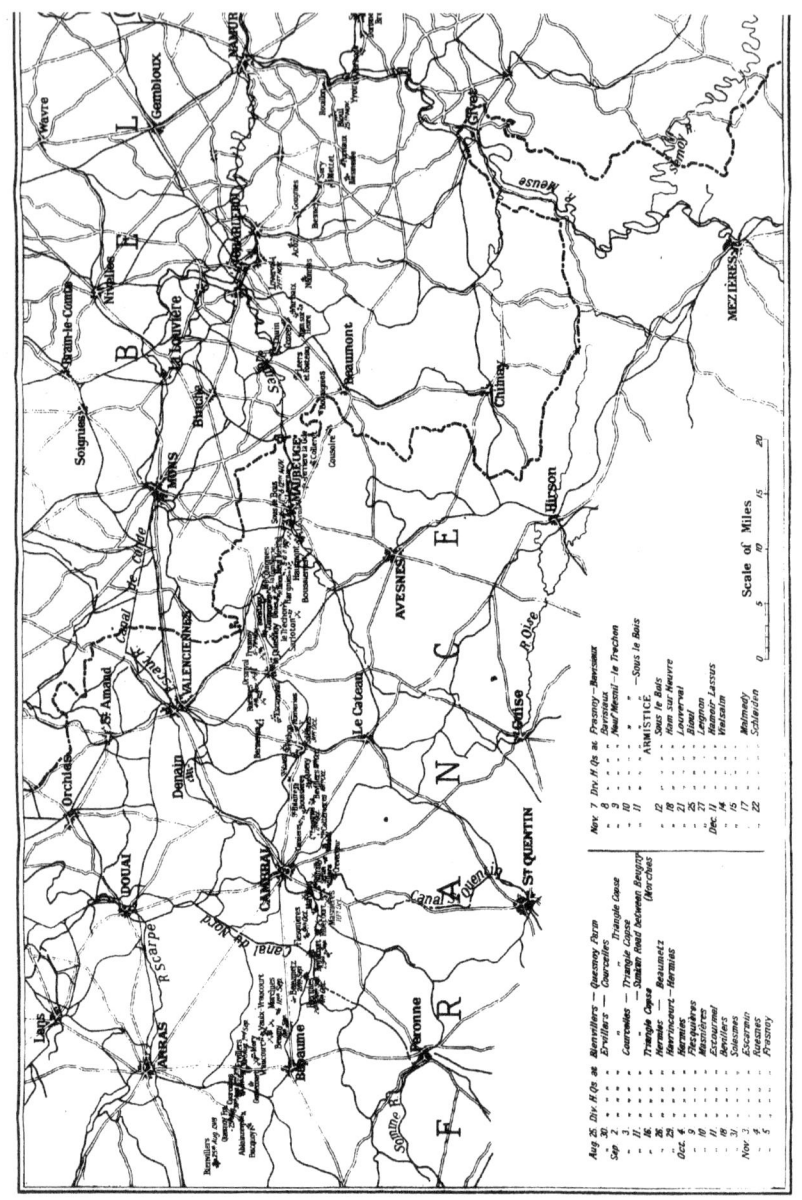

LINE OF ADVANCE OF THE DIVISION FROM 25TH AUGUST TO 11TH NOVEMBER, 1918.
The red crossed swords indicate Villages captured by the Division
For details of captures during advance see Appendix V

CONTENTS

VOLUME II.

		PAGE
I.	Vraucourt and Vaulx-Vraucourt	1
II.	The Battle of the Drocourt-Quéant Line—2nd-3rd September, 1918	23
III.	Of the 62nd Divisional Artillery, from 21st August to 6th September, 1918..	33
IV.	The Battle of Havrincourt, 12th September, 1918	39
V.	The Battle of the Canal du Nord and Breaking of the Hindenburg Line—27th September to 1st October, 1918 .. I. Operations of 27th September	67
VI.	The Battle of the Canal du Nord and Breaking of the Hindenburg Line—27th September to 1st October, 1918 .. .. II. Marcoing and Masnieres	85
VII.	Solesmes: I.	107
VIII.	Solesmes: II.	121
IX.	Orsinval and Frasnoy	125
X.	Maubeuge	143
	Conclusion	151
	The Unveiling of the 62nd Divisional Memorial at Havrincourt	154
	Appendices	168
	Index	212

ERRATUM.

In Map II., facing page 23, the British and German lines are printed in opposite colours to the reference in error.

ILLUSTRATIONS

VOLUME II.

	PAGE
Lieut.-General Sir Robert D. Whigham, K.C.B., K.C.M.G., D.S.O.	*frontispiece*
Sergeant L. Calvert, V.C., M.M., 5th K.O.Y.L.I.	*facing* 49
Artillery crossing the Canal du Nord	,, 54
Scene in the Canal du Nord	,, 72
The Guns moving up through the Canal du Nord	,, 88
The Ruined Church, Marcoing	,, 90
Private H. Tandey, V.C., D.C.M., M.M., 5th Duke of Wellington's Regt.	,, 93
Troops moving up on the morning of 29th September, 1918	,, 98
Sergeant J. Daykins, V.C., 2/4th York and Lancaster Regt.	,, 117
The Canal near Maubeuge, November, 1918	,, 146
Unveiling of the 62nd Divisional Memorial at Havrincourt	,, 154
Général Berthelot—Lieut.-General Sir R. D. Whigham	,, 164
A Message of Greeting from Général Girard, commanding the 62nd French Division, being read out to the representatives of the 62nd (W.R.) Division	,, 167

LIST OF MAPS

VOLUME II.

		PAGE facing
I.	Vraucourt and Vaulx-Vraucourt	1
II.	The Battle of the Drocourt-Quéant Line	23
III.	Barrage Map: Battle of the Drocourt-Quéant Line	32
IV.	The Battle of Havrincourt, 1918	39
V.	The Battle of the Canal du Nord and Breaking of the Hindenburg Line	67
VI.	Marcoing and Masnieres	85
VII.	Solesmes: I.	107
VIII.	Solesmes: II.	121
IX.	Orsinval and Frasnoy	125
X.	Maubeuge	143
XI.	Line of Advance of 62nd Division from 25th August to 11th November, 1918	v.

APPENDICES

I. Order of Battle of the 62nd (W.R.) Division when Major-General Sir R. D. Whigham assumed command on 28th August, 1918.

II. Extract from "London Gazette," 15th November, 1918.

III.   ,,   ,,   ,, 14th December, 1918.

IV.   ,,   ,,   ,, 6th January, 1919.

V. Casualties and captures of the 62nd Division from 24th August to 11th November, 1918.

VI. Report on Bridging Operations carried out by 62nd (West Riding) Divisional R.E. on the night of 19th/20th October, 1918.

VII. Citations of Award of Croix de Guerre to 8th Battalion West Yorkshire Regiment.

VIII. Casualties of officers of 62nd (W.R.) Division from January, 1917, to November, 1918.

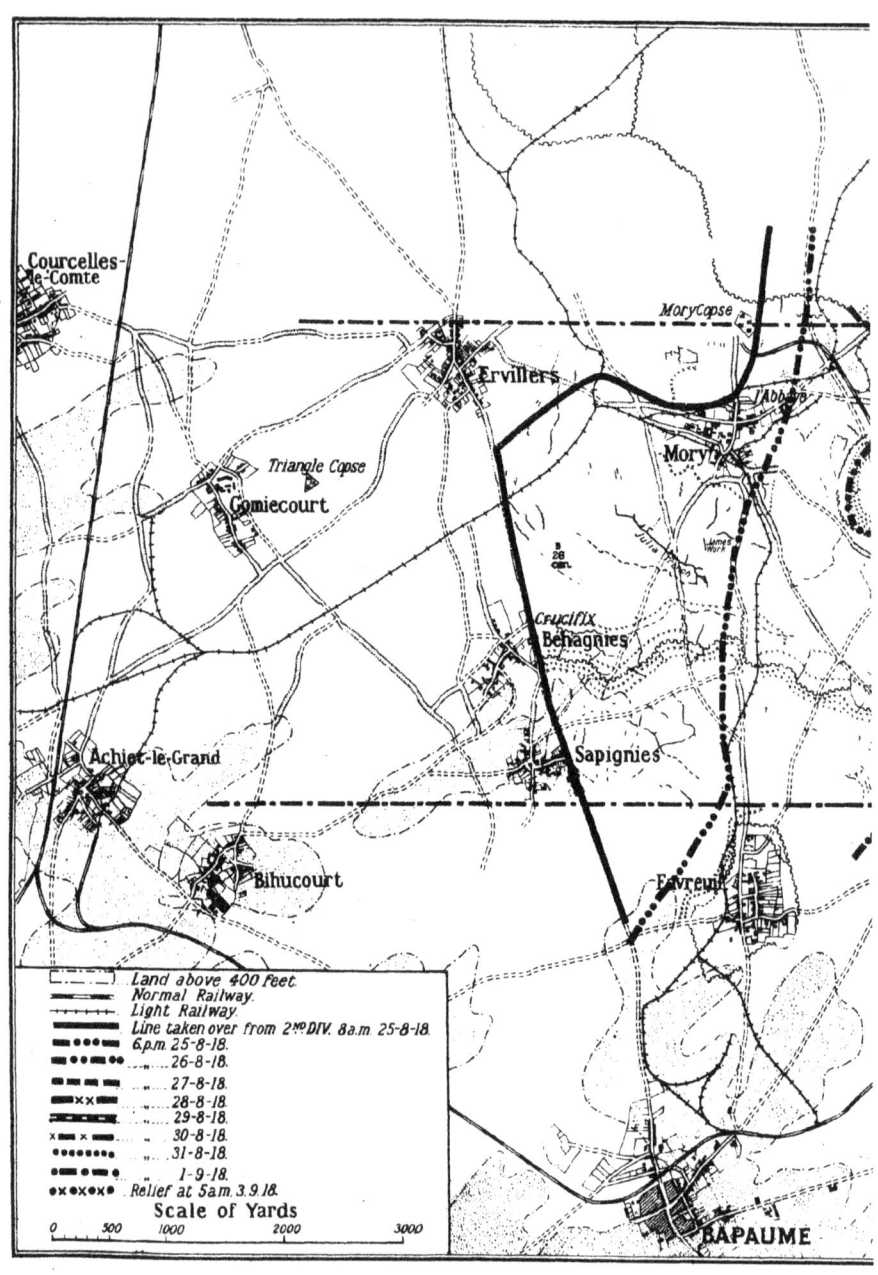

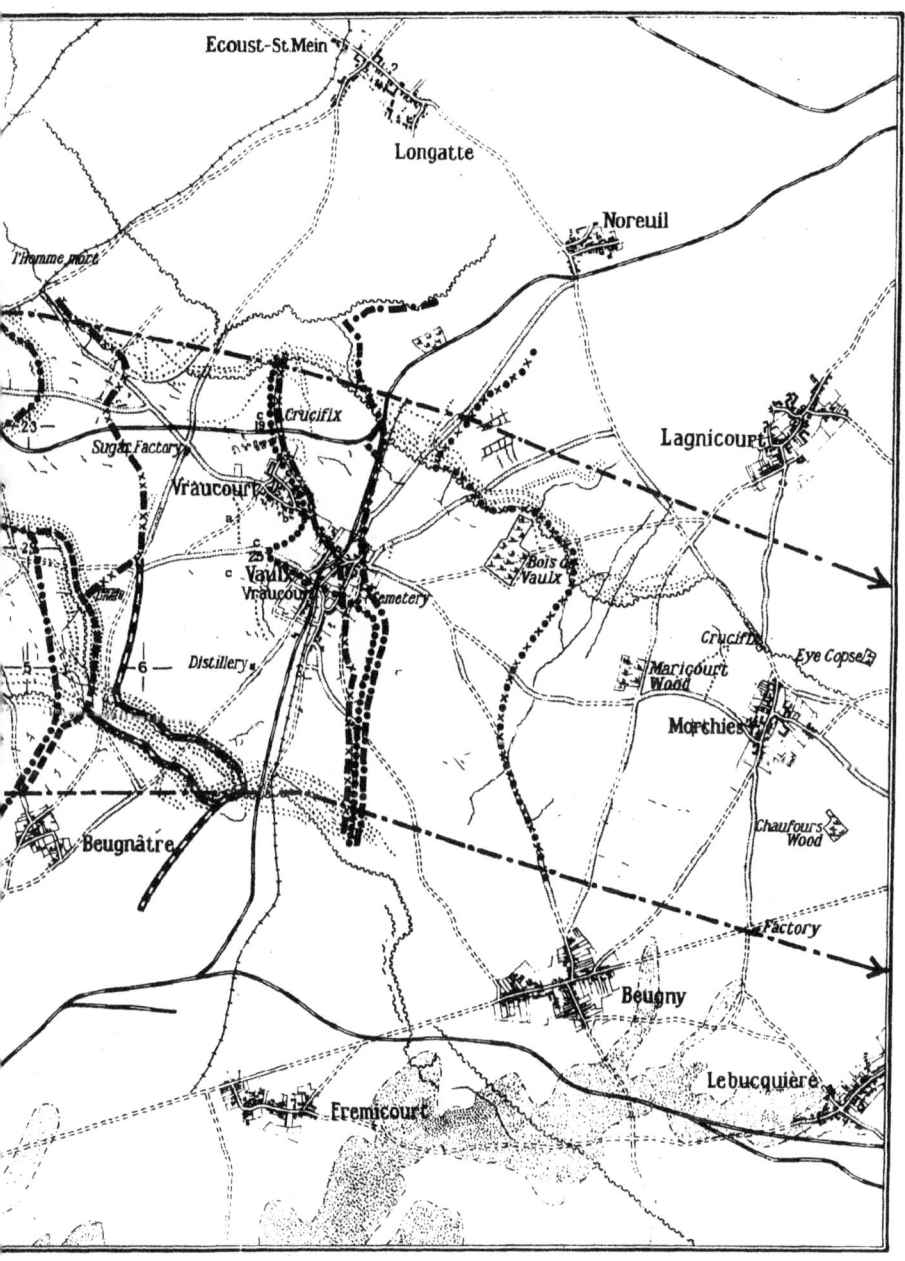

VAULX-VRAUCOURT.

Chapter I.   1918.

VRAUCOURT AND VAULX-VRAUCOURT

WARNING orders concerning further opera- 25TH AUG. tions to take place on 26th August were issued at 4-30 p.m. on the 25th. Briefly, these operations were designed to secure a firm footing in the old Third Army Line, along the Divisional front from north of Beugnatre to east of Mory Copse. Having secured this line and re-organized it for defence in depth, reconnaissances were to be made with a view to further advances. On the right of the 62nd Division, the IVth Corps had been ordered to clear Bapaume and Favreuil, whilst the Guards Division, on the left, was to establish itself on the line—Banks Trench and St. Leger Ravine. This warning order was confirmed at 10-5 p.m.

The 186th Infantry Brigade, on the right, and the 187th Infantry Brigade, on the left, were again to carry out the attack by the 62nd Division; the 185th Infantry Brigade was still in Divisional Reserve. Of the former Brigade, the 2/4th Hants. Regt. (Lieut.-Col. F. Brook) was to assault the old Third Army Line and the high ground in Squares No. 29 and 5. The Hampshires were to attack on a two-company front—D, right, B, left, with C and A, right and left reserve Companies respectively. D and B Companies were detailed to attack the first objective and C and A Companies were to leap-frog D and B. A creeping barrage was to cover the attack, Zero hour being 6 a.m. on 26th.

Owing to Zero hour for the attack of the Guards Division not being fixed when the time came to issue orders, the G.O.C., 187th Infantry Brigade, decided to push forward his right flank only—5th K.O.Y.L.I.—the attack of the left Battalion being postponed so as to take place simultaneously with that of the Guards Division. The brief respite thus afforded the 2/4th K.O.Y.L.I. and the 2/4th York. and Lancs. (Hallamshires) was very welcome, for both Battalions had suffered heavy casualties during the operations of the 25th.

26TH AUG.   At 5-45 a.m. on the morning of the 26th August, the 37th Division reported that Favreuil had been finally cleared of the enemy, and that the 5th Division had taken over that place and would be on the right of the 62nd during the forthcoming operations. Owing to rain and darkness and lack of guides the Hampshires had considerable difficulty in reaching their assembly positions along the Favreuil—Mory Road. But at Zero hour—6 a.m.—D and B Companies followed close on the heels of the barrage and gained the line of the first objective, which was roughly a north and south line, 500 yards west of the Squares No. 29 and 5. The two Companies had passed through the enemy's barrage, but were not held up by it. C and A Companies now advanced through D and B (respectively). Heavy machine-gun fire from the Beugnatre—Mory Road and the high ground along the Brigade front, just beyond the final objective, met these two Companies as they advanced. The fire was especially heavy on the left Company. The O.C. Company (Capt. Cave), however, handled his Company with considerable skill and by 9 o'clock all objectives had been gained and the Battalion settled down to reorganize its newly-won line.[1]

On the left of the Hampshires the 5th K.O.Y.L.I. of the 187th Infantry Brigade, had experienced very little difficulty in advancing their line in conformity with the first-named Battalion, the final objective being reached by 6-20 a.m.

The 2/4th K.O.Y.L.I., however, did not attack, for the Guards Division had postponed operations ; as a consequence, the assault by the 2/4th was cancelled.

At dusk the 2/4th Hants. advanced their line slightly to conform to the left flank of the 13th Infantry Brigade, 5th Division, which ran from the west of Beugnatre, north-east towards the old Third Army Line.

The night of the 26th was spent in consolidating the positions gained during the day.

The warning order for next day's operations was received from VIth Corps at 2 p.m. Pressure was to be maintained on the enemy by the 62nd Division in the direction of Vaulx-Vraucourt, and by the Guards Division towards Ecoust.

On receipt of these instructions orders were issued for operations on the 27th. The 186th Brigade was ordered to push forward along spur running north-east towards Vraucourt and attempt to get patrols

---

[1] Casualties :—One officer (Capt. J. F. Bennett), nine other ranks killed, one officer and twenty-five other ranks wounded, seven other ranks missing.

into Vaulx-Vraucourt, the 187th to push forward along spur running 26TH AUG. north of Vraucourt and to capture Banks Trench.

The C.R.A. was ordered to push the Artillery well forward so as to be close at hand to support the advance.

The 185th Infantry Brigade, was to have relieved the 187th Brigade in the left sector of the Divisional front on the night of 26th, but the G.O.C. of the latter asked permission to make the attack on the following day and the relief was therefore postponed twenty-four hours. In view, however, of impending operations by the 62nd Division, General Reddie was instructed not to use more than one Battalion in his attack.

At 7 a.m. on the 27th, under a creeping barrage, the 187th 27TH AUG. Infantry Brigade advanced, with two Companies of the 5th K.O.Y.L.I. (D in the front line, B in support) on the right, and two of the 2/4th K.O.Y.L.I. (C on the right, D on the left) on the left. On the right of the 187th Infantry Brigade the 186th pushed out patrols to gain the line of the Beugnatre—Ecoust Road. The Guards Division was attacking on the left.

"The artillery barrage," the record states, "was practically perfect and the attack moved forward steadily, our troops keeping close to the barrage." But the leading Companies came almost immediately under a murderous machine-gun fire principally from the direction of l'Homme Mort and the cross roads south-east of that place. The right Brigade of the Guards Division also came under heavy fire.

The advance of the 5th K.O.Y.L.I. was covered by a steady barrage, running immediately south of the light railway in front of the Battalion. The 5th K.O.Y.L.I., though subjected to a heavy machine-gun fire, collected a large number of prisoners from dugouts and trenches north-west of the Sugar Factory. Their progress was, however, stopped in this position, hostile machine guns in Bank Trench and in l'Homme Mort bringing the leading Companies to a standstill. A hostile machine gun nest in rear, which had been overlooked in the advance, suddenly opened fire on the two Companies as they were engaged in clearing the captured trench. This gun was soon put out of action.

On the left, the 2/4th K.O.Y.L.I. also came under the same heavy machine-gun fire, though C Company, on the right (Lieut. Rodger) succeeded in reaching the old Third Army Trench (Mory Switch) with scarcely a casualty. D Company was, however, less fortunate; the Company commander—Capt. G. Skirrow—was

27TH AUG. killed, and the Guards on the left being held up also, the attack of D Company was brought to a standstill.

Hostile machine-gun fire now became more intense and it was evident that the enemy had reinforced his line with additional guns. Orders were now issued for the Brigade to consolidate its positions along the old Third Army Line, this being the limit of the advance made by the 186th Infantry Brigade and the Guards Division.

When darkness fell two small parties of men of 5th and 2/4th K.O.Y.L.I., who had progressed to the Sunken Road, east of the old Third Army Line, managed to get back to their Companies. They had gone forward under the barrage, but had been forced to lie down all day, being too weak to attack the enemy.

The patrols sent out by the 186th Infantry Brigade were unable to make headway, and no further progress was made beyond the old Third Army Line.

Prisoners captured during the day numbered eight officers and 150 other ranks.

Orders were received during the afternoon from the VIth Corps, giving new Corps boundaries, the southern boundary becoming the grid line running east through I.8 central. Corps Headquarters also directed that, owing to the success of the turning movement by the XVIIth Canadian Corps, every opportunity must be taken of the weakening of the enemy on the Corps front, to push out patrols.

During the night of the 27th/28th the 185th Infantry Brigade moved up and took over the left of the Divisional front from the 187th Infantry Brigade, the latter marching back to the Railway Line east of Courcelles.[1]

28TH AUG. The relief was completed at 3 a.m. on the 28th, the 1/5th Devons taking over the line on the right, held by the 5th K.O.Y.L.I. and the 8th West Yorks. the left sub-section of the Brigade front; the 2/20th Londoners were in reserve south and south-east of Ervillers.

Both the 186th and 185th Infantry Brigades pushed out patrols during the day, with the object of keeping touch with the enemy.

---

[1] The casualties of the 187th Infantry Brigade for 26th/27th August were as follows :—5th K.O.Y.L.I.—Officers, four wounded ; other ranks, twenty-four killed, 114 wounded, fifteen missing ; 2/4th K.O.Y.L.I.—Officers, three killed, eight wounded ; other ranks, twenty-one killed, 160 wounded, eighteen missing ; 2/4th York. and Lancs. Regt.—Officers, one killed, six wounded, one missing ; other ranks, nineteen killed, 168 wounded, twenty-seven missing. The Brigade had captured nine officers and 221 other ranks, numerous machine guns and trench mortars.

The 2/4th Hampshires had several encounters in their en- 28TH AUG. deavour to establish posts along the Bapaume—Vraucourt Road. B Company had compelled the enemy to withdraw from the Horse Lines between the old Third Army Line and the Bapaume—Vraucourt Road. This Company was, however, unable to hold the Lines as the enemy firing from the north from concealed positions swept the position with rifle and machine-gun fire. C Company patrolled south of the Horse Lines, but could make no headway.

The 1/5th Devons did not gain touch with the enemy until the night 28th/29th, when enemy machine-gun posts were located along the Beugnatre—Sugar Factory Road, north-east of the Horse Lines.

Patrols from the 8th West Yorks. pushed forward and cleared Banks Trench along the Battalion front.

The forward area of both Brigades was shelled persistently by the enemy throughout the day.

At 1 p.m., Major-General Sir Robert Whigham, K.C.B., D.S.O., arrived in order to take over command of the 62nd (W.R.) Division from Major-General W. P. Braithwaite, C.B., who had been appointed to command an Army Corps, reported temporarily to the XXIInd Corps, while Lieut.-Gen. Godley was employed in the Fourth Army.[1]

The fine record of success gained by the Division between January, 1917, and August, 1918, was due very largely to General Braithwaite's personality. That his officers and men shall trust him implicitly is perhaps the first of all necessary attributes in a Commander; and General Braithwaite had the absolute confidence of all ranks of his Division. His humane sympathy and never-failing cheerfulness, even under the most adverse conditions, won from his Yorkshiremen the best that was in them. More, no commander could obtain. On leaving the Division, General Braithwaite sent the following message to all ranks : " It is a matter of great regret to me that I cannot see the battle out as commander of the Division, but my orders are to hand over this afternoon and proceed to take command of an Army Corps.

" I have commanded the Division since December, 1915, so saying good-bye to it is no easy matter. I am, and always shall be, very, very proud of the 62nd West Riding Division, and the memories of its fighting at the Ancre, Bullecourt, Cambrai, Bucquoy, the Marne, and in the present battle, can never fade.

[1] For Order of Battle of 62nd Division when General Whigham assumed command, see Appendix I., p. 168.

28TH AUG. "I hope it may be my good fortune to have the Division under my command in the future, but until that time comes I must say good-bye.

"I take this opportunity of thanking every officer, warrant officer, N.C.O., and private soldier for their unfailing support and their matchless gallantry, which has made the Division what it is—a fighting force of the first rank."

(Sd.) Walter Braithwaite,
Major-General,
Commanding 62nd (W.R.) Division.

It was very natural that the Division should feel very keenly the loss of its beloved commander, nevertheless it was not long before its new chief won the confidence and whole-hearted co-operation of all ranks; for the surest way to a soldier's heart is never to ask him to do an impossible thing.

29TH AUG. Touch was maintained with the enemy during the night of 28th by means of patrols. Early on the morning of 29th the Guards Division, on the left of the 62nd, was relieved by the 3rd Division.

Patrols, both from the 186th and 185th Infantry Brigades, were unable to make much progress owing to the activity of the enemy. The latter was posted very strongly in the vicinity of the Sugar Factory and Banks Trench.

At 1 p.m. orders were issued to the 186th Brigade to cover an attack of the 13th Infantry Brigade (5th Division) on Beugny, by capturing the two lines of trenches north-east of Beugnatre, *i.e.*, running from north-west to south east between Beugnatre and Vaulx-Vraucourt. Zero hour for the attack was to be 4 p.m., and two Companies of the 5th Duke of Wellington's Regt. were detailed for the operation.

A creeping barrage, and a smoke barrage to screen the operations from Vaulx-Vraucourt, were to be put down before the assault.

At 2 p.m. the 2/4th Hampshires again attacked the Horse Lines. The attack was carried out by one platoon from A Company, under 2nd Lieut. H. Brierly. As the platoon approached its objective, the enemy was seen to be in possession, but with the assistance of another platoon, sent up as reinforcements, the Horse Lines were cleared and held, and two platoons consolidated a position immediately east of the Beugnatre—Sugar Factory Road.

Simultaneously with the Hampshires attack two platoons of the 1/5th Devons (Lieut. R. Bedford), on the left, attacked the enemy along the Sugar Factory Road, north of the Horse Lines. Heavy machine-gun fire swept the front of the platoons as they advanced, and was so strong that the Devon men were forced to dig in when a distance of from 100 to 150 yards from their objective.

Owing to the 13th Infantry Brigade, on the right of the 186th Infantry Brigade, having received too short notice of the attack ordered for 4 p.m., Zero hour was altered to 5-30 p.m.

D Company of the 5th Duke of Wellington's Regt., under Capt. C. G. H. Ellis, was detailed for the attack, with A Company in close support, also under his command. The forming-up operations were completed by 3-30 p.m., at which hour the Companies held a jumping-off position immediately north-west of the trenches to be captured.

At 5-30 p.m. the barrage fell north and south of the trenches creeping forward at 100 yards in four minutes. On the northern side of the trenches the smoke barrage successfully screened the advance of the 5th Duke's from observation from Vaulx-Vraucourt.

The organization of this attack is of interest. Two bombing platoons worked down each trench towards the trench junction, the first party to reach it firing three red lights, in order to prevent one party bombing the other. On each side of each trench a Lewis-gun team kept pace with the bombing platoons, forcing the Germans by their fire to keep their heads down and shooting Germans who attempted to get out of the trench. Two platoons, at a distance of 150 yards, in rear of the bombing parties in each trench, followed for the purpose of establishing section posts about every 100 yards, to protect the flanks as the attack advanced. Two more Lewis-gun sections (4 guns) of the Support Company, were distributed fifty yards north and south of each trench and 100 yards in rear of the leading company.

As D, followed by A Company, advanced close on the heels of the barrage, the enemy at first put up a stiff fight, but the Lewis guns disorganized his bombing parties, who were unable to throw their bombs with any accuracy. And at bayonet work the Yorkshiremen were infinitely superior.

Between the two lines of trenches were a number of derelict huts, which were organized by the enemy as posts. These were dealt with by the Support Company—A. On reaching the final objective heavy machine-gun fire was opened on the 5th Duke's from the direction of the light railway, east of the two trenches. But a small bombing party was sent out with instructions to work round

B

29TH AUG. the enemy in rear. This was done and twenty Germans were captured. Thirty-five of the enemy were killed in the trenches and ninety-three were taken prisoner, together with fifteen machine guns and one trench mortar.

The success of this small operation was due to the rapidity with which the bombers and Lewis gunners swept along the trenches, giving the enemy no time in which to organize a defence.

The attack was over by 6-30 p.m. and the positions won were consolidated, touch on the right being obtained with the IVth Corps. A threatened counter-attack at 8 p.m. did not develop, the Divisional Artillery placing an accurate barrage on the enemy's assembling troops, completely breaking up the attack.

Meanwhile, during the afternoon, orders had been issued by the 185th Infantry Brigade to clear Banks Trench as soon as arrangements for the attack could be made. Brigadier-General Viscount Hampden fixed 8-15 p.m. for this attack.

About 5 p.m. the enemy was seen advancing in lines to counter-attack from a position about 500 yards east of the Horse Lines. This attack was broken up by rifle and Lewis-gun fire, the enemy also coming under the artillery barrage. As a result of this counter-attack twenty-one more prisoners were captured.

A little later, whilst at a conference, the G.O.C., 185th Infantry Brigade, received a message that the right Battalion of the 3rd Division (on the left flank of the 186th Brigade) would not be ready to attack alongside the 8th West Yorks. at 8-15 p.m. The G.O.C., however, decided that his attack should take place.

Just prior to Zero hour the enemy put down a heavy barrage, including gas, on the trenches where two platoons of D Company, 8th West Yorks. (the attacking part) were assembled. At 8-15 p.m., assisted by a barrage of light field guns, the two platoons advanced, but from the first the attack was met by determined opposition from a number of machine guns, which swept the ground over which the West Yorkshiremen were advancing. Six of these guns were established in Banks Trench, immediately in front of the attacking party. Two gallant attempts were made to clear the trench, but both failed; finally the survivors returned to their assembly positions.

The night of the 29th/30th passed quietly.

During the afternoon on the 29th, orders had been received from the VIth Corps to capture the villages of Vaulx-Vraucourt and Vraucourt at dawn on the 30th.

The 3rd Division was at the same time to capture the villages of Longatte and Ecoust. 29TH AUG.

As the time available for preparing the attack was very limited, a staff officer from Divisional Headquarters, and the Brigade Major R.A., were sent to the Headquarters of the 186th Infantry Brigade to arrange the details of the attack with the Brigadiers 185th and 186th Infantry Brigades.

Orders were sent out during the evening confirming the arrangements made at the conference.

The attack was to be made at dawn (5 a.m.) under cover of a creeping barrage by the 185th and 186th Infantry Brigades, assisted by eight Mark V Tanks, four tanks being allotted to each Brigade—objectives, the villages of Vraucourt and Vaulx-Vraucourt and the high ground east of the latter village. Dividing line between Brigades B.26 Central—Cross roads at C.26 c.o.4—Morchies.

The 2/4th Duke of Wellington's Regt. (left), with one Company of the 5th Duke of Wellington's Regt., on the right, were detailed by the G.O.C., 186th Infantry Brigade for the right attack; whilst the 2/20th Londoners were ordered to carry out the left attack by the G.O.C., 185th Infantry Brigade. The 8th West Yorks. were to follow up the attack by the Londoners and establish posts on the left flanks along Vraucourt Trench.

The 2/4th Duke's had relieved the 2/4th Hants. during the night 29th/30th, the relief being completed by 4 a.m., whilst on their right the 5th Duke's still held the trenches captured on the 29th. 30TH AUG.

The 5th and 2/4th Duke's were ready in their jumping-off positions when, at 5 a.m., the barrage came down on the line of the Bapaume—Ecoust Road and remained there for three minutes; then moved forward at the rate of 100 yards in three minutes, until it reached the line of the first objective, the railway between I.7. central and C.26.c.o.4. B Company of the 5th Duke's had been detailed as the attacking Company, C being in close reserve. A and D Companies remained in the trenches captured on the day previous.

B Company had been organized into three platoons, the first advancing in line on the first objective, the two remaining platoons following in columns behind the leading platoon, with instructions to " leap-frog " the latter and capture the second objective, a line from I.8.a.7.8. to I.8.a.7.2.

Keeping well under the barrage the leading platoon advanced and, with very little opposition, reached the line of the first objective, after capturing a few prisoners. The remaining two platoons then "leap-frogged" the leading platoon and extending, passed on towards the second objective. No opposition was experienced until within a short distance of the objective, when a hostile machine gun suddenly opened fire and continued active until a Lewis gun of the 5th Duke's came into action and quickly silenced the hostile gun. The second objective was then reached and consolidated. The casualties of the 5th Duke's had been very light, but 100 Germans and one machine gun had been captured. Touch had been maintained throughout on both flanks.

The first objective of the 2/4th Duke's was also the line of the railway, west of Vaulx-Vraucourt, high ground some 500 yards east of the village being the second objective. The advance to the second objective involved the capture of the southern half of the village.

At Zero, A (right) and B (left) Companies of the 2/4th Duke's advanced to the attack. The creeping barrage was very effective, and although the enemy put up a strong resistance, the attack was successful and the first objective was reached. C and D Companies then advanced through A and B (respectively) towards the second objective.

C Company, having only a small portion of the southern half of the village to traverse, had little difficulty in fighting its way through and reaching the second objective. But D Company became involved in very severe fighting and progress was slow, especially as the 2/20th Londoners (185th Infantry Brigade), attacking the northern half of the village, was experiencing great difficulty in making headway.

At this stage B Company came to the assistance of D, and, together, the two Companies gradually forced their way through to the eastern exits of the village. Well-concealed machine guns had held up the advance, and it was necessary to locate and silence them before definite progress could be made.

On emerging from the eastern exits of the village to the ridge, beyond the line of the second objective, both Companies again came under heavy frontal machine-gun fire; moreover a harassing fire from the cemetery and the northern half of the village, enfiladed the attack. In face of this opposition it was only possible to gain a line some 200 yards east of the village and here the two left Companies consolidated. B Company was then withdrawn and placed in support of D Company, but the position taken up was a poor one for defence purposes and finally B was brought back to a trench behind the village.

A heavy counter-attack by the enemy now gained the northern 30TH AUG.
end of the village, which necessitated an adjustment of the Battalion
front. The left flank was swung back to form a defensive flank,
and this line was maintained throughout the night of 30th/31st.

In the meantime what had happened to the 2/20th Londoners
of the 185th Infantry Brigade, attacking on the left of the 2/4th
Duke of Wellington's?

The attack on Vraucourt and Vaulx-Vraucourt is of particular
interest to the 2/20th Londoners, for it was the Battalion's first action
since it landed in France from Egypt and Palestine. " A combination
of circumstances," said an officer of the Battalion,[1] " made the operation a difficult one. The attack had to be made without reconnaissance; the Battalion had never previously advanced under a
creeping barrage, and many of the men had never seen a Tank. The
only guides to the line were the officers who had visited Col. Bastow's
(5th Devons) Headquarters on the previous day."

The frontage allotted to the Battalion included the northern
half of Vaulx-Vraucourt, the whole of Vraucourt, and a line running
directly north as far as Vraucourt Trench. The latter ran at right
angles to the line of attack, and therefore, the 8th West Yorks. had
been ordered to deal with this trench in order to keep down enfilade
fire and secure the left flank of the advance. The Sugar Factory
and the four cross roads west of Vraucourt were the principal strong-
holds in the enemy's defences in front of the village. A light railway,
running east and west and parallel with Vraucourt Trench, was
another obstacle in the line of advance. These three features—the
Sugar Factory, the cross roads and the light railway—were the principal points on which the three attacking Companies were to advance.

At 4-10 a.m. the Battalion moved forward to its position of
assembly, a line running directly north and south, about 1,700 yards
due west of Vraucourt.

The attack was to be made by A Company (2nd Lieut. P. S. R.
Marshall) on the right, with orders to capture part of Vaulx; by C
Company (Capt. Hunt) in the centre with orders to capture Vraucourt; and by B Company (Capt. Jones) on the left, having its left
on the light railway, with orders to move straight through to the
final objective,[1] the ridge overlooking Vaulx-Vraucourt and Vraucourt from the east. D Company (Capt. Reynolds) was in reserve,
with orders to " leap-frog " through A and C Companies, when the

[1] " The Second Twentieth," by Capt. W. R. Elliot, M.C.

30TH AUG. latter had gained Vaulx-Vraucourt and Vraucourt respectively, and to join with B Company in consolidating the final objective.

The "jumping-off" line had been taped out by the Brigade Intelligence Officer (Lieut. C. Friend), and to this line the Companies moved forward in pitch darkness. Progress was slow, the men having to file through a single trench, and just before Zero the enemy became unpleasantly active with gas shells, which necessitated the men putting on their gas respirators. It was all vastly different from the sands and plains of Egypt and Palestine.

At 5 a.m. the barrage fell heavily upon the enemy's line. The Sugar Factory and the cross roads being specially dealt with.

With considerable spirit the three attacking Companies moved forward. "A" Company, after experiencing opposition from the sunken road, soon broke down the enemy's resistance and the road was cleared and several prisoners taken The Company next came up against a thick belt of wire (which ran along the front of both villages) raked by enfilade machine-gun fire. Men were then sent forward to cut the wire, whilst their comrades dropped into shell holes and waited until it was possible to continue the advance. Too much praise cannot be given to the brave fellows who thus prepared the way for the attack, which, sweeping on, carried the dangerous points. Thirty more prisoners had been captured when the line was once more held up about 400 yards from Vaulx. Nothing, up to this period, had been seen of the 186th Infantry Brigade on the right, and very heavy shelling and machine-gun fire had opened from the direction of Vaulx.

C Company, on the left of A, had, from the start, made rapid progress. The Sugar Factory was cleared in dashing style and the men pressed on towards Vraucourt, close on the heels of the barrage. A halt was called just west of the village, until the "crash" had finished and the barrage had lifted. The leading waves of the Company then jumped to their feet and went straight through Vraucourt, occupying the sunken road beyond.

The advance of C Company had been so rapid that there were still many Germans in the scattered buildings in the outskirts of the village. These now opened fire in rear of the Company, and also opened heavy rifle and machine-gun fire from some hutments north of the village. Arrangements were then made with D Company, which had followed close behind C, to attack these hutments. The former Company with splendid dash was completely successful and cleared the hutments, taking two officers and seventy other prisoners.

The Company then moved into line on the left of C Company, 30TH AUG. occupying the sunken road running north from the village. There was, however, a gap of some 300 yards between the two Companies. B Company (on the left) had, however, met with misfortune. Very soon after the Company had gone forward the attack was held up by a nest of machine-gun posts. Capt. R. G. Jones was killed, and many other ranks became casualties. The Lewis gunners then came into action and by their initiative and gallantry the posts were knocked out and ten machine guns captured. But the Company had lost so heavily that, with the delay caused through having to break down opposition, the advance was held up and further progress was impossible. This was the position when, at 10 a.m., a runner reached Battalion Headquarters (in a quarry just south of Mory) stating that Sergeant F. W. Cook of B Company was in charge of thirty men in a sunken road, which proved to be about 1,000 yards behind D Company.

At 7-30 a.m., with the exception of the gap between C and D Companies, the line from right to left was continuous, though on the right A was not in touch with the right of the 3rd Division. D Company, therefore, formed a defensive flank, touch being gained shortly afterwards—at 8 a.m.—with troops of the 3rd Division, who were occupying Vraucourt Trench.

A and B Companies of the 8th West Yorks., detailed to clear Banks Trench and protect the left of the 2/20th Londoners as the latter attacked, succeeded in carrying out the former task. But as the advance of B Company of the Londoners had been held up the West Yorkshiremen were unable to make further progress, and the position gained was consolidated, posts being formed in accordance with orders.

The enemy's artillery now concentrated on the new line of the 185th Infantry Brigade, the sunken road north of Vraucourt, held by D Company of the Londoners, the cross roads and the Sugar Factory and the line held by A Company being heavily barraged. But the 2/20th clung tenaciously to their ground, though the inferno created by the enemy's shell fire was terrific. Communications were cut between Battalion Headquarters and the front line, and visual signalling was impossible. Yet volunteers were not wanting amongst the signallers to go out and repair the wires, though each one knew it was death to linger in that living hell. In the early afternoon the enemy began to assemble opposite C Company for a counter-attack, but the guns answered promptly to the " S.O.S." and the threatened attack was broken up.

30TH AUG.

At 4-15 p.m. a message from the VIth Corps was received at Divisional Headquarters containing the following instructions : if Vaulx-Vraucourt had not been captured by the morning of the 31st August, a fresh attack was to be organized with the object of gaining the whole of the high ground east of the village ; the 3rd Division, on the left, was to co-operate by capturing Ecoust and the Noreuil Switch.

On receipt of these instructions arrangements were made for 185th Infantry Brigade to attack Vaulx-Vraucourt with the assistance of Tanks working up from the southern portion of the village to the northern exits. The final objective of the attack was the western end of Vaulx Trench and the ridge east of the village.

The 186th Infantry Brigade was also ordered to co-operate in this attack by pushing forward along the spur running north-east towards Vraucourt. Zero hour for the attack was fixed for 5-30 a.m.

During the evening of the 30th the villages of Vaulx and Vaulx-Vraucourt were heavily shelled.

The story of the attack on Vaulx-Vraucourt, on 31st August, is told from right to left. It may be difficult to follow the progress of the action for there are gaps and inconsistencies in the official reports which it is impossible to set right.[1]

31ST AUG.

On the night of the 30th/31st August, shelling on both sides was severe and little rest was possible, though there were some comparatively quiet spots in the line.

The 5th Duke of Wellington's state that, at 5 a.m., the " S.O.S." signal went up on the right and a hostile counter-attack was completely repulsed. The enemy then heavily shelled the area H.6. and the forward area of the 5th Duke's. On the left of the latter Battalion the 2/4th Duke of Wellington's had, on the night of 30th August, occupied the line I.8.a.7.5.—I.2.c.6.3.—I.1.b.8.2.—I.1.b.0.7, where it remained throughout the night.

Six Tanks, which were to assist in the capture of the village were, at Zero hour, assembled at I.7.central, where also B and D Companies of the 1/5th Devons (Lieut.-Col. Bastow), on a jumping-off line from I.2. central to L.7. central, awaited the order to go forward.

At 5-30 a.m. the barrage fell on a line running west to east

---

[1] The Diary of the 186th Infantry Brigade Headquarters of 31st August contains only the following words :—

"August 31st : Fairly quiet day, with the exception of shelling of Vaulx-Vraucourt."

practically through the centre of Vaulx-Vraucourt, and remained 31st Aug. on this line until 6 a.m.

As the barrage fell the Tanks and Devons moved forward to attack through the line held by the 2/4th Duke of Wellington's.

Two of the Tanks broke down soon after starting; three more having moved on ahead, penetrated the village from south to north, and were then lost sight of. But the sixth Tank (under Lieut. Paton, 15th Tank Battalion) kept well with the Devons as they advanced and rendered most valuable assistance.

Up to 7-30 a.m. all had gone well with the Devons. D Company had established itself on the ridge, east of Vaulx-Vraucourt, whilst B Company had won as far north as the small trench just in front of Vaulx Trench. Both Companies had traversed the village from south to north and small clearing parties had been left behind to round up Germans hidden, with their machine guns, in cellars and buildings.

In conformity with the advance of the Devons, B and D Companies of the 2/4th Duke's pivoted on their right and moved through the village, clearing as they went, taking up a position, finally, on the right of D Company of the first-named Battalion.

Thus the ridge east of the village was occupied and Vaulx Trench was under attack.

But now the trouble began. Owing to the speed of the Tanks and, probably, to the attack being carried out in insufficient depth, the village of Vaulx-Vraucourt had not been thoroughly cleared of the enemy. The ruined village formed a most intricate piece of country, the crumbled houses and walls and innumerable cellars offering the enemy countless hiding places in which to conceal machine guns and parties of infantry.

As a result, no sooner were the leading waves of the attack clear of the village, and were establishing themselves on the ridge east of Vaulx-Vraucourt than hostile machine guns opened fire on them from behind from numerous positions in the village, and they began to suffer heavy casualties.

Touch had also been lost with all but one of the six Tanks which accompanied the attack. They had fulfilled their primary task in helping the infantry forward through the village to their objective, the ridge east of the village, but most careful organization is required in an attack with Tanks, especially over such intricate terrain as a large ruined village presents; and this was the first experience the Devons had had of operating with Tanks.

31ST AUG.
After holding on to their positions until 9 a.m., the two Companies were forced to retire to the Sunken Road on the western edge of Vaulx, about C.25.a. and I.2.a., where they established posts linking up on the right with B Company of the 2/4th Duke of Wellington's, which had also been involved in the retirement, and had thrown back its left flank in conformity with the right of the Devons.

The line established by the Duke's and the Devons ran, apparently, from I.1.b.9.2.—I.1.b.5.4—I.1.b.2.9. to C.25.d.7.6, the nearest post of the Devons being at C.25.a.9.1.

Meanwhile, on the left of the Devons, the 2/20th Londoners, who had been ordered to clear Vraucourt Trench, had similarly made good progress.

On the previous evening the Londoners held a line running from C.25.b.9.1. to C.19.b.4.0. At 11 p.m. orders were issued for 2nd Lieut. Barnes to take a bombing party from B Company out along Vraucourt Trench in order to dislodge enemy snipers. He was to advance behind the creeping barrage which had been ordered for the attack by the 185th Infantry Brigade at 5-30 a.m. on 31st.

At 5 a.m. D Company moved up and occupied the sunken road (which runs directly north from Vraucourt) from the German cemetery to the junction of the road and Vraucourt Trench.

A certain amount of progress had been made by the bombing party along Vraucourt Trench, when heavy machine-gun fire was opened from an enemy gun securely posted on the top of the trench, and protected by a thick belt of wire. Under this fire it was impossible to go on, or even maintain the position already won and, having reached a point at C.20.a.3.9. the party withdrew. Had this party successfully cleared Vraucourt Trench to its junction with Vaulx Trench, the Londoners would have joined hands with the Devons, and thus prevented the retirement of the latter.

By 5-30 p.m. the Battalion had reorganized and held a line from C.25.b.9.4. to the junction of the sunken road with Vraucourt Trench. B Company was in support in the sunken road north of the Sugar Factory. At dusk D Company pushed out posts in front of the left flank.

The results of the attack on Vaulx-Vraucourt, on 31st August, were disappointing, but the troops were becoming exhausted and there is a limit to human endurance. For five or six days the Division had been on the move, each day advancing its line in an easterly direction, which meant the digging of fresh trenches and all the work of consolidating new positions. This, in addition to heavy fighting. 31ST AUG. Moreover, the enemy had a large number of machine guns which he sited, as usual, with great skill and fought with dogged determination. In many cases a single gun crew appeared to have two or more guns sited in depth, and when driven from one gun the detachment fell back and manned its second or third gun.

At 6·5 p.m. on the 31st the 185th Infantry Brigade was again ordered to complete the capture of Vaulx-Vraucourt on the morning of 1st September. The attack was to be on lines similar to those which had governed the operations of 31st, *i.e.*, from the south under a creeping barrage. The " Heavies " were to bombard Vaulx Trench, the Noreuil Valley and selected points, ahead of the Field Artillery barrage. Zero hour was fixed for 6 a.m.

The attack was to be carried out by the 8th West Yorks. Regt., who were to assemble in I.7.central, *i.e.*, the line from which the Devons had advanced on the village.

About 4 a.m. on the 1st September the West Yorks. arrived in 1ST SEPT. their assembly positions—I.7.central—and formed up for the attack. To D and C Companies had been allotted the task of clearing the village; A and B Companies passing through when the clearing operations had been completed, A to capture Vaulx Trench between the three sunken roads running north-east from the village, B the high ground running south from Vaulx Trench. If these objectives were obtained, C Company was to swing east and come up between B Company on the left and 186th Infantry Brigade on the right.

About twenty minutes before Zero hour the enemy put down a heavy barrage on the valley south of Vaulx, searching the ground thoroughly over which the advance was to take place. But although the shells fell with uncanny precision over the very line of advance the West Yorkshiremen escaped with only a few casualties and when, at Zero hour, the Divisional barrage fell on Vaulx, the two leading Companies went forward rapidly and with fine dash.

Vaulx was cleared without much trouble, for the place had become a veritable death trap, and even the deep dug-outs and cellars which had, at first, sheltered the enemy during the early stages of the attack, were blocked by fallen débris or rendered quite untenable.

Clear of Vaulx, A and B Companies made gallant efforts to reach Vaulx Trench and the high ground east of the village, but once again a murderous machine-gun fire swept the line of advance, and all that A Company could accomplish was the occupation of the

1ST SEPT. small trench north of the village, running parallel with Vaulx Trench.

B and C Companies were similarly held up on the eastern exits of the village. These two Companies had, however, secured a good jumping-off position for future attacks, but apart from the final clearing and capture of Vaulx-Vraucourt this was the only tangible result of the attack.

The ridge east of the village had indeed proved a hard nut to crack. The enemy's machine guns, dug into carefully concealed positions had again held up the advance. For the barrage, heavy though it had been, was still insufficient to smash up the German machine-gun nests.

At 8 a.m. the line held ran along the eastern outskirts of Vaulx-Vraucourt, along the railway line to the trench running parallel with Vaulx Trench. The Sunken Roads, east and north-east of the village had been cleared by the enemy, but after a heavy bombardment, he counter-attacked the West Yorkshiremen and succeeded in getting back into the roads.

Thus, so far as can be ascertained from the official diaries, ended the attack of 1st September. The 8th West Yorks. lost two officers killed, five officers wounded, eighteen other ranks killed, eighty-seven wounded and eleven missing. At nightfall a line of posts was established east and north of the village.

Between 12 noon and 1 p.m., Divisional Headquarters received warning from VIth Corps Headquarters that the Corps, in conjunction with the IVth Corps on the right, was to renew the attack on the 2nd September, when both Corps were to assault the Beugny—Morchies—Lagnicourt line and the high ground east of those villages.

From the foregoing narrative of operations, from the 25th August (when the Division took over the front line from the 2nd Division) to the 1st September, it will be apparent that the Division was engaged in operations which might be described as tactically supplementary to the Battle of the Scarpe; the fighting was of a severe nature. To maintain pressure on an already-shaken enemy was essential and although the area of the Battle of the Scarpe, 1918,* ran from just north of the 62nd Division, yet the continuance of attacks on the southern flank of the main operations must have contributed to the success of the latter.

---

* The official area of the Battle of the Scarpe, 1918, is thus given in the Report of the Battles Nomenclature Committee :—" Noreuil (ex)—St. Leger (ex)—Boisleux-au-Mont—Roclincourt—Bailleul—Oppy."

Splendid results had followed closely on the victorious offensives of 8th and 21st August. On 27th August, the 18th Division had won Trônes Wood after heavy fighting. The 28th saw the 12th and 58th Divisions in possession of Hardecourt. On both these dates the 38th Division made progress about Longueval and Delville Wood, in company with the 17th Division attacking towards Flers over the old Somme Battlefield of 1916. Bapaume was evacuated by the enemy on 29th, the New Zealanders forcing the enemy to quit the town. On this date also the 18th Division entered Combles, whilst north of Bapaume the 56th and 57th Divisions penetrated as far as Riencourt-lez-Cagnicourt.

1ST SEPT.

By the night of the 30th the line of the Fourth and Third Armies north of the Somme ran from Clery-sur-Somme past the western edge of Marrières Wood to Combles, Lesboeufs, Bancourt—Frémicourt—Vraucourt (held by the 62nd Division) and thence to the western outskirts of Ecoust, Bullecourt and Hendecourt.

Thus a further advance of the victorious British would threaten the German line south of Peronne along the east bank of the Somme, to which position the enemy had been forced to retreat by the progress of Sir Douglas Haig's armies north of the River. Brilliant fighting on the night 30th-31st August and on the 1st September by Australian troops had resulted both in the capture of Mont. St. Quentin and Peronne. Attacks by the left of the Fourth Army and along the Third Army front on 31st August/1st September, in support of operations further south, resulted in the British line north of the Somme being carried forward to Sailly-Saillisel, Morval, Beaulencourt and Riencourt-les-Bapaume, whilst on the ridges east of Bancourt, Frémicourt, Vaulx-Vraucourt and Longatte a footing had been obtained ready for the next advance. Bullecourt and Hendecourt, and later Riencourt-lez-Cagnicourt fell to troops of the XVIIth Corps.

The following paragraph from the official despatches gives an excellent idea of the situation at this period :—" The 1st September marks the close of the second stage in the British offensive. Having in the first stage freed Amiens by our brilliant successes east of that town (the Battle of Amiens, 8th—11th August), in the second stage the troops of the Third and Fourth Armies, comprising twenty-three British Divisions, by skilful leading, hard fighting and relentless and unremitting pursuit, in ten days (21st—31st August) had driven thirty-five German Divisions from one side of the old Somme Battlefield to the other, thereby turning the line of the River Somme.

1ST SEPT. In so doing they have inflicted upon the enemy the heaviest losses in killed and wounded and have taken from him over 34,000 prisoners and 270 guns. For the remarkable success of the Battle of Bapaume, the greatest credit is due to the excellence of the staff arrangements of all formations, and to the most able conduct of the operations of the Third Army by its commander—General Byng."

The obstinate fighting which had taken place between 21st and 31st August had not yet forced the enemy back to his old defences of the Hindenburg Line. His evident intention was to retire slowly from one outstanding position to another, until he could withdraw his hard-pressed Divisions behind the Hindenburg defences, which were being strengthened in feverish haste. The high ground about Beugny and Rocquigny afforded him opportunities of making a stand, whilst a little further south the line of the Tortille River and the high plateau about Nurlu offered still further opportunities for withdrawing his artillery to safe positions and securing the much-needed material stored in his forward dumps.

But his *morale* had been badly shaken. German rearguards left behind in important positions to hold up the British advance had surrendered as soon as isolation threatened them. Nevertheless it is only fair to state that this lack of staying power was not general in the German armies, for as has already been shown, the troops opposed to many British Divisions, stoutly defended their positions and ground was won from them only after hard fighting; the 62nd Division experienced many instances of the desperate efforts of German Divisions to hold their ground.

One of the principal factors in the demoralization which gradually permeated the whole German Army was the uncertainty as to where the next blow would fall. The Allied attacks had been spread over such a wide front that the enemy was forced to throw in his reserves, piecemeal, as they arrived, Divisions were split up and what *esprit de corps* remained was dissipated. It is, however, well to remember what Ludendorff said of the troops at his disposal in 1918 :—" Our relative strength in Divisions was more formidable at the beginning of September than it had been in the previous year (1917), but some of our Divisions were very weak."[*] Many British Divisions were also deplorably weak, though Sir Douglas Haig could never have said as Ludendorff said a little later, after the above comparisons of his strength :—" Shirking at the front became more prevalent, especially

---

[*] " My War Memories, 1914—1918." General Ludendorff.

among men returning from home leave. Over-staying of leave 1ST SEPT. increased and the fighting line got thinner and thinner."

It was, of course, obvious that the enemy could not be allowed to establish himself once more in the Hindenburg Line, and before he had even reached it, the next blow fell up him : " A sudden and successful blow of weight sufficient to break through the northern hinge of the defences to which it was his design to fall back, might produce results of great importance." This " northern hinge " was the powerful trench system running from the Hindenburg Line at Quéant to the Lens defences about Drocourt. If this position should fall the whole of the enemy's organized positions, on a wide front southwards, would be turned.

The Battle of the Scarpe, 1918, which ended on the last day of August, had prepared the way for this next operation, *i.e.*, against the Drocourt—Quéant line, planned for the 2nd September. And although the official area of the battle excluded the operations of the 62nd Division (and, indeed the attacks of the Third and Fourth Armies) they cannot be separated from the general attack.*

---

* The official area of the Battle of the Drocourt—Quéant line (2nd—3rd September) is :—Moeuvres (exclusive)—Noreuil (inclusive)—St. Leger (exclusive)—Monchy-le-Preux—Pelves, thence to the River Scarpe.

The Report of the Battles Nomenclature Committee is seemingly in need of revision for, as the official despatches stated in the Battle of the Drocourt—Quéant line :—" Troops of the Third and Fourth Armies prolonged the line of attack as far south as Peronne. At all important points progress was made though fighting was severe."

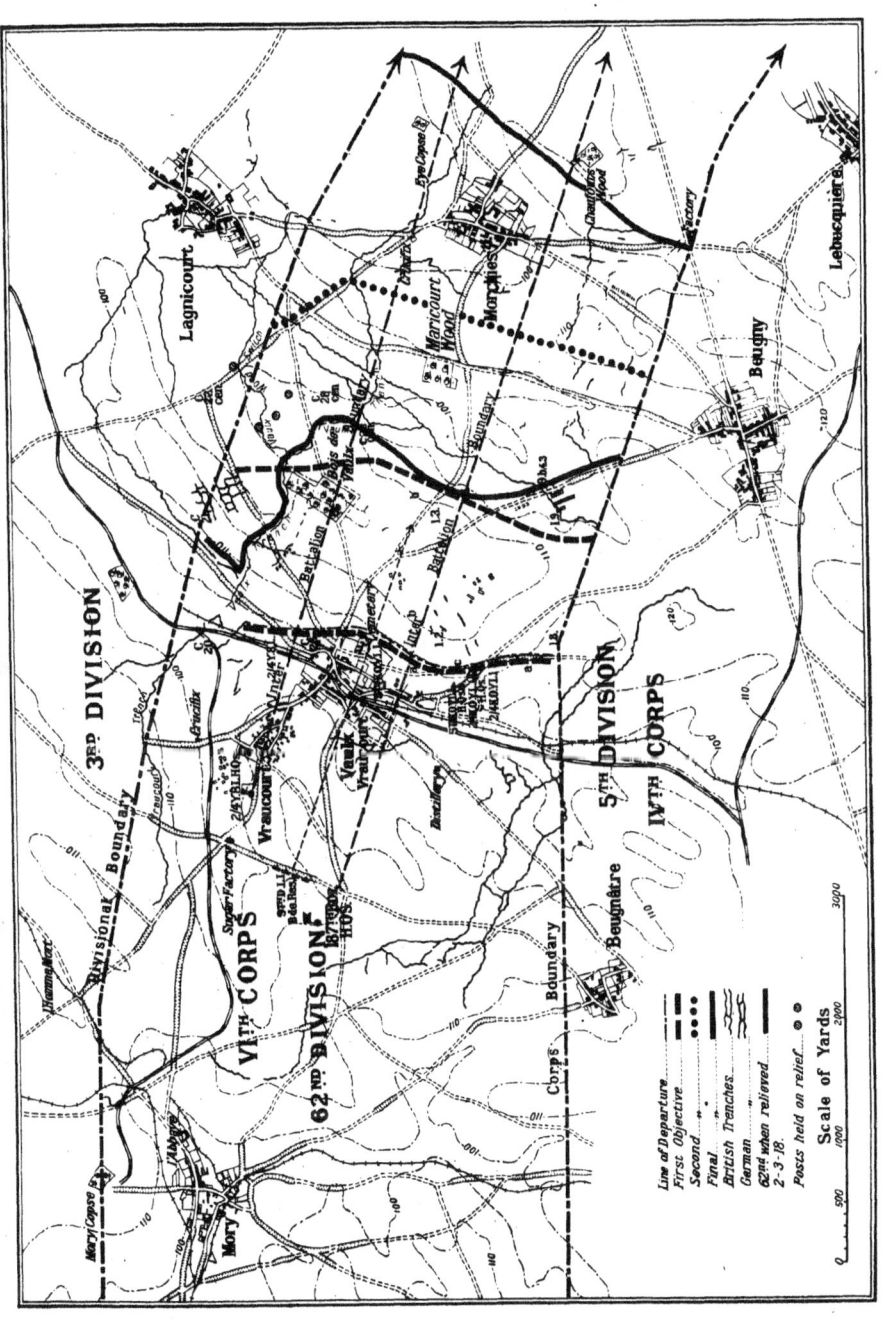

The Battle of the Drocourt-Quéant Line.

Chapter II.   1918.

THE BATTLE OF THE DROCOURT—QUÉANT LINE, 2nd—3rd September

BETWEEN 12 noon and 1 p.m. on the 1st September, as 1ST SEPT. the troops of the 185th Infantry Brigade were consolidating themselves in Vaulx-Vraucourt, and on the eastern outskirts of the village, General Whigham received orders from VIth Corps Headquarters stating that the attack would be renewed on the following day—the 2nd September.

In conjunction with the IVth Corps, on the right, the VIth Corps was to capture Beugny—Morchies and Lagnicourt with the high ground east of the three villages. Beugny was in the IVth Corps area; Morchies lay in the direct line of advance of the 62nd Division, while Lagnicourt was in the area of the left flank Division of the VIth Corps.

The G.O.C. discussed the plan of operations with the Brigadier, 187th Infantry Brigade, who had been previously summoned to Divisional Headquarters. It was decided that the 187th Infantry Brigade reinforced by the 9th Durham Light Infantry should carry out the attack on the Divisional front, and details for the artillery barrage were worked out. Eight Mark IV Tanks were available for the operation and at the close of the conference the Tank commanders accompanied General Reddie (G.O.C., 187th Infantry Brigade) to the latter's Headquarters to settle details for the attack. The 62nd Battalion M.G.C. and a Company attached to the 186th Infantry Brigade were also placed at the disposal of the G.O.C., 187th Infantry Brigade. On receipt of orders from Divisional Headquarters the 185th and 186th Infantry Brigades were to be prepared to move forward a Battalion each, in order to relieve troops of the 187th Infantry Brigade on the line of the first objective. If the line of the final objective (east of Morchies) was gained, the 62nd Division was to exploit success in the direction of Beaumetz-lez-Cambrai. Six

1ST SEPT. whippet Tanks, in VIth Corps reserve, had received similar orders, *i.e.*, to exploit success in the open country in front of the 62nd Division.

The Battalions' objectives and barrage lines are shown on the map :—the 2/4th K.O.Y.L.I. were detailed for the right attack, the 5th K.O.Y.L.I. for the centre and the 2/4th York. and Lancs. Regt. for the left.

The artillery programme included a creeping barrage (100 yards per three minutes), commencing at Zero, and a protective barrage 500 yards in depth and moving forward with the creeping barrage on the left flanks of the 187th Brigade, the jumping-off line of the 3rd Division being in echelon in rear of the 187th Infantry Brigade. It was anticipated that the right brigade of the 3rd Division would experience difficulty in crossing the Noreuil Valley and, as a further protection to the left flank of the 187th Infantry Brigade, the 2/4th Battalion York. and Lancs. was ordered to form a defensive flank along Vaulx Trench as the attack progressed.

One section of the 187th Trench Mortar Battery was allotted to each of the centre and left Battalions, while B Company on the right, and A Company on the left, of the 62nd Battalion M.G.C. were to assist the advance.

On the right of the 62nd the 5th Division (IVth Corps) was attacking Beugny, whilst the 3rd Division (on the left of the 62nd) had Lagnicourt and the ground east of it as final objectives.

Zero hour for the 62nd and 3rd Divisions was fixed for 5-30 a.m. ; the 5th Division was attacking at 5-15 a.m.

It will be remembered that after the successful clearing of Vaulx-Vraucourt on the morning of the 1st September the line of the Division ran as follows :—186th Infantry Brigade (right) almost directly north from I.8a—I.2.c and a., and the eastern outskirts of Vaulx-Vraucourt, where the left of the Brigade joined up with the right of the 185th Infantry Brigade, the latter carrying the line thence along the Railway Line to the trench running parallel with Vaulx Trench, C.20.d. When the attack was planned, the units of the 187th Infantry Brigade were disposed in depth between the villages of Sapignies and Behagnies, where old existing trenches and posts had been organized as a defensive line of the Division. The Brigade, therefore, had some distance to traverse before reaching its assembly and jumping-off positions. Moreover the situation along the Divisional front was by no means clear, and it was 6 p.m. on the 1st before a suitable jumping-off line was selected, which gave very little time for C.O.'s and company commanders to reconnoitre the positions. Considerable credit was therefore due to officers and N.C.O.s for the skilful manner in which each unit reached its allotted position in the line of battle.

1ST SEPT.

At 10-30 p.m. on the night 1st/2nd September, the 2/4th K.O.Y.L.I. (Lieut.-Col. C. B. Chaytor) set out along the track running east from Sapignies, guides from the 186th Infantry Brigade meeting the Battalion on the Bapaume—Ecoust Road. The night was very dark, but, well-led, the 2/4th reached their assembly positions without incident and formed up for the attack—A and B Companies each on a two-platoon frontage, forming the first wave, C and D Companies the second wave, with orders to " leap-frog " the first two Companies on the line of the second objective, and go through to the final objective.

1ST/2ND SEPT.

The 5th K.O.Y.L.I. (Lieut.-Col. F. H. Peter), though hampered by heavy shelling falling to the south of Vaulx-Vraucourt, formed up successfully on the left of the 2/4th K.O.Y.L.I. along the road skirting the Cemetery, at the eastern exits of Vaulx-Vraucourt.

The Hallamshires (2/4th York and Lancs.) —Lieut.-Col. L. H. P. Hart—arrived at their forming-up line—the Sunken Road in C.19.b. and d. (running north by north-east of Vraucourt) at 2-30 a.m., the line being about 1,000 yards in rear of the first barrage line. B Company (right) and D Company (left) were to form the first two waves of the attack, A Company on the left and C Company on the right forming the third and fourth waves.

The 9th Durham Light Infantry (Pioneers), in Brigade reserve, moved up to the Sunken Road in B.30, ready to go forward if called upon. Few were the opportunities these gallant fellows had of fighting as infantry men, but when it did occur, as in March during the Great German Offensive, they responded splendidly to whatever calls were made upon them.

Throughout the very early hours of the 2nd September the enemy was particularly " nervy " and the ground west of Vaulx-Vraucourt was intermittently shelled, a considerable amount of gas being used. A little after 5-15 a.m., when the 5th Division, south of the 62nd Division, had launched its attack, a heavy hostile barrage fell in front of the sunken road in which the 2/4th K.O.Y.L.I. had formed up for the attack. All accounts agree that the fifteen minutes difference between the Zero hours of the IVth and VIth Corps was sufficient to allow the enemy time to arrange a barrage on the latter. it being more than probable that the attack of the former would be

2ND SEPT.

2ND SEPT. followed almost immediately by an assault by the 62nd and 3rd Divisions.

The enemy's barrage fell almost immediately after VIth Corps Zero—5·30 a.m.—but until the high ground of the first objective was reached casualties were remarkably light, considering the volume of machine-gun and shell fire which met the troops as they moved forward from their jumping-off positions.

With commendable gallantry the Company commanders of the 2/4th K.O.Y.L.I. led their men through the enemy's barrage close on the heels of the Divisional screen of fire, for the Battalion Diary stated :—" the men were only too anxious to leave this barrage and get under our own." The leading waves of the Battalion came immediately under a heavy close-range machine-gun fire, but these guns, however, were soon put out of action and on the whole the attack commenced very favourably.

Shortly after the attack began a number of the enemy were seen about the hutments on the west side of the sunken road, in which the Battalion had formed up. How they got there or where they had concealed themselves, it was impossible to say, but they attacked the left flank of the 2/4th K.O.Y.L.I., which for a little while became disorganized. But the right of the 5th K.O.Y.L.I., moving down towards the left of the 2/4th Battalion, caught these Germans, and a desperate fight ensued and numbers of the enemy were killed and captured. The inner flanks of the two Battalions had, however, become mixed, but without staying their advance for reorganization the move forward was continued and presently an old trench, running through I.9.b to where it cut the road from Beugny, was reached, and, a little later, the road going southwards towards the village. In these positions the advance was stayed and the Battalions attempted to dig in. But eventually a short retirement had to be made to the forward slopes of the ridge in I.8 and I.9., hostile machine guns south of Maricourt Wood sweeping the Beugny—Vaulx road and the old trenches just west of it.

In spite of the heavy hostile barrage falling in front of the road skirting the Cemetery, along which the Battalions had assembled, the 5th K.O.Y.L.I. went forward punctually at 5·30 a.m. The Battalion Diary states that " up to 6·30—7 a.m. reports received to the effect that the attack was going splendidly." That was so. Vaulx Wood had been passed, and the troops were well on their way towards Maricourt Wood, beyond which lay the line of the second objective. But trouble was brewing. From Vaulx Trench, the left of the 5th K.O.Y.L.I. came suddenly under a very heavy enfilade 2ND SEPT. machine-gun fire, which compelled the troops to seek shelter in an old trench running southwards from Vaulx Trench (C.28.c.7.3.), but which, fortunately, was situated on fairly high ground and on the forward slopes of the hill. Here the 5th K.O.Y.L.I. gallantly maintained themselves, though in a perilous position. For by now the enemy was all round their left flank, and the majority of the men of B, C and D Companies were cut off, communication between them and Battalion Headquarters being impossible. The enemy next began to dribble back (westwards) along the Vaulx Trench, and to push men out into Vaulx Wood, parts of which he re-occupied. A Company (still in communication with Battalion Headquarters) was then ordered " at all costs " to hold on to the Vaulx-Lagnicourt and Vaulx-Morchies roads, and access to Vaulx itself was to be refused the enemy, who was making desperate efforts to regain the ground lost. With splendid tenacity and gallantry, though practically surrounded, the three isolated Companies of 5th K.O.Y.L.I. clung to their positions. Their desperate condition was the result of the hard luck which had befallen the left flank of the attack launched by the 2/4th York and Lancs. Regt.

Of the tasks allotted to the three Battalions of the 187th Infantry Brigade, on that September morning, that given to the Hallamshires was the most difficult. To begin with, their forming-up line was 1,000 yards in rear of the first barrage lines and the two first waves (of B Company on the right and D Company on the left) began to move forward at 5 a.m., half-an-hour before Zero, in order to conform to the line of attack. On their left, the right Brigade of the 3rd Division was echeloned in rear of the Hallamshires, and therefore the protective barrage (already mentioned), 500 yards in depth, was placed on the left flank of the 187th Infantry Brigade. Finally, the 2/4th York and Lancs. had been ordered to form a defensive flank along Vaulx Trench as the attack progressed. From the map it will be seen that Vaulx Trench ran practically the whole length of the Battalion frontage, *i.e.*, from the jumping-off line to beyond the second objective.

Though the barrage was falling when the Hallamshires moved forward at Zero hour, few casualties were sustained, and for the first 500 yards all went well. But on topping the high ground, which ran northwards and southwards directly in the line of advance and across which Vaulx Trench was sighted, considerable opposition was experienced from enemy machine guns and 77mm. guns. Nothing

2nd Sept. daunted, however, the Hallamshires, with gallantry and determination, overcame the enemy's resistance and the line of the first objective was captured.

An aeroplane message, timed 6-50 a.m., reached Divisoinal Headquarters. It contained information that flares had been " seen all along Vaulx Trench to C.28 central, thence in a south-south-east direction to I.9.b.4.3., thence along the road to Beugny." This apparently was the correct situation at this period.

Meanwhile, as had been feared, the 3rd Division had found the crossing of the Noreuil Valley a very difficult task. The Hallamshires were thus forced to form a defensive flank along Vaulx Trench or that portion of it from which they had cleared the enemy. But now as they advanced towards the second objective the enemy began to appear on the left flank of the Battalion and, about 7 a.m., he opened heavy artillery fire, from short range, principally along Vaulx Trench. This was followed by violent counter-attacks from the north and east, forcing the Hallamshires to withdraw to the sunken road in C.26 and that portion of the Vaulx Trench in C. 21 and 20. The forward garrison of Vaulx Trench had become casualties. The left flank of the 187th Infantry Brigade was thus left unprotected. Until 9-30 a.m., the official narrative records that reports received concerning the situation on the left flank of the Divisional front were " conflicting." Twenty minutes later another message was received from an aeroplane, which had been working with the Tanks, reporting the Divisional front line east of Maricourt Wood, but this was not confirmed. A staff officer was sent out from Divisional Headquarters, to clear up the situation and the positions of the three attacking Battalions which appeared to be as follows :—the 2/4th K.O.Y.L.I., on the right, were dug in along the ridge in I.9 and I.8, in touch with troops of the 5th Division on the Beugny—Vaulx Road, and the 5th K.O.Y.L.I. on the left. Of the last Battalion, B, C, and D Companies were practically cut off, though maintaining their positions splendidly in the old trench running south from Vaulx Trench in C.28.c. with Maricourt Wood on their front and Vaulx Wood behind ; the latter again in possession of the enemy. A Company of the 5th K.O.Y.L.I. was holding on to the Vaulx—Morchies and Vaulx—Lagnicourt Roads and covering the eastern exits of Vaulx itself. The Hallamshires (2/4th York and Lancs.) held Vaulx Trench in C.20.a. and C.21.c. and the sunken road in C.26.b. and d.

The G.O.C., 187th Infantry Brigade, was then ordered to recapture Vaulx Wood and Vaulx Trench, between the left of the 5th

K.O.Y.L.I. and the right of the Hallamshires, the attack to take place from the south as soon as arrangements could be made. The 9th Durham Light Infantry (Pioneers) were detailed for this operation.

At 6 a.m., half-an-hour after Zero hour, the Durhams moved forward to the ridge east of Vaulx, in support of the attack then going forward, and which at this period had gained the line of the first objective. At 7-45 a.m., the O.C. was ordered to move two Companies up to the line of the first objective in I.3.b. and d., and one Company to I.2.a. and b. The two forward Companies promptly set to work and dug themselves in, consolidating the line they held behind the 2/4th and 5th K.O.Y.L.I. on the right and centre front of the Pioneers. These two Companies were well disposed for their strenuous work, for a little later hostile machine guns swept their position with such violence that all communication with the front line Battalions was severed. Several men of the 2/4th and 5th K.O.Y.L.I. were seen to leave their positions in a gallant attempt to carry back messages, but all were shot down. Under such conditions the 9th Durham Light Infantry passed the morning, until the C.O. received a message from 187th Infantry Brigade Headquarters ordering him to attack Vaulx Wood and Vaulx Trench, and, after obtaining a footing in the latter, to work westwards and join up with the Hallamshires, and south-east along the trench to where the leading troops of the 5th K.O.Y.L.I. were reported.

C Company was detailed for the attack, Zero hour being 2-30 p.m. The very modest account contained in the Battalion Diary of the 9th Durham Light Infantry conveys but little idea of this completely successful and gallant enterprise. " C Company," said the Battalion Diary, " attacked Vaulx Wood and Vaulx Trench, which had been recaptured by the enemy, and took them with but few casualties, after beating down machine-gun fire which commanded the place." That is all! But those who knew what it meant to beat down hostile machine-gun fire in 1918, will know also that no easy task was accomplished by these Pioneers,* whose ordinary functions were to dig trenches and work generally with picks and shovels in the consolidation of ground already won by infantry.

So Vaulx Wood and Vaulx Trench were once more captured and, working east and south-east as directed, the 9th Durham Light

---

* It should be remarked that the 9th Durham Light Infantry had been Pioneers only a few months—that as infantry they were a very gallant and hard-fighting Battalion. The Battalion was originally trained and commanded by Brig.-Gen. Bradford, V.C., who lost his life at Cambrai in 1917, whilst serving with the 62nd Division.

2ND SEPT. Infantry joined up with the Hallamshires and 5th K.O.Y.L.I. respectively. In this attack the Durhams had four officers wounded (two evacuated to hospital and two remaining " at duty "), two other ranks killed and forty-one wounded.

The Hallamshires in Vaulx Trench were shortly afterwards relieved by troops of the 185th Infantry Brigade, who took over the trench as far as the junction of Vaulx Wood Switch inclusive, thus relieving sufficient men of the 9th Durham Light Infantry to fill adequately the gap between this junction and the left of the 5th K.O.Y.L.I.

By 5 p.m. the whole line was successfully established, at which hour General Reddie (G.O.C., 187th Infantry Brigade) was informed that during the night 2nd/3rd September the 2nd Division would take over his front line and continue the attack.

Finally at 5-30 p.m. the Hallamshires worked along Vaulx Wood Switch and gained touch with the 3rd Division on the left flank C.22 central—the Brigadier's report ending with the words :— " this concluding a most satisfactory day's fighting."

Once again the doggedness and determination of this Yorkshire Division had turned what, at one period of the day, looked like failure, into a distinct success. True, the final objectives had not been reached, but the high ground east of Morchies had been won, the enemy turned out of a difficult and somewhat intricate system of trenches and an excellent jumping-off position gained for the relieving Division.

The two sections of Tanks working with the Division after having given great assistance to the leading Battalions in gaining the high ground immediately east of Vaulx had been stopped, principally by anti-tank rifle fire. A number of these weapons were found during the day in the captured trenches.

Although the Division was not supported by its own artillery, glowing tributes are contained in the official narrative to the splendid assistance given by field and heavy guns of the batteries under the command of Brigadier-General Anderson (the C.R.A.). Battery commanders lost not a single opportunity and pushed their guns forward east of Vaulx in order the more effectively to cover and support the attacking infantry, who were often in desperate need of assistance. The close liaison maintained between Battery and Battalion Commanders contributed largely to the success of the day and increased to a marked extent the number of casualties inflicted on the enemy.

Throughout the operations the 62nd Battalion M.G.C. and the T.M. Batteries lent effective support. 2ND SEPT.

The prisoners captured by the 187th Infantry Brigade on 2nd September numbered nine officers and 470 other ranks. Three field guns intact, six Heavy Trench Mortars (which being too large to move were left on the field), eleven Light Trench Mortars and seventy-three machine guns were collected and brought back to Brigade Headquarters. The Brigade's casualties were nineteen officers and 576 other ranks, killed, wounded and missing.

At 3 a.m. on the 3rd September, the 6th and 99th Infantry Brigades of the 2nd Division passed through the line held by the 187th Infantry Brigade and the latter, in high spirits, set out to march back to a well-earned rest in the Ervillers—Behagnies area; the 185th Infantry Brigade was withdrawn to Behagnies and Sapignies, while the 186th Infantry Brigade moved back to the railway east of Courcelles. Command of the sector passed from G.O.C., 62nd Division, to the G.O.C., 2nd Division at 5-20 a.m. on the morning of the 3rd September. 3RD SEPT.

The West Riding Division was now in VIth Corps Support.

The operations in which the Division had taken part between 24th August and 3rd September had resulted in the capture of thirty-nine officers and 1,418 other ranks, three field guns, 277 machine guns, fifty-five Trench Mortars, and thirty-five anti-Tank rifles. The total casualties suffered by the Division were ninety-four officers and 2,329 other ranks.*

The general results of the Battle of the Drocourt—Quéant Line were that the strong maze of trenches, at the junction of that Line and the Hindenburg Line, were broken into and the enemy thrown back in a precipitate retreat on the whole front southwards. The 1st and 4th Canadian Divisions (Canadian Corps) and the 4th (English) Division of the First Army and the 52nd, 57th and 63rd Divisions of the XVIIth Corps, Third Army, had achieved this splendid feat and, when night fell on the 2nd September, positions had been won to a depth of three miles along the Arras—Cambrai Road, and the outskirts of Buissy reached. Cagnicourt, Villers-les-Cagnicourt and Dury had also been taken from the enemy. As already shown the 3rd and 62nd Divisions of the VIth Corps, Third Army, and troops of the Fourth Army had prolonged the line of attack as far south as Peronne.

¹ Officers: nineteen killed, seventy-four wounded, one missing; other ranks 302 killed, 1,702 wounded, 325 missing.

3RD SEPT. During the night of 2nd/3rd September the enemy fell back rapidly on the whole front of the Third Army, and the right of the First Army, and by the evening of the 3rd he had taken up positions along the general line of the Canal du Nord from Peronne to Ypres, and thence east of Hermies, Inchy-en-Artois and Ecourt St. Quentin to the Sensee east of Lecluse.

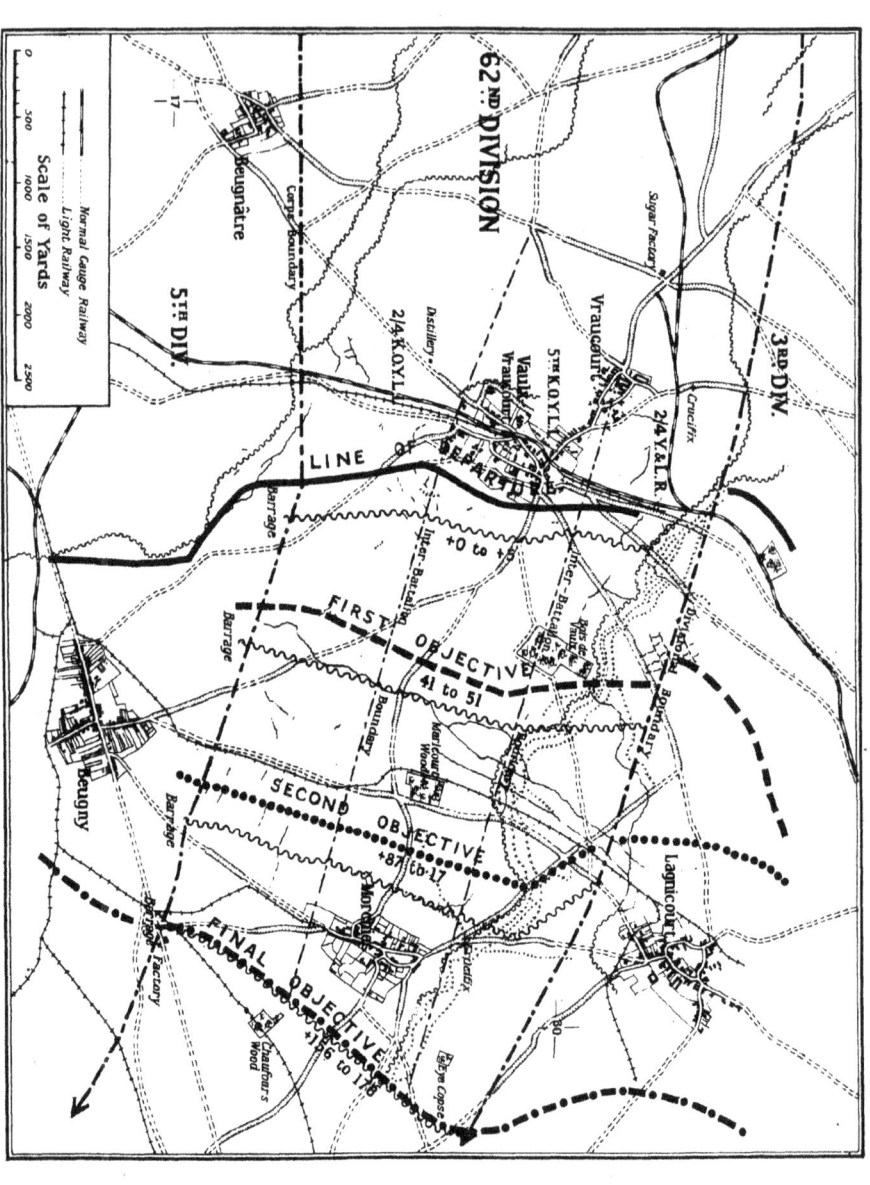

Barrage Map: The Battle of the Drocourt-Quéant Line.

Chapter III.

1918.

OF THE 62nd DIVISIONAL ARTILLERY, from 21st August to 6th September, 1918

" We are the guns, and your masters ! Saw ye our flashes ?
Heard ye the scream of our shells in the night, and the shuddering crashes ?
Saw ye our work by the roadside, the grey wounded lying,
Moaning to God that he made them—the maimed and the dying ? Husbands or Sons,
Fathers or lovers, we break them ! We are the guns ! "
Gilbert Frankau.

ONE of the outstanding characteristics of the 62nd (West Riding) Division was the fraternal spirit which existed between all ranks of every unit of the Division. Physical exhaustion, hunger or thirst or that terrible " played out " feeling, from which from time to time every officer and man suffered, were not sufficient to deter one unit from going to the assistance of another, if that other was in need of succour. And for the guns, which supported, covered him, nay ! almost fathered him, the infantryman had an altogether extraordinary affection. It was, therefore, with something akin to disappointment, that when the operations between 24th August and 3rd September began, the infantry of the 62nd Division learned that their beloved guns were not to support them during the stiff fighting obviously ahead. And, although the superb gunners of those two Old Army Divisions—the 2nd and 3rd—had covered the attack of the 62nd Division most gallantly, there was just that one difference, they were not the Division's own gunners.

From supporting the 37th Division of the Fourth Army in the early hours of 21st August, in its attack on Bucquoy, the 310th and 312th Brigades, R.F.A. had, during the afternoon of the same day, supported the 63rd Division attacking Achiet-le-Petit. On the 22nd the two Brigades came under the orders of the 5th Division, the 310th

21ST AUGUST

22ND AUGUST

22ND AUGUST moving forward during the morning to take up gun positions between Hannescamp and Bienvillers, the 312th remaining all day north-west of Bucquoy and just east of Essarts, until the evening, when the Brigade moved off to new positions immediately north-east of Puissieux. On the 22nd both Brigades fired in the creeping barrage, covering the attacks of the 5th Division on Miraumont, Irles and Achiet-le-Grand.

23RD AUGUST Late in the afternoon of the 23rd* both the 310th and 312th Brigades received orders to rendezvous that night at Bertrancourt, where they were to come under the C.R.A., 38th (Welsh) Division. The guns were pulled out of the line during the evening and late that night the two Brigades bivouacked at Bertrancourt. The march was

24TH AUGUST continued at 8 a.m. on the 24th, and Colonel Sherlock (commanding 310th Brigade, R.F.A.) and Colonel Eden (commanding 312th Brigade, R.F.A.) met the C.R.A. of the 38th (Welsh) Division between Englebelmer and Forceville, where it was decided that the 62nd Divisional Artillery should move south to just north of Albert, where both Brigades were to come into action. On reaching Bouzincourt, Battery Commanders went forward to reconnoitre positions on the eastern bank of the River Ancre, which had been gained during the night by the 38th Division. The four batteries of the 310th Brigade came into action just north-east of Albert. Immediately west of Usna Valley, the guns of the 312th Brigade, crossing by the temporary bridge at Aveluy, came into action west of Athuille Wood. The enemy was then holding Tara and Usna Hills, which overlooked Albert from the east.

25TH AUGUST At 7.30 am.. on the 25th the 38th Division attacked towards Contalmaison, and Tara and Usna Hills were captured. The 310th and 312th took part in the creeping barrage, covering the attack and lending effective support to the attacking infantry of the Welsh Division. A few hours later the guns were again limbered up and both Brigades moved forward, the enemy retiring slowly before the victorious Welshmen.

Heavy fighting and continuous hard work were borne willingly by the gunners, whose devotion was never more marked than in these strenuous days of the Advance to Victory. On the afternoon of the 25th the 310th Brigade came into action near the crest of the hill north-east of La Boisselle, whilst the 312th Brigade moved to new positions about 1,000 yards north of Pozieres.

---

* Lieut. J. C. Massey-Beresford, 310th Brigade, R.F.A., was killed in action on this date.

Splendid work was again done by the two Brigades on the 26th, when the 38th Division wrested High Wood, Trônes Wood and Bazentin from the enemy and forced him back still further.

26TH AUGUS

The 310th was in action in the valley between Contalmaison and Pozieres and during the morning B/310 and D/310 carried out a combined shoot on two companies of 3rd Grenadiers Regt., which had counter-attacked the right brigade of the 38th Division. As the Germans emerged from Trônes Wood B/310 caught them beautifully; forty dead were counted there next morning. During the evening the 38th Division, which had attacked Longueval and had gained a footing in the village, were forced out again. That night the guns of the 310th Brigade were located in the vicinity of Contalmaison Wood.

The 312th Brigade had opened at 3.20 a.m. with twenty minutes destructive and harassing fire on Bazentin-le-Petit and Longueval in preparation for the attack of 114th Infantry Brigade, 38th Division. On the success of the attack being reported the guns moved forward to positions near Martinpuich and Bazentin.

The two Brigades were again in action on the morning of the 27th. The 38th Division had been ordered to attack the line Flers—Longueval—Delville Wood—Guillemont, " Zero " hour being fixed at 5.30 a.m.

27TH AUGUE

The 310th Brigade supported the right of the attack in the Longueval—Guillemont area. Under cover of a creeping barrage the infantry assaulted and captured both Longueval and Delville Wood, but during the afternoon the enemy counter-attacked heavily and both these places were lost again. Throughout the night the 310th fired continuously on the village and on the Wood.

On the left of the attack, the 312th Brigade supported the 114th Infantry Brigade (38th Division) attacking towards Flers and Longueval, first by firing a creeping barrage and later by harassing fire at intervals on reported targets.

The situation was obscure all day, but A Battery moved forward to east of Bazentin and D Battery to about 1,000 yards south of High Wood.

On the 28th, the 310th Brigade appears to have remained in its gun positions of 27th, harassing fire being carried out throughout the day and night. B Battery of the 312th Brigade moved to positions immediately north-west of Bazentin-le-Grand.

28TH AUGUE

At 5.15 a.m. on 29th, the 310th Brigade put down a creeping barrage from a line running north and south through the centre of

29TH AUGUE

29TH AUG. Longueval Village, moving east to a north and south line 500 yards east of Ginchy. Under this barrage the infantry swept forward, capturing both Ginchy and Guillemont.

The 312th Brigade covered the attack towards Morval. Both Flers and Delville Wood were occupied by the 38th Division and the line advanced to the high ground half way between Lesboeufs and Ginchy. Morval, however, was still strongly defended and an attack on the village during the evening accomplished nothing. At nightfall on 29th the guns of the 310th Brigade occupied positions just north of Trônes Wood, the 312th Brigade being also moved forward to the high ground half way between Lesboeufs and Guinchy.

2nd SEPT. For several more days the two Brigades did yeoman service with the 38th Division, following close on the heels of the harassed enemy, and giving him no rest. To every call upon them the guns responded splendidly, though all ranks were by now greatly worn out, under the constant moving and fighting. "Reconnoitring the long forward slope down to the Canal du Nord at Manancourt on the 2nd September," said the Battery Commander of B/310, " was a nasty job, and some 38th Division batteries who were pushed out in front of us here, had a bad time. Meanwhile, my Battery moved up close behind Sailly-Saillisel.

3RD SEPT. On the evening of the 3rd September, we moved up close to the Canal. I went in rear of B/310 about 800 yards from the Canal, which our infantry was to cross in the morning. By bad luck I came under a German gas concentration, which lasted from 10 p.m. to 6 a.m. I had to stay there to fire a barrage and consequently got about 90 per cent. of my men at the gun positions gassed. We were digging and carrying ammunition all night; the position was close to Manancourt."

The night of the 3rd September was particularly hazardous, for the enemy's shell fire was intense and the guns were close up to the front line. With great determination the officers moved amongst their men, encouraging them. Two guns of one battery received direct hits but, removing the casualties himself the section commander kept the guns in action, and by his splendid example enabled his men to keep the guns firing. During the same night one of the guns of D/312 burst, killing two and wounding two of the gun detachment, and setting fire to the pit. Nothing daunted, however, the section commander, with a gunner, went to the assistance of the wounded men. With great gallantry and fine disregard of their own safety officers and men remained burying charges which had been blown into the ammunition recess, preventing an explosion and keeping down the fire until with further help it was put out. 3RD SEPT.

On the 6th September, the 310th and 312th Brigades were withdrawn, Batteries then being east of the Canal du Nord and rejoined the 62nd Division on the 8th September. They had advanced 18 miles, almost as the crow flies, and for thirteen days had been moving and fighting across the old German battlefields of 1916. And well indeed had they upheld the honour and high distinctions already gained by the 62nd Division. 6TH SEPT. 8TH SEPT.

After the two Brigades had rejoined the 62nd Division, General Whigham received the following letter from the G.O.C., 38th Division :—

" I have experienced the great honour and privilege of having under my command from 21st August to 5th September, 1918, the artillery of your Division.

" The Division has attacked on a 3,000 yards front for 16 days continuously with a truly remarkable success. I attribute this success to a great degree to the magnificent support I have received from the Field Artillery. On many occasions batteries of your artillery have literally moved parallel with my advancing infantry. Their dash, determination and staying power are above all praise. I wish especially to bring to your notice the gallant and distinguished conduct of Lieut.-Col. D. J. Sherlock, D.S.O. and Lieut.-Col. A. G. Eden."

The generous appreciation of the work of the Divisional gunners contained in the above letter was hailed with delight by all ranks of the 62nd—the guns had not failed them. Moreover, they had returned, covered with glory, to their own !

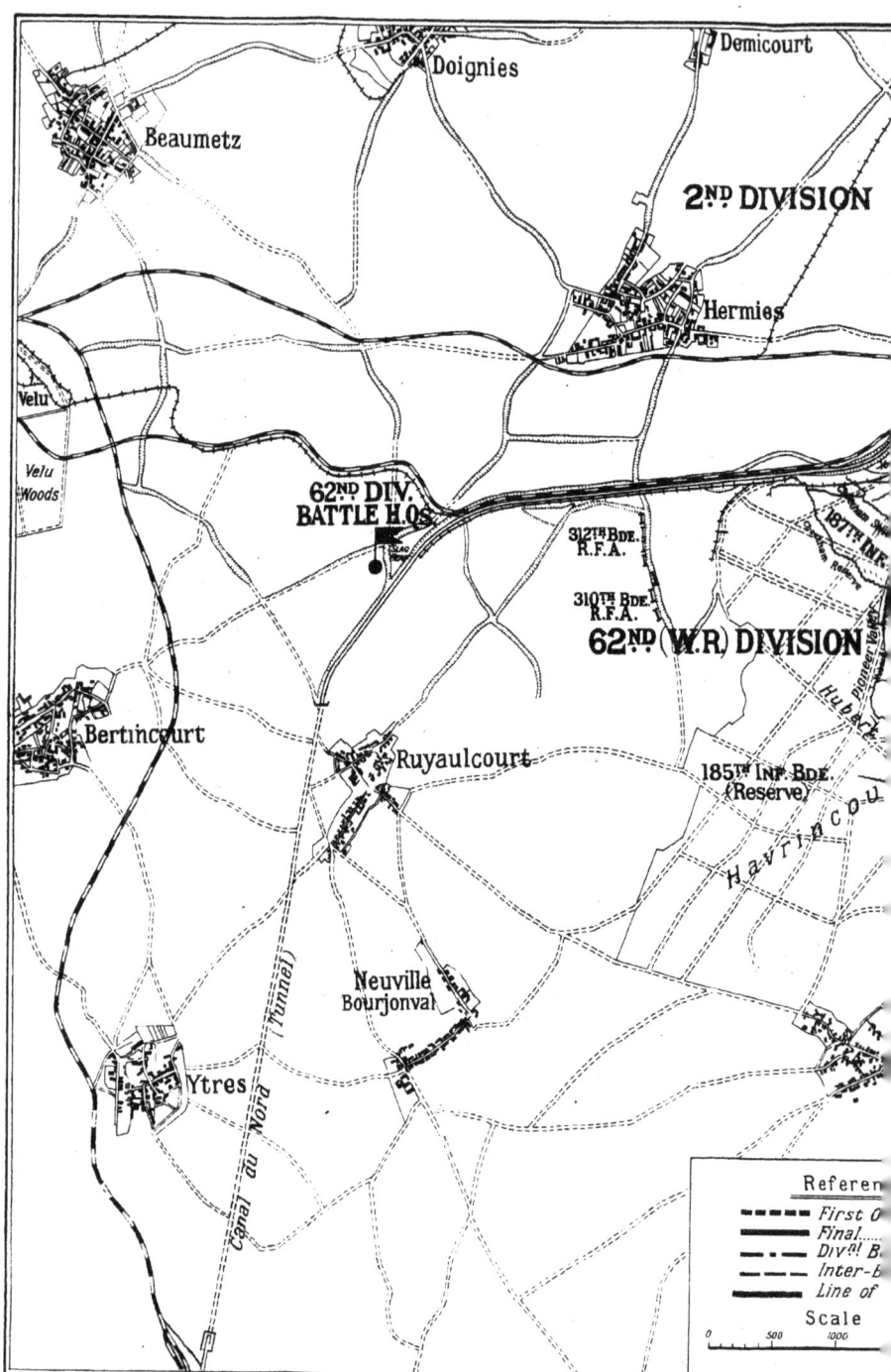

THE BATTLE OF H

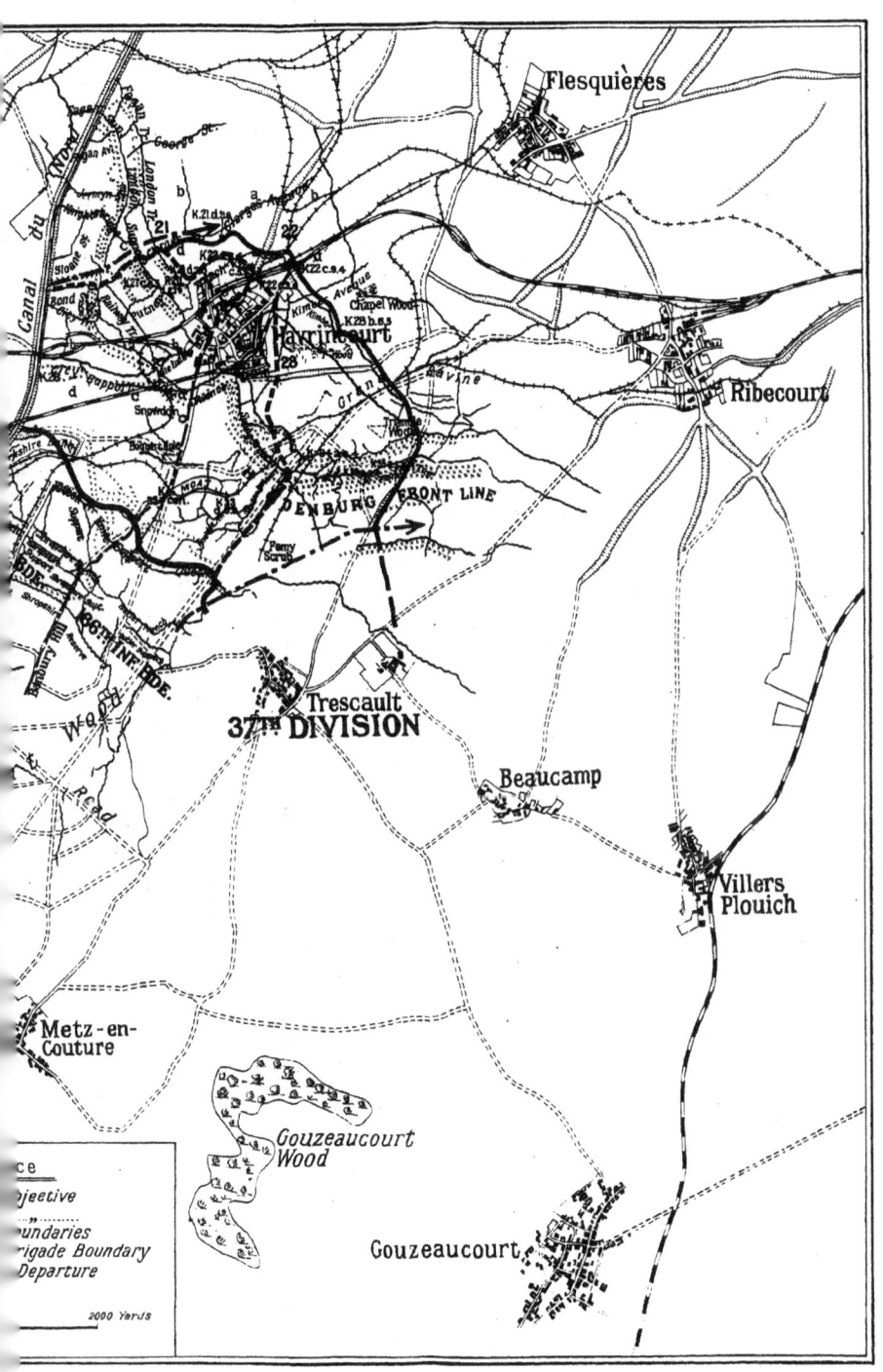

Chapter IV. 1918.

THE BATTLE OF HAVRINCOURT*
12th September, 1918

" The 62nd Division has borne a brilliant share in the operations on the Marne in July, and more recently in nine days hard fighting near Mory and Vaulx. It captured Havrincourt on the 20th November last year, and a second capture of the strong positions in the Hindenburg Line will add fresh lustre to the splendid record of the Division."

From a Divisional Order, by the G.O.C., Major-General Sir Robert Whigham, K.C.B., on 10th September, 1918.

ON the very day—8th September—on which the guns returned to the Division, the Corps Commander called at Triangle Copse, where General Whigham had his Headquarters and told the G.O.C. it had been decided that on 11th September the 62nd Division should attack and capture Havrincourt. Havrincourt village was not, according to Corps Boundaries, on the front of the VIth Corps, nevertheless the Division had the honour of being selected to carry out the attack on this strong position, which they had captured so brilliantly the previous November in the Cambrai battle, and Corps boundaries were adjusted accordingly.

8TH SEPT.

The Corps Commander thought at first that tanks would be available to assist the Division in the attack, but on the following day, September 9th, he informed the Divisional Commander that all available tanks were required for another operation and that none could be spared for the 62nd Division. A strong force of artillery had been detailed to support the attack and the operation was postponed to September 12th; the extra twenty-four hours gave the Brigades carrying out the attack an opportunity to rehearse the

---

* The title adopted in the Report of the Battles Nomenclature Committee. In the official despatches this operation is known as the Battle of Havrincourt and Epehy, 12th—18th Sept., 1918.

8TH SEPT. manœuvre, which was complicated, thus helping considerably towards the success of the operation.

The news spread quickly and soon all ranks were aware of the task allotted to them—Havrincourt—the most brilliant capture of the many captures which had fallen to the Division, re-occupied by the Germans during their great offensive and ever since held by them, was to be recaptured. In the officers' messes and tents occupied by the " other ranks," the success of the previous year was debated with fresh interest. Many there were who knew all about it; of the tense feeling throughout the Division on the night of 19th/20th November, 1917, during which the troops had formed up in grim silence, whilst the guns and tanks moved into position in Havrincourt Wood, fearful lest the sound of the wheels and the snorting of the tanks should disclose their presence to the vigilant enemy; of the absence of artillery preparation and the sudden crash at dawn on 20th as the guns belched flame and sent screaming bursts of shells into the enemy's positions; of the mad terror of the enemy as the tanks advanced and hurling their fascines on to the hostile trenches, passed over and up and down the enemy's lines, crushing into the sodden ground machine guns and their teams and those brave Germans who, with less discretion than valour tried to hold up the advance of the steel monsters; of Yorkshire Bank and Boggart's Hole and of the three huge craters, Etna, Vesuvius and Snowden, and the hard fighting which had taken place in Havrincourt Park; of how, one company of a certain battalion on the morning of the 21st November, had gone " over the top " smoking captured German cigars; of the tussle for Havrincourt itself, Graincourt and Anneux, and of Bourlon Wood, place of evil repute and much bloody fighting. Ten short months only had passed since that dim November morning and yet how changed was the 62nd! Time had laid a heavy hand on the Order of Battle of the Division; several units had ceased to exist, whilst others had joined. In *personnel*, scarcely a C.O. remained of those who commanded the gallant battalions when Havrincourt had been captured the first time. Brigadiers had left to take up higher commands and General Braithwaite was now a Corps Commander.

Many brave and true soldiers had " passed over " for the last time and had become numbered with the " Great Battalion."

The task before the Division was very different from that which had faced it in November, 1917.

In that operation the Division formed part of a large force approximately on an East and West line which was to sweep forward

in a northerly direction. A large number of tanks took part in the 8TH SEPT.
attack, which was prepared secretly and came as a complete surprise
to the enemy.

In the present operation, the capture of the Havrincourt Salient
was the first move in a general advance eastward for forcing the Canal
du Nord and Canal de St. Quentin. No tanks were available, and
the element of surprise was necessarily to a great extent, absent.

To understand the reasons for the plan of attack, a short description of the topography of the Havrincourt Salient is necessary.

Two features affected this plan very materially : (1). The Canal
du Nord on the west of Havrincourt, runs due north and south as far
as Yorkshire Bank where it makes a sharp turn to the west. In this
section the Canal runs through a deep cutting, the sides are high and
steep and there were no bridges across it. (2). The moat bounding
the southern edge of the Chateau grounds, was known from previous
experience to form a serious obstacle in the way of an attack from the
South.

Although the general direction of the attack was from west to
east, the first of these two features, the Canal, prevented the attack
from being launched in this direction, whilst the second feature, the
Chateau Moat, made it undesirable to attack the Chateau grounds
from the south. The ground available, therefore, over which the
initial stages of the attack could be launched was restricted to the
space between the western boundary of the Chateau grounds and the
Canal, a front of about 1,200 yards.

A third feature which influenced the plan of attack was Havrincourt village, which stood on commanding ground overlooking the
approaches from the south and west, and was known to contain
strongly built houses and substantial cellars.

It was very desirable to keep the village, especially the eastern
half, under artillery bombardment for as long as possible and not to
attempt to push troops through until it was outflanked by other
troops on its north and south.

After a careful reconnaissance of the ground by the Divisional
and Brigade Commanders, the following plan of attack was decided 9TH SEPT.
upon at a conference held at Divisional Headquarters on September
9th.

The attack to be carried out by two brigades, the 186th Brigade,
to which was attached the 9th Battalion Durham Light Infantry, on
the right, and 187th Brigade on the left, supported by a powerful
artillery and machine-gun barrage.

9TH SEPT.

Both Brigades were to assemble in and in rear of, the front line trenches between the north-west end of Havrincourt Wood and the Canal at Yorkshire Bank.

At zero hour, which was fixed for dawn the 187th Brigade was to advance and capture the western half of Havrincourt village and the high ground between the village and the Canal.

At the same hour the right Battalion of the 186th Brigade was to advance and clear the thickly wooded country south of Havrincourt Chateau Moat known as Femy Scrub. The remainder of the 186th Brigade was to follow behind the right flank of the 187th Brigade (protecting the right flank of that Brigade) until reaching the southern end of the village; one Battalion was then to face to the right and clear the Chateau grounds from the west, and another Battalion to capture the eastern half of the village from south-west to north-east, both battalions advancing behind a creeping barrage, which was to remain stationary on the edge of the Chateau grounds and the southern edge of the village until the hour fixed for the attack of the two battalions.

The final objective, to be captured by the reserve troops of the two Brigades, was the high ground east and north-east of Havrincourt.

On the right of the 62nd Division, the 37th Division of the IVth Corps was to advance at zero and capture the village of Trescault, whilst on the left, the 2nd Division of the VIth Corps was to secure the Canal du Nord to the north of the 62nd Divisional front during the evening of September 11th, and join hands with the left of the 62nd Division, east of the Canal as the attack progressed.

The artillery barrage to cover the operation was necessarily complicated, as the attack entailed a change of direction from north to east. It included the guns of eight Brigades of Field Artillery, reinforced with a Machine Gun Barrage of four Machine Gun Companies.

Three groups of heavy artillery also supported the attack and were used to deepen the Field Artillery Barrage, to bombard Havrincourt village and certain other selected points, beside the guns detailed for counter battery work.

One company of the Machine Gun Battalion was allotted to each attacking Brigade, the remaining two companies and two Companies sent by the 2nd and Guards Divisions being used to put down a barrage in front of the Field Artillery barrage, from the northern edge of Havrincourt Wood and from positions west of the Canal respectively.

It was decided to move the Division on September 10th and to concentrate as far forward as possible so as to enable officers to reconnoitre the positions of assembly and the roads to them, and finally to move into the assembly positions during the night of September 11th/12th.

9TH SEPT.

Very careful traffic control arrangements had to be made as both attacking Brigades, the 62nd Battalion Machine Gun Company and four Brigades of Field Artillery, besides troops of the IVth Corps, had all to pass through Bertincourt.

Such was the plan of attack decided upon at Divisional Headquarters, after which detailed instructions were issued by Brigadier Generals to all units of their Brigades.

The 186th Brigade, the right of the attack, had to advance over very difficult country, and in order to avoid the moat of the Chateau grounds, it was necessary (as already explained), for the bulk of the attacking troops of this Brigade to follow, at first, the advance of the 187th Brigade and then turn to the right and attack from west to east.

The 186th Brigade was to dispose its battalions in line thus: the 5th Duke of Wellington's (less two companies) on the right; 2/4th Duke of Wellington's in the centre and the 2/4th Hants. (less one company) on the left. The 5th Duke's were to attack at zero hour under a creeping barrage moving from south to north, the 2/4th Duke's were to wait until zero plus 55 minutes, before attacking the Hindenburg Line and Chateau Grounds, under a barrage running from west to east; the attack of the 2/4th Hants. was timed to begin at zero plus 90 minutes, at which hour the Battalion was to attack Havrincourt village, the standing barrage lifting off the village in three sections from south-west to north-east at intervals of a quarter of an hour as the advance proceeded. The attack on the final objective was to be carried out by the 9th Durham Light Infantry on the right and one Company 2/4th Hants. on the left, the Durhams passing through the 5th and 2/4th Duke of Wellington's, and the Reserve Company 2/4th Hants. Regt., through its own leading companies.

The attack of the 187th Infantry Brigade was more straightforward; one Battalion (5th K.O.Y.L.I.) plus one Company of 2/4th K.O.Y.L.I. was to attack on the right and capture the high ground west of Havrincourt village and the western half of the village itself. On the left the 2/4th York and Lancs. (Hallamshires) were to advance in a northerly direction east of the Canal and secure the enemy's trenches in K.26 b and d; the 2/4th K.O.Y.L.I. (less one company) was to be in Brigade Reserve and if the attack progressed satisfactorily, pass through and in conjunction with the 5th K.O.Y.L.I. capture the final objective.

Thus, it will be seen that not only was the attack of the 186th Infantry Brigade entirely dependent on the measure of success gained by the 187th Infantry Brigade, but during the advance the right flank of the latter Brigade was exposed to flanking fire from the Chateau grounds. This was guarded against by a standing artillery barrage on the western edge of the Chateau grounds and, as the Brigade gradually advanced, by flank protection afforded by the 186th Brigade. The distance between the western edge of the Chateau grounds and the Yorkshire Bank Spoil Heap was only about 700 yards and formed a " bottle-neck " through which the attacking troops had to pass. To reduce congestion and avoid confusion very careful timing was therefore necessary.

D Company of the 62nd M.G.C., which had been allotted to accompany the 186th Infantry Brigade, was to be disposed as follows : two sections were to follow the attack of 2/4th Duke of Wellington's Regt., one section covering the front of that Battalion during consolidation and one section on its flank. As the 2/4th Hants. (on the left of the 2/4th Duke's) advanced through Havrincourt, the latter section was to swing round to cover consolidation of the village. A proportion of the guns of these two sections was to be pushed forward after the capture of the second objective in order to cover consolidation. A third section was to follow the advance of the 9th Durham Light Infantry to cover consolidation of that Battalion ; the fourth section was to be held in Brigade Reserve.

A Company of the M.G. Battalion was detailed to assist the 187th Infantry Brigade.

It is not possible to give details of the artillery barrage, but the Divisional narrative states : " The artillery barrage to cover the operations was complicated. This could not be avoided as the plan of attack entailed a change of direction from north to east ; there was, however, sufficient time to work out the barrage with great exactitude. The plan of attack was adopted as the best means of circumventing the obstacle of the Moat and the Chateau and of utilizing the ground available for forming up the assaulting troops."

The C.R.A., 62nd Division had under his command for this

attack no lesss than twenty-four 18-pounder Batteries and eight 4.5 Howitzer batteries.¹

On the 10th September, before the battle, General Whigham issued a special Order of the Day to his troops :

10TH SEPT.

" The 62nd (West Riding) Division has been called on to make a big effort to capture the high ground on which the village of Havrincourt stands.

" The early capture of this important tactical feature is regarded as essential to the success of larger operations in the near future. Every day given to the enemy to strengthen his positions there is a day gained for him.

" There are no Tanks available for this attack on Havrincourt, which will be carried under intense bombardment.

" The 62nd Division has borne a brilliant share in the operations on the Marne in July, and more recently in nine days' hard fighting round Mory and Vaulx. It captured Havrincourt on the 20th November last year, and a second capture of this strong position in the Hindenburg Line will add fresh lustre to the splendid records of the Division.

R. Whigham, Major-General."

The importance of this operation is described in the official despatches : "From the neighbourhood of Havrincourt, southwards, the enemy's main line of resistance was the well-known Hindenburg Line which, passing through the village, ran south-east across the Beauchamp, La Vacquèrle and Bonavis Ridges to the Scheldt Canal at Bantouzelle, whence it followed the line of the Canal to St. Quentin. In front of this trench system strong German forces held formidable positions about Havrincourt and Epehy, *which had to be taken before a final attack on the Hindenburg Line could be undertaken.*"

It has already been stated that on the night of 11th September, the 2nd Division (on the left of the 62nd Division) was to carry out a preliminary attack and secure crossings over the Canal du Nord, from which on the morning of the 12th it could advance and bomb down London Trench and London Support in order to gain touch with the West Riding Division, north-west of Havrincourt village.

During the afternoon of 10th September, the 62nd Division began to move forward from the VI Corps Support area. The

¹ Right Group : Lieut.-Col. Mair, 40th and 42nd Brigades, R.F.A. and 93rd (Heavy) Brigade, R.F.A. ; left group : Lieut.-Col. Sherlock, 310th and 312th Brigades, R.F.A. and 7th (Heavy) Brigade, R.F.A. ; No. 3 group : Major Bernerslee, 5th and 232nd (Heavy) Brigade, R.F.A.

10TH SEPT.	186th Infantry Brigade, marching via Gommecourt, Ribecourt, Bancourt, Haplincourt and Bertincourt, reached the south-west corner of Havrincourt Wood before midnight, where they were joined by the 9th D.L.I. (Pioneers). The 187th Infantry Brigade, moved forward via Favreuil, Beugnatre, Frémicourt and Laboucquière to Vélu Wood, where the Brigade was to concentrate. The 185th Infantry Brigade (the Reserve Brigade of the Division) from Sapignies and Behagnies moved up to hutments east of Frémicourt.
11TH SEPT.	From early morning until dusk of the 11th September was spent in making careful reconnaissance of assembly positions, in taping routes and in laying out cable communications, but as the dark hours
11TH/12TH SEPT.	of the night of 11th/12th crept on, units of the two attacking Brigades with their attached troops began to move forward to their assembly positions.

To deal with Brigadier-General J. G. Burnett's Brigade (186th) first : B and D Companies of the 5th Duke of Wellington's Regt. (Lieut.-Col. J. Walker) relieved a Company of the 8th Somerset Light Infantry (37th Division) in the front line about Queer Street, Butler Trench and Butler Support. A and C Companies were located in Havrincourt Wood, about 2,000 yards in rear of the front line, *i.e.*, Queer Street. The forming-up operations were successfully accomplished by 11 p.m. with only one casualty.

The 2/4th Duke of Wellington's Regt. (Lieut.-Col. P. P. Wilson) moved up to assembly positions in the vicinity of Shropshire Trench and Shropshire Reserve. The 2/4th Hants. (Lieut.-Colonel F. Brook) did not move forward until 1 a.m. on the 12th, but by 3 a.m. the Battalion lay between Banbury Hill and Hubert Avenue, formed up on a three-company front, A on the right, C in the centre and D on the left. B Company in support. Each Company was drawn up on a one-platoon front.

Brigadier-General A. J. Reddie's Brigade (187th) moved forward to its assembly positions without a hitch. The 5th K.O.Y.L.I. (Lieut.-Colonel F. H. Peter) set out from Vélu Wood at 7.30 p.m. All four Companies (C on the right, B on the left, D in rear of C, and A in rear of B) were located in Shropshire Trench and Shropshire Support.

The Hallamshires (2/4th York and Lancs. Regt.) under Lieut.-Colonel L. H. P. Hart, left Vélu Wood half-an-hour after the 5th K.O.Y.L.I. and marching along the bank of the Canal du Nord to Cheetham Switch, were in position by 1 a.m. The 2/4th K.O.Y.L.I. (Lieut.-Colonel C. A. Chaytor), greatly assisted by the well-picqueted roads and carefully taped tracks, successfully formed up two companies in Cheetham Reserve and the other two companies partly in Shropshire Reserve and partly in Hubert Avenue.

11TH/12TH SEPT.

The 9th D.L.I. (Pioneers), commanded by Lieut.-Colonel E. Crouch, who had been accommodated in Nissen Huts just west of Bertincourt, paraded at 4 a.m. and marched to their assembly position, about 1,300 yards south-west of Cheetham Reserve.

The 310th (Major C. A. Eeles) and 312th (Major F. A. Arnold Forster) Brigades, R.F.A. occupied gun positions west of High Wood. Headquarters of the 312th were in the same dug-outs as the Brigade had occupied during the Battle of Cambrai, 1917, whilst the gun positions of both Brigades were a little to the left of those occupied during the first attack on Havrincourt. " I had hoped," said Brigadier-General A. T. Anderson, the C.R.A. " that our gunners would have a rest after their fine work with the 38th Division, but it was not to be, for on the day of their arrival we received orders to be prepared to attack and capture Havrincourt, the scene of our former triumph, in a few days. The Brigades and D.A.C. accordingly moved on the 9th to the area round Beugny, and the work of reconnoitring positions for the coming battle began at once."

Thus the stage was set for the second attack on Havrincourt. No Tanks were available to assist the Infantry, and yet the defences of the village and the area surrounding it were not less powerful than in 1917. By 3 a.m. on the morning of the 12th, both attacking Brigades were reported in position and command of the front passed to General Whigham. Everything had gone without a hitch, reflecting great credit upon the Staff responsible for the forming-up operations.

12TH SEPT.

One hour before Zero, the outpost troops of the 37th Division, who were holding the line Queer Street and Kitten Trenches, were withdrawn. Just prior to Zero hour the enemy opened a counter-preparation bombardment and inflicted a number of casualties on the assembled troops, but not sufficient to cause any real disorganization. At 5-25 a.m. (Zero hour) all 18-pounder Batteries of the Left Group and five 18-pounder Batteries of the Right Group opened fire on the front line of the creeping barrage.[1] Under this barrage the infantry attack was launched.

[1] From K.34.c.1.1. to K.32.b.4.0 and K.37.c.0.0. to K.26 d.0.5. The gun positions of Artillery Brigades other than those of the 62nd Divisional Artillery are not given in the official diaries.

12TH SEPT. Within a very few minutes, the enemy's barrage fell heavily upon the line of Butler's Trench, and although the leading ranks of D and B Companies of the 5th Duke's went forward quickly, the rear ranks suffered somewhat heavily. The ground over which the advance was going forward was covered by a thick scrub, which impeded progress, and direction was difficult to maintain. Nevertheless, D Company, in spite of heavy machine-gun fire, gained the line of its first objective and the trench between Shropshire Spur Road and Knuckle Trench. The Company then began bombing its way down Kangaroo Avenue. Half-way along this trench a machine gun and eight prisoners were captured. On reaching Swing Trench several hostile bombing squads were encountered and driven eastwards towards the Femy Line, whilst a number of the enemy were seen retiring up the valley towards Havrincourt, where they were captured by the 2/4th Duke's. On reaching the point K.34 a.9.4 a block was formed in the trench and a post established, a similar post was made about thirty yards down Kin Lane, and more posts along the Shropshire Spur Road. Meanwhile B Company on the left of D had also reached its objective (K.33 central to K.33 d. 9.9.), obtaining touch on both flanks.

Thus the right assaulting Battalion of the 186th Infantry Brigade had reached the line of its first objective without serious loss and was consolidating its gains.

The 187th Infantry Brigade, the left of the attack, had suffered from the enemy's counter-preparation bombardment, troops of the 2/4th K.O.Y.L.I. assembled in Cheetham Reserve, having thirty casualties in one Company before Zero hour. But punctually at 5-30 a.m. (Zero hour for the Battalion being Zero plus 5) the 5th K.O.Y.L.I. on the right, advanced, keeping close on the heels of the creeping barrage. Colonel Peter had, with great care, organized the attack to be carried out by his Battalion. Each Company had a specified and clear objective: to C Company (Capt. T. A. M. Oliphant) on the right of the two leading Companies, had been allotted the task of clearing and consolidating the triangle in the south-west corner of the village formed by Knat Avenue and Mile End Road; B Company (Lieut. E. S. French, who was killed during the advance) was ordered to capture Putney Avenue from K.21 d. 3. 0 to K.22. c.2.2, with instructions to push on to the Trench from K.22. c.0. 4. to K.22. c. 9.4. (railway) inclusive. B Company's position between K.21. d. 3. 0 and K.22. c. 0. 4 was to be occupied by a Company of the 2/4th K.O.Y.L.I. (Lieut. Swanson), then

SERGT. L. CALVERT, V.C., M.M., 5th BN. K.O.Y.L.I.

Face p. 49.

moving up in close support. D Company (Lieut. C. H. Wilson) marched in rear of C Company and was allotted the quadrangle in the village formed by Railway Trench, Mile End Road and a line drawn across the village square north-west to where London Trench cuts the railway ; A Company (Capt. W. Crow) moving in rear of B Company, was to make good the triangle formed by the railway (through K.27 b. and K.27. a) and the main (north and south) road through the Village and a line drawn across the Village Square, northwest to where London Trench cuts the railway. B Company's orders were very explicit. The Company Commander was ordered to push on whatever happened, so that if C Company experienced any difficulty, the fact of B coming round its flanks might assist considerably, and finally D Company was ordered to " go through " C Company, if possible, but if that was impracticable, to push round C's left flank ; A in the meanwhile was ordered to keep on the move and follow B closely.

" For the purpose of this narrative " (states the Diary of the 5th K.O.Y.L.I.), " four objectives must be considered : of C (No. 1), D (No. 2), A (No. 3) and B (No. 4) Companies, and in that order."

The first three of these objectives were taken without great loss, but the credit was due almost entirely to the great gallantry of an N.C.O. of C Company—Sergeant L. Calvert. In the line of advance lay Boggart's Hole, even more strongly defended than in 1917. Heavy machine-gun fire was coming from this stronghold, catching the advancing troops not only in front but in enfilade also. Nothing daunted, Calvert, single-handed, rushed the machine guns mounted in the Hole, bayonetting three and shooting four of the team of Germans. This feat so dumbfounded the enemy that the whole crew was captured without further resistance, four officers and eighty other ranks, besides machine guns and six trench mortars, being taken. For this fine deed Sergeant Calvert was awarded the Victoria Cross,[1] the second gained by the 5th K.O.Y.L.I.

The capture of the first objective by B Company was not attained without considerable loss and some delay. Early in the advance B Company lost all its officers and became somewhat disorganized, but Captain Crow (A Company) with splendid initiative, realizing that something serious had happened, after taking his own objective, pushed on and made good also the objective allotted to B. All four objectives were thus reported taken, with under 100 casualties.

[1] London Gazette. See Appendix.

12TH SEPT. On the right of the 5th K.O.Y.L.I. two Platoons of the 2/4th Duke of Wellington's Regt. (186th Brigade) had moved forward at Zero in touch with the right flank of the former Battalion, successfully covering its advance by forming a defensive flank along the western edge of the Chateau Grounds.

The way was now clear for the advance of the centre Battalion of the 186th Infantry Brigade, *i.e.*, the 2/4th Duke of Wellington's Regt. (less two platoons), which at Zero plus 10, following behind the 5th K.O.Y.L.I., pushed on steadily, advancing in shallow columns, and reached a point 200 yards north of the Crater Snowden, the time being Zero plus 60, *i.e.*, 6-25 a.m. The right flank of the Battalion was protected by posts which had taken up positions during the advance of the 5th K.O.Y.L.I. In this position by turning to the right the Battalion was brought into fighting position, two companies in the front line (D on the right, C on the left) and two in support (B on the right, A on the left), each on a two-platoon frontage. This difficult movement made (be it remembered) in actual battle was most successfully carried out and the attack on the Chateau Grounds from the west was begun. The barrage in this area had changed at Zero plus 55, and pivoting on the south-west corner of Havrincourt Village, was advancing at the rate of 100 yards in six minutes, and in an easterly direction.

The two leading Companies of the 2/4th Duke's, following close behind the barrage attacked the line of the first objective, a line about 300 yards east of the road in the Wood south of the Chateau. Clearing the trenches as they advanced, these two Companies reached their objective, where B and A Companies, passing through C and D, pressed on towards the Hindenburg Line. But the wire and undergrowth in this part of the Wood impeded the advance. This obstacle combined with machine-gun fire from the front and also from the Village caused the advance to come, temporarily, to a standstill. But eventually the enemy's resistance was overcome and the final objective secured and consolidated. Five officers, 168 other ranks, four trench mortars and two machine guns had been captured by the Battalion in its advance. Meanwhile, north of the 2/4th Duke's the 2/4th Hants. appeared to have passed through the Village and were engaged in consolidating their position.

At Zero plus 20, the Hampshire men left their assembly position between Banbury Hill and Hubert Avenue, and although the enemy's barrage fell almost as the Battalion started and several casualties were suffered, the men went steadily forward until the south-west corner of Havrincourt Village was approached. Thirty prisoners had been captured in Knat Avenue, but heavy machine-gun fire was opened on the Hampshires from the direction of the Village Square. The Battalion now swung to the right and at Zero plus 70 (6-35 a.m.) was formed up south-west of the Village waiting for the barrage to lift. A Company was on the right, C in the centre, and D on the left, the three Companies being disposed on a one-platoon frontage, two platoons to take the first half of the Village, the remaining two platoons passing through to the eastern edge ; B Company was in support.

Owing to the bombardment by the heavy artillery the attack could not begin until about Zero plus 110, and at Zero plus 120, when the assaulting troops had gone forward, heavy howitzer shells were still falling in the Village Square causing many casualties to the left Company (D). With very little opposition, A Company captured Havrincourt Chateau, but heavy machine-gun fire was opened on the men as they pressed on towards the eastern exits of the Village. These guns were, however, successfully dealt with, one officer and twelve other ranks, with the machine gun being taken and another officer and several other ranks killed. The O.C. Company, shortly afterwards received information that two hostile machine guns were holding up the attack of the 2/4th Duke of Wellington's Regt. (on the right of the Hampshires). He immediately detailed one Platoon to engage these guns. This Platoon, with commendable gallantry, succeeded in killing or capturing the crews of both guns, and the 2/4th Duke's were able to continue their advance.

Presumably the Divisional barrage was still falling when the above actions took place, for on this point the Battalion Diary of the 2/4th Hants. contains the following record : " On the barrage lifting, A, C and D Companies went forward through the Village, clearing cellars and dug-outs and taking a number of prisoners."

Near the Church, C Company (in the centre) met with considerable opposition, and before reaching its objective had some hard fighting. On the left, D Company's advance was also temporarily held up by two machine guns, but these guns were also engaged and their crews either killed or captured.

The general situation along the front of the 2/4th Hants. was then, as follows : D Company held positions about K.22 c. 3.1 (just north of the Village), C and A Companies carried the line southwards, C covering the south-east corner of the Village. Touch on the left with the 5th K.O.Y.L.I. (187th Infantry Brigade) had been obtained.

Thus everywhere along the front of the Brigade the 186th had reached the line of its first objectives.

Meanwhile the attack of the left Battalion of the 187th infantry Brigade, the Hallamshires (2/4th York and Lancs.) had progressed splendidly. The advance of the right Battalion (5th K.O.Y.L.I.) has already been described, Colonel Peter's Battalion having reached the line of its first objective.

The objective given to the Hallamshires was the line Bond Street (from the junction with the Canal du Nord) and K.27 a. o. 9. and K.21. c. 8.5, thence down London Trench to K.21 d. 2.1. A and C Companies formed the first and second waves, B and D the third and fourth waves, the latter Companies each supplying one platoon as to clear up the trenches behind A and C Companies.

The Battalion Diary merely states that " The attack was successful and all objectives were gained by 7-30 a.m. Communication was difficult but was maintained by visual to an advanced visual post." It is a pity that full details of the Hallamshires attack are not given, for though the task set the 187th Brigade did not entail such a complicated manœuvre as that allotted to the right Brigade, its attack was made against a naturally formidable and strongly held position over an intricate trench system.

Touch between the Hallamshires and troops of the 2nd Division in London Trench was reported at 9 a.m., the left Company of the former having cleared London Trench and London Support as far north as Knight's Bridge; the right Company of the Hallamshires had similarly obtained touch on the right with the 5th K.O.Y.L.I.

The time had now arrived for the advance to the second objective and for this operation, the right attack was to be carried out by the 9th Durham Light Infantry (on the right) and one Company of the 2/4th Hants. Regt. (on the left). The Pioneers were to pass through the 5th and 2/4th Battalions, Duke of Wellington's Regt., and the Company of Hampshires through the three Companies of the Battalion advancing on the line of the first objective.

On the 187th Brigade front the assault on the second objective was to be carried out by the Battalion in Brigade Support (less one Company), *i.e.*, 2/4th K.O.Y.L.I., in conjunction with the 5th K.O.Y.L.I.

At Zero plus 60, the 9th Durham Light Infantry (Pioneers) left their assembly positions west of Cheetham Reserve and advanced to the line of the first objective from which their attack was to be made, *i.e.*, through the 5th and 2/4th Duke of Wellington's Regt. This advance, over most difficult ground, was of a very trying nature. The right Company (A) meeting with numerous obstacles, natural and artificial, having to traverse trenches, ditches, old wire and barbed-wire entanglements, and when at last the forming up line was reached, both leading Platoon Commanders had become casualties. The difficult country over which the Company had to pass had delayed the advance considerably, and the platoons had not reached their jumping-off point when the barrage moved forward at Zero plus 160. It was not surprising, therefore, that after advancing about 200 yards beyond the line of the Shropshire Spur Road, A Company was held up by the Hindenburg Main Line and unable to make further progress.

12TH SEPT.

The left Company C, however, reached its starting point up to time, and was able to advance covered by the barrage to the final objective, capturing *en route*, in the Sunken Road, sixty prisoners and ten machine guns. The leading platoon of the Company, in spite of considerable machine-gun fire, maintained by the enemy though the Divisional barrage was falling heavily upon his trenches, pushed on and occupied Kimber Support Trench.

Hardly had the two platoons of C Company occupied the latter trench, when from the direction of " T " Wood and Triangle Wood, the enemy attacked in force. With splendid tenacity, the Durhams, though greatly weakened (the two platoons now numbered only sixteen men), beat off the attack with heavy loss to the enemy. But it was evident that with so small a number of men it would be impossible to withstand another heavy attack. This, in point of fact, came shortly afterwards; the enemy again attacked heavily and the survivors of the two platoons of Durhams, were forced to withdraw down the Ravine.[1]

B Company of the 2/4th Hants. should also have " gone through" the three front Companies of this Battalion and attacked the final objective. But unfortunately during the preliminary advance the Company had lost heavily and consequently was unable to reach the " jumping-off " line before the barrage crept eastwards, thus losing the advantage of cover afforded by the guns. The attack of B Company was, therefore, held up and all that could be done was to reinforce the two Companies advancing to the railway cutting and the eastern edge of the village.

Reference to the action of the 2/4th K.O.Y.L.I. has been delayed because two objectives were allotted to this Battalion : the relief of

[1] The Grand Ravine apparently.

the 5th K.O.Y.L.I. in Putney Trench (the first objective) after the latter had been taken, and the capture of Clarges Avenue (the final objective), as soon as an opportunity arose, but which depended on the progress of the attack.

As already stated, two Companies of the 2/4th K.O.Y.L.I. had assembled in Cheetham Reserve and the remaining two Companies in Shropshire Reserve and Hubert Avenue. This area was very congested with troops and just before Zero, the enemy's shell fell heavily, causing a number of casualties. At Zero, however, C Company moved forward in support of the left rear Company of the 5th K.O.Y.L.I., with the object of taking over Putney Trench when captured by the latter Battalion. A Company then moved up the Cheetham Switch and B Company into Shropshire Trench. D Company, less one platoon which had been detailed as a carrying party to the machine-gunners, was left in reserve in Cheetham Reserve.

Advancing in four waves at intervals of about 100 yards, C Company reached City Support Trench at about 6-15 a.m. Here a short halt was called in order to reorganize. Little opposition had been met with and the enemy's barrage caused no inconvenience. At 6-30 a.m. an advance was made to Putney Trench and most of it was occupied by 6-45 a.m.; the 5th K.O.Y.L.I. being already in part occupation.

At this stage as it was apparent that little opposition was being met with, A Company was ordered to move forward as soon as possible. This Company, when assembled in Cheetham Reserve, had been subjected to heavy shell fire just before Zero and had sustained a number of casualties including an officer, but on receipt of orders went forward *via* Railway Trench to London Support, which was rapidly cleared, and thence on to London Trench. Here one platoon, which had earlier lost direction by going too far to the left, after losing its Commander and platoon sergeant, killed, now rejoined the Company. A. Company now established touch with A Company of the 5th K.O.Y.L.I. in Putney Trench, and with 2nd Lieut. Champion (of C Company) who with some of his men was holding London Trench and Clarges Avenue as far as the road in K.21. d., with a party of men from all three Battalions (5th and 2/4th K.O.Y.L.I. and 2/4th York and Lancs.) of the Brigade, which he had collected and reorganized.

Captain Spencer, commanding A Company, then reconnoitred the first objective allotted to him *viz.*: from a point where the road

ARTILLERY CROSSING THE CANAL DU NORD, SEPTEMBER, 1918.

in K. 21. d. cuts Clarges Avenue to K.21. d. 9.9., and thence to K.22. c. 5.5. He decided that, although his casualties had been heavy, he could hold the line and moving his Company forward he formed a series of posts on the objective. It was impossible, however, to consolidate the ground between K.21. d. 9.9. and K.27. c. 5.5. in daylight, for hostile machine guns and snipers kept the intervening space under a heavy fire. Before this move took place the enemy made several attempts to bomb down Clarges Avenue and some stiff fighting ensued. One hostile bombing party was led by a German officer, but the latter was killed and the bombers driven back. Every attempt made by the enemy shared a similar fate.

At this period, about noon, the situation (so far as can be gathered from the Divisonal Diaries) was roughly as follows : the right Brigade (186th) had established itself firmly along the line of the first objective, but had failed to secure the ultimate objective (Kimber Trench). It was then decided not to renew the attack on this Trench until the following day. The left Brigade (187th) was reported to be " definitely on the final objective." Havrincourt Village had been cleared of the enemy and the inner flanks of both Brigades were in touch at the north-east corner (about the railway and light railway) of the village. As soon as information reached Divisional Headquarters of the capture of the first objectives a Supply Tank, carrying two trench mortars and ammunition as well as a large supply of S.A.A., Lewis gun drums and bombs was sent forward to Boggart's Hole. This was the first occasion on which Supply Tanks were used by the Division. Those who remembered the enormous difficulties and delays in getting forward supplies during the previous battle of Havrincourt in November, 1917, were much impressed by the simplicity and ease with which supplies were passed forward in these Tanks right up into the fighting zone. The Boggart's Hole dump proved of great value. The trench mortars were moved up to that section of the Hindenburg Line occupied by the 2/4th Duke of Wellington's Regt., and came into action, engaging hostile machine-gun positions most successfully.

At 3-30 p.m. the situation of the 187th Infantry Brigade was more clearly defined : " 5th K.O.Y.L.I. holding a trench line and dug in from K.22. c. 9.3 in touch on the right with the 186th Infantry Brigade, thence along Kimber Trench to its junction with Putney Trench at K.22 c. o. 4., with supporting troops in Putney Trench in touch with the 186th Brigade at its junction with the railway at K.22. c. 3.2.

E

12TH SEPT. "2/4th K.O.Y.L.I. in touch with 5th K.O.Y.L.I. at K.22. c 4.5 and dug in, in shell hole positions to Clarges Avenue at K.21. d. 9.9., thence Clarges Avenue to junction with London Trench, in touch with troops of the 2nd Division in London Trench and London Support.

"Forward Battalions consolidating in depth.

"The 2/4th York and Lancaster Regt. (Hallamshires) being gradually withdrawn to London Support, Railway Trench and City Trench."

During the afternoon, the Divisional Commander visited 186th Brigade Headquarters and, after consulting with Brig.-Gen. Burnett, decided to reduce the front of the 186th Infantry Brigade, which was unduly extended, and at 5-20 p.m. orders were sent to the G.O.C. 187th Infantry Brigade to take over the whole of the village of Havrincourt, relieving the 186th Infantry Brigade as far south as the Flesquieres Road. Two Companies of the Reserve Brigade (185th Infantry Brigade) were placed at the disposal of the G.O.C. 187th Infantry Brigade in close support.

On receipt of these orders General Reddie proceeded personally to Battalion Headquarters of the 5th K.O.Y.L.I., and explained the situation of the 186th Infantry Brigade as far as was known. The 5th K.O.Y.L.I. had been detailed to side-step and take over the line held by the 2/4th Hants. Regt.—the left Battalion of the 186th Infantry Brigade.

The difficulties of the relief might have been overcome aided by semi-darkness, for night was falling. But just before 7 p.m. the enemy opened a violent bombardment of Havrincourt Village. His aeroplanes, flying low, bombed and machine-gunned the Divisional front line, whilst from his trenches heavy machine-gun and rifle fire swept the front of the 186th Infantry Brigade and the right line of the 187th. The bombardment was followed immediately by a heavy and determined counter-attack from the direction of "T" Wood and the Chapel, against the eastern exits of the village. Two fresh German battalions, belonging to the 20th Division,[1] had been brought up with the intention of recapturing Havrincourt Village, but as they advanced the 2/4th Hants. and the 5th K.O.Y.L.I. swept their ranks with a murderous rifle, Lewis gun and machine-gun fire. However, at 7.3 p.m. the S.O.S. was sent up, and a heavy and accurate barrage

[1] The 20th had always been a good fighting Division and was one of the original Divisions of the Xth Army Corps of the Second German Army, von Bülow's, of 1914.

was placed by the Divisional Artillery on the advancing enemy. The result was that the attack was broken up and although a few gallant Germans succeeded in penetrating the eastern defences of the village, they were either killed, wounded or taken prisoner, or promptly ejected.

12TH SEPT.

By the time this counter-attack had been beaten off darkness had fallen ; " the night," reports the 187th Infantry Brigade Diary, " was one of the darkest we had experienced and enemy shell and machine-gun fire increasing." Moreover, at dusk heavy rain had begun to fall and the line on the right of the 5th K.O.Y.L.I. was even more indefinite seeing that a certain measure of disorganization always existed after an attack. The relief of the 2/4th Hants. was therefore carried out by a series of fighting-patrols, one Company of the 5th K.O.Y.L.I. assisted by troops of the 2/4th York and Lancs. Regt. working down in a south-easterly direction from Putney Trench, and another Company of the 5th K.O.Y.L.I. moving due east from the vicinity of the junction of Knat Avenue and Railway Trench, along the southern Brigade boundary to join up with the Company moving down from the north-east. The latter Company of 5th K.O.Y.L.I. was then replaced by one Company of the Hallamshires (2/4th York and Lancs. Regt) from the neighbourhood of City Trench.

Two Companies of the 1/5th Devon Regt. (185th Brigade) were then moved up to City Support Trench at the disposal of the G.O.C., 187th Brigade.

During the relief the 5th K.O.Y.L.I. suffered very heavy casualties,[1] the enemy's shell-fire sweeping the village and ground over which the troops were moving to take up their new position.

By 9-30 p.m. the 5th K.O.Y.L.I. reported completion of the relief and two hours later, the 187th Brigade had successfully taken over the defence of Havrincourt Village.

" The difficulty of carrying out this relief can hardly be appreciated by anyone not actually on the spot. The time it took runners to find company officers, the condition of the ground with mud and wire and broken down houses, making it a three hours' task for a runner to reach Company Headquarters from Advanced Battalion Headquarters, a total distance of only 1,000 yards."

Thus, for the second time Havrincourt Village had been captured by the 62nd Division, and on both occasions large numbers of prisoners and war material had been taken from the enemy.

[1] The 187th Divisional Diary, from which this statement was taken, gives no figures, neither were they obtainable from the Battalion Diary.

12TH SEPT. At midnight on the 12th September,[1] the disposition of the 62nd (West Riding) Division after the complicated operations during the day and subsequent reorganization of the Divisional front at night was as follows : The right Brigade (186th) was now re-organized in depth, the left Company of the 9th Durham Light Infantry having been withdrawn from the eastern edge of the Chateau grounds to trenches in the Knuckle, the Support Company side-stepping to the right and occupying Kangaroo Alley[2] and the trench immediately east of the latter. The Pioneers were thus re-organized in depth along the right front of the Brigade Section. The 5th Duke of Wellington's remained in the position they had captured on the morning of the 12th, and on their left the 2/4th Duke's held the line as far north as the road running due east and west, along the southern exits of Havrincourt Village. This was the northern boundary of the 186th Infantry Brigade.

The 2/4th Hants. on being relieved by the 5th K O.Y.L.I. had moved down to Shropshire Trench.

Of the 187th Infantry Brigade (on the left of the 186th) the 5th K.O.Y.L.I. carried the line northwards, along the eastern extremities of Havrincourt Village to K.22. c. 4.5 where touch was maintained with the 2/4th K.O.Y.L.I., the latter " dug in," in shell hole positions to Clarges Avenue at K.21. d. 9.9., thence along Clarges Avenue to the junction with London Trench in touch with troops of the 2nd Division in London Trench and London Support. Thus the line taken by the Hallamshires (2/4th York and Lancs.) had been incorporated into the Divisional area. The Hallamshires were then formed up in depth behind the two Battalions of K.O.Y.L.I.

Throughout the day the 185th Infantry Brigade had not taken part in the operations, though the Battalions were moved forward as the line of the first objective was gained to positions of readiness. At midnight on the 12th the Brigade was disposed as follows : Two Companies of 1/5th Devons had (as already explained) been lent to the 187th Infantry Brigade and were in City Support. The two remaining companies, with the 8th West Yorks. were at Cheetham Trench, Yorkshire Bank and Shropshire Trench; the 2/20th Londoners were in the south-west corner of Havrincourt Wood.

[1] The official date of the Battle of Havrincourt as laid down in Report of the Battles Nomenclature Committee is 12th September, the close of the Battle being fixed at midnight, though it will be seen that certain attacks were reported on the 13th.

[2] Kangaroo Avenue ?

Both on the right and left flanks the 62nd Division was in touch with the 37th and 2nd Divisions respectively.

With the exception of intermittent shell fire which continued with more or less violence, the night of the 12th/13th passed without any further attacks. A patrol of the 9th Durham Light Infantry reconnoitring during the dark hours had reached " T " Wood and Kimber Trench south of it, without encountering the enemy, who appeared to have vacated both positions. On sending word back to the 2/4th Duke of Wellington's Regt., the latter sent forward a platoon soon after dawn, but by that time the enemy had returned and the platoon after suffering several casualties was forced back to its own line. The Durhams, however, were able to occupy the sunken road just east of Femy Wood, where two platoons established themselves. But the first streak of dawn had hardly started across the sky before it became evident that the enemy intended making another attempt to regain the lost village. For three hours (from 4 to 7 a.m.) very heavy artillery fire was opened on Havrincourt and the trenches west of it. Communication became impossible, the wires being cut and the village streets an impasse. Next came a violent shrapnel barrage, under cover of which the enemy again advanced with the intention of wresting from the Yorkshiremen, the village which he had twice lost, on each occasion to the 62nd Division.

12TH/13TH SEPT.

13TH SEPT.

Exactly what happened during the counter-attack is not clear, for communications being cut between forward units and Battalion, Brigade and even Divisional Headquarters it was impossible to send back reports, which otherwise would have been preserved with the Diaries. From the somewhat scanty reports available it appears certain that the enemy reached the immediate eastern outskirts of Havrincourt and pushed the line back some 200 yards inside the village. The G.O.C. 187th Brigade immediately organized a counter attack with the two Companies 1/5th Devons lent him from the 185th Brigade, and these companies succeeded by a vigorous attack in driving the enemy out of the village once more, and completely re-established the line.

The enemy, however, managed to hold on to a Machine Gun Post in the Cemetery[1] which gave considerable trouble all day until it was finally captured about 10 p.m. by a skilfully planned turning movement by Lieut. Townend with a platoon of the 5th K.O.Y.L.I. and elements of the two Companies 1/5th Devons.

---

[1] This cemetery is not shown on any map, but it appears to have been at the N.E. Corner of Havrincourt, just S. of the Railway.

13TH SEPT. The 62nd Division M. G. Corps also lent splendid support, the crews of two machine guns mounting their guns in the south-east corner of the village, inflicting heavy casualties on the enemy as he advanced. A small party of Germans approached the point in which these two crews were established. With his revolver the N.C.O. in charge of the two guns shot the leading German, and at nightfall when the body was searched, it was discovered that the dead man was a battalion commander of the 240th I.R.

After the first hostile attack at dawn the remainder of the day passed without hostile action except of a desultory nature.

At 10 a.m. the 5th Duke of Wellington's who had been ordered to capture the double trench system forming a part of the Hindenburg Front Line, east of the Battalion (approximately from Kin Lane to the connecting trench south of Triangle Copse) made a bombing attack on the two trenches, supported by Lewis guns, but without artillery assistance. A Company set out to attack the southern trench, while C Company tried to bomb down the western trench. Considerable opposition was immediately met with, but after stiff fighting A Company succeeded in forcing its way along the Femy Line and established a post, some sixty yards only from the enemy at about K.35 a. 2.4. Further than this it was impossible to go. C Company was less fortunate. The road just east of Kin Lane, which cut the northern trench, was strongly held by the enemy, and although one platoon got through (and was for a time isolated), the Company was held up just west of the road.

These two Companies held to their gains with fine tenacity, for they were in no enviable position. From the direction of " T " and Triangle Woods, the enemy's machine guns swept the Hindenburg Line. Other hostile guns firing in enfilade down the trenches just captured by the 5th Duke's made movement impossible. Moreover, the area in the neighbourhood and just east and south-east of Kin Lane was heavily shelled by the enemy's artillery, and altogether the Duke's were in a difficult position. A Company obtained touch on its right with the 9th Durham Light Infantry, who held the Sunken Road south of the Femy Line. The 37th Division on the right of the Pioneers had also gained touch with the latter.

At 2 p.m. it was decided to break off the attack down the two trenches and to consolidate the ground gained. One hostile machine gun had been captured and many Germans killed. The 5th Duke's lost two officers (one killed) and 25 other ranks.

Throughout the day considerable movement had been observed

in the enemy's lines. Small parties of Germans had begun to dribble forward and establish themselves nearer the Divisional front. The Divisional Artillery and the Lewis gunners took heavy toll of these Germans, but did not stay their advance.

At 5 p.m., after a conference with the Brigadiers, the Divisional Commander decided to attack and capture Kimber Trench, the Green Line from the Hindenburg Line at K.35. a. 5.5., Triangle Wood and Kimber Trench to the Railway, on the morning of the 14th September. The attack was to be made by the 185th Brigade, through the 186th and 187th Infantry Brigades, then holding the Divisional front line. " Zero " was to be 5-30 a.m., the troops advancing under a creeping barrage, the heavy artillery firing on selected targets ahead of the Field Artillery. The 186th Infantry Brigade was to clear the Hindenburg Line in rear of the 185th Brigade as the latter advanced.

On the capture of the objective the G.O.C. 185th Infantry Brigade was to take over the left section of the Divisional front at an hour to be arranged mutually by G.O.C.'s 185th and 187th Infantry Brigades, whilst the 186th Infantry Brigade was to relieve the attacking troops of the 185th Brigade up to the late Brigade Boundary during the day or early evening of September 14th.

Arrangements were made with the 37th Division on the right to complete the capture of Chapel Wood Switch, and with the 2nd Division to prolong the barrage on the left.

The 2/20th London Regt. was detailed for the attack. The plan was given verbally by Lieut.-Col. W. St. A. Warde-Aldam to his Company Commanders; D Company on the right was to form up just east of Kin Lane and Star Trench, two platoons of the Company advancing east along the two trenches forming the Hindenburg Front Line, and two platoons across the open to Triangle Wood and Keating's Lane; C Company in the centre, was to form up on a jumping off line on the eastern edge of Chateau Wood and capture Kimber Trench, south of B Company as far as the Grand Ravine, one platoon being specially detailed to clear " T " Wood; B Company on the left was to form up just east of Havrincourt Village and capture Kimber Trench from the left boundary (approximately the railway) to K.28. b. 6.5. (the point of junction with C Company); A Company to be in rear at the junction of Kangaroo Avenue and Swing Trench.

At the north and north-east edge of Havrincourt Village the situation, when these orders were issued, was obscure, the enemy

13TH SEPT. being still in possession of the Cemetery. At about 10 p.m., however, elements of two Companies of the 1/5th Devons, and a platoon of 5th K.O.Y.L.I. went out with the intention of clearing the enemy from this stronghold. Under 2nd Lieut. Townend the Devons, aided by the dark night, gradually worked round the Cemetery and succeeded in capturing it together with a German officer and ten other ranks. "Too much," reported the 187th Infantry Brigade Diary, "cannot be said for the determination of the Devons who succeeded in clearing this point, which undoubtedly contributed largely to the success of the advance of the 185th Infantry Brigade later in the morning."[1]

14TH SEPT. Meanwhile the Londoners at 11 p.m. had begun to move up to their "jumping-off" position, from the south-west corner of Havrincourt Wood. Three subaltern officers, one from each Company, had already reconnoitred and marked out the jumping-off places and under their guidance the men were led with great skill to their respective positions. All these attacking Companies had passed Battalion Headquarters (south of Chateau Park) by 3 a.m. It was fortunate they did so, for at 3-15 a.m. the enemy suddenly put down a heavy barrage, which increased in intensity along the two railway lines and the front line trenches.

At 5-20 a.m., the guns opened fire and immediately the 2/20th went forward, all three Companies keeping close under the barrage. The enemy's barrage which fell in No Man's Land shortly afterwards, in no way stayed the advance of the Londoners who, advancing rapidly and with great dash captured all their objectives by 6 a.m., though it was not until 8-15 a.m. when a contact aeroplane reported having seen British flares east of Triangle Wood, that the exact location of D Company became known. Several small parties of the 2/20th had gone on beyond the Green Line and had brought back prisoners. Numbers of prisoners were also taken, mostly in batches from dug-outs. Throughout the day the inevitable hostile bombardment fell on the captured trenches, the forward trenches of the Division, and all approaches, and at 2 p.m. the enemy counter-attacked, but was beaten off, an S.O.S. barrage promptly put down by the Divisional Artillery smashing up his advance. A few of the enemy reached Kimber Trench near "T" Wood, but were speedily dealt with by a bombing section of the Reserve Company of Londoners. Some slight trouble was also experienced from a party

---

[1] The report of the capture of the cemetery was not received at Brigade Headquarters until 3 a.m. on the 14th.

of Germans who had hidden themselves in a dug-out near " T " 14TH SEPT. Wood, which had been overlooked by the " clearing-up " party. A Company of the 5th Duke of Wellington's Regt. which had been detailed to clear the Hindenburg Line on the southern borders of the attack, did so without suffering a single casualty, though capturing three German officers and seventy-three other ranks and two machine guns.

No less than thirty machine guns and two trench mortars were captured by the 2/20th London Regt., and the number of prisoners totalled approximately 250. Casualties suffered by the Battalion were four officers (two killed and two died of wounds) and twenty-one other ranks killed and 114 other ranks, wounded and missing.

During the night, the 185th Infantry Brigade took over the left sub-sector of the Divisional front from the 187th Infantry Brigade, one Battalion of the latter, the 2/4th K.O.Y.L.I., remaining in the sub-sector and coming under the orders of the G.O.C. 185th Infantry Brigade. The area occupied by the right Company of 2/20th London Regt. was taken over by the 186th Infantry Brigade. " One Company of the 8th West Yorks. was placed by the G.O.C. 185th Brigade at the disposal of the O.C. 2/4th K.O.Y.L.I. and one Company of the same Battalion under the orders of the O.C. 2/20th Londoners." Two Companies of the 1/5th Devons who were in the village were withdrawn to west of the Canal du Nord. Thus the whole Divisional front was reorganized, but it was not for long, for already orders had been issued for the relief of the 62nd Division by the 3rd Division.

The 15th September was passed in comparative quietitude and 15TH SEPT. without any incident of importance. During the day a personal letter from the General Officer Commanding the Third Army (General Sir Julian Byng) was received by General Whigham, in which the former said :

" I set the 62nd Division a very hard task yesterday (12th), but the importance of it was so great that I determined to try it. The Division has done it and done it splendidly, and so I write to let you know how proud I am of their achievement."

On the night of 15th/16th, the relief was carried out, command 15TH/16TH of the section passing to the G.O.C., 3rd Division at 3-10 a.m., SEPT. 16th September. Divisional Headquarters moved back to Triangle Copse, east of Gomiécourt and the three Infantry Brigades were disposed in the Béhagnies—Sapignies area.

But as usual the hard-worked gunners remained in the line

15TH/16TH SEPT.

under the orders of the C.R.A., 3rd Division. There was no opportunity of giving them the rest and relief they so badly needed. How well they had supported their own infantry during the Battle of Havrincourt, is evident from the Diaries of the latter, the guns had never failed them.

And now, at this period, the middle of September, 1918, what was the general situation? Havrincourt had again fallen to the 62nd Division, whilst the 37th Division had captured Trescault. On the right flank of the latter the New Zealand Division had continued the advance. Away on the southern extremities of the British Line, which joined hands with the French, north of St. Quentin, the IXth and Australian Corps captured Holnon village and Wood, and Massemy on the 17th September, and were approaching Le Verguier and Templeux-le-Guérard. On the 18th the Battle of Epéhy opened, the Fourth and Third Armies attacking in a heavy rain on a front of about 17 miles from Holnon to Gouzeaucourt. The first French Army co-operating south of Holnon. Once again the British and French troops bit deeply into the enemy's positions, penetrating to a depth of three miles through the deep, continuous and well-organized defensive belt formed by the old British and German lines. Heavy fighting ensued all day, the enemy's resistance being very determined. But nothing could stay the advance of troops who had before their eyes the almost certain prize of victory. Epéhy fell, and during the succeeding days the remainder of the positions required from which to make an attack upon the main Hindenburg defences, were secured.[1]

Everywhere along the front the position of the German Army was becoming more and more desperate. The clumsy efforts of the enemy to obtain a one-sided peace had borne no fruit; the submarine campaign, terribly destructive and disturbing to the Allies as it had been, had not brought forth those overtures which the German Government had hoped would be forthcoming; the rain of bombs on London and other towns in England had alike failed to shake the British people. " Our position," said Ludendorff, " was

[1] The front line of the British Armies in France and Flanders on the morning of the 18th September, 1918, ran approximately from right to left as follows:—Holnon (the junction of the French and British Armies) west of St. Quentin—west of Epéhy and Gouzeaucourt, just east of Trescault and Havrincourt—Moeuvres—Marquion, west of Sauchy and Pailuel—Etaing—Gavrelle, through Bailleul to Lens, thence to immediately west of La Bassée—east of Givenchy—Festubert—Neuve Chapelle to Fleurbaix, thence west of Armentières in a slightly north-east direction to east and north east of Ypres, where (approximately at St. Jean) the British front line joined hands with French and Belgian troops under H.M. King Albert.

now so serious that General Headquarters could not hope that air raids on London and Paris would force the enemy to make peace. *Permission was refused for the use of a particularly effective incendiary bomb (expressly designed for attack on the two Capitals), sufficient supplies of which were ready in August. The large amount of damage that they were expected to do would no longer have affected the course of the war. Destruction for its own sake had never been permitted. Count Hertling, too, had asked General Headquarters not to use these incendiary bombs on account of the reprisals on our own towns that would follow."* Cold fear had at last gripped the Germans. Ludendorff probably knew that huge bombing planes for the purpose of flying over Berlin and other German towns were being constructed by the Allies. He knew also that once he had used those incendiary bombs, the wholesale bombing of Germany would probably have followed. He had experienced what happened when the Allies took reprisals!

15TH/16TH SEPT.

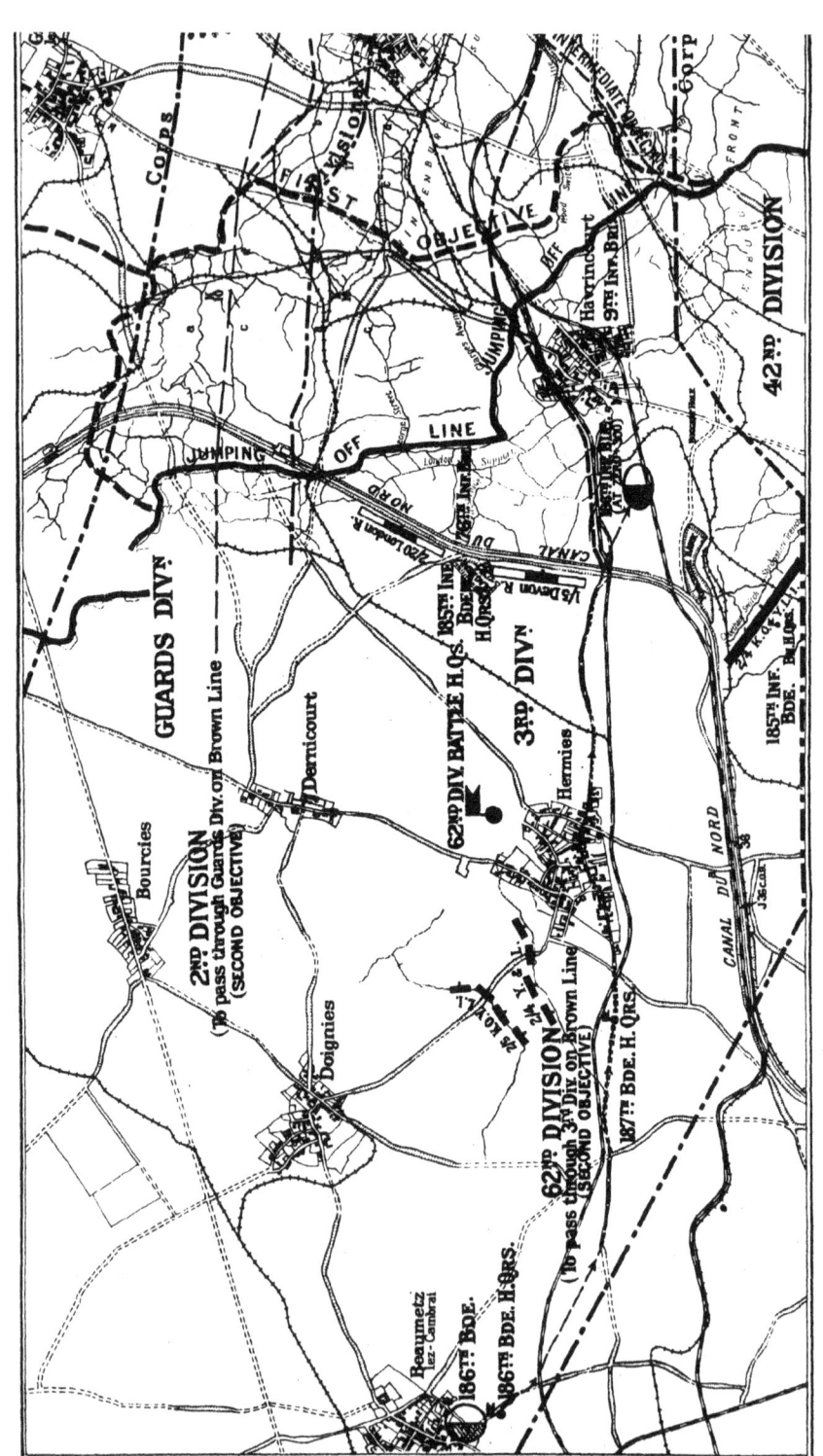

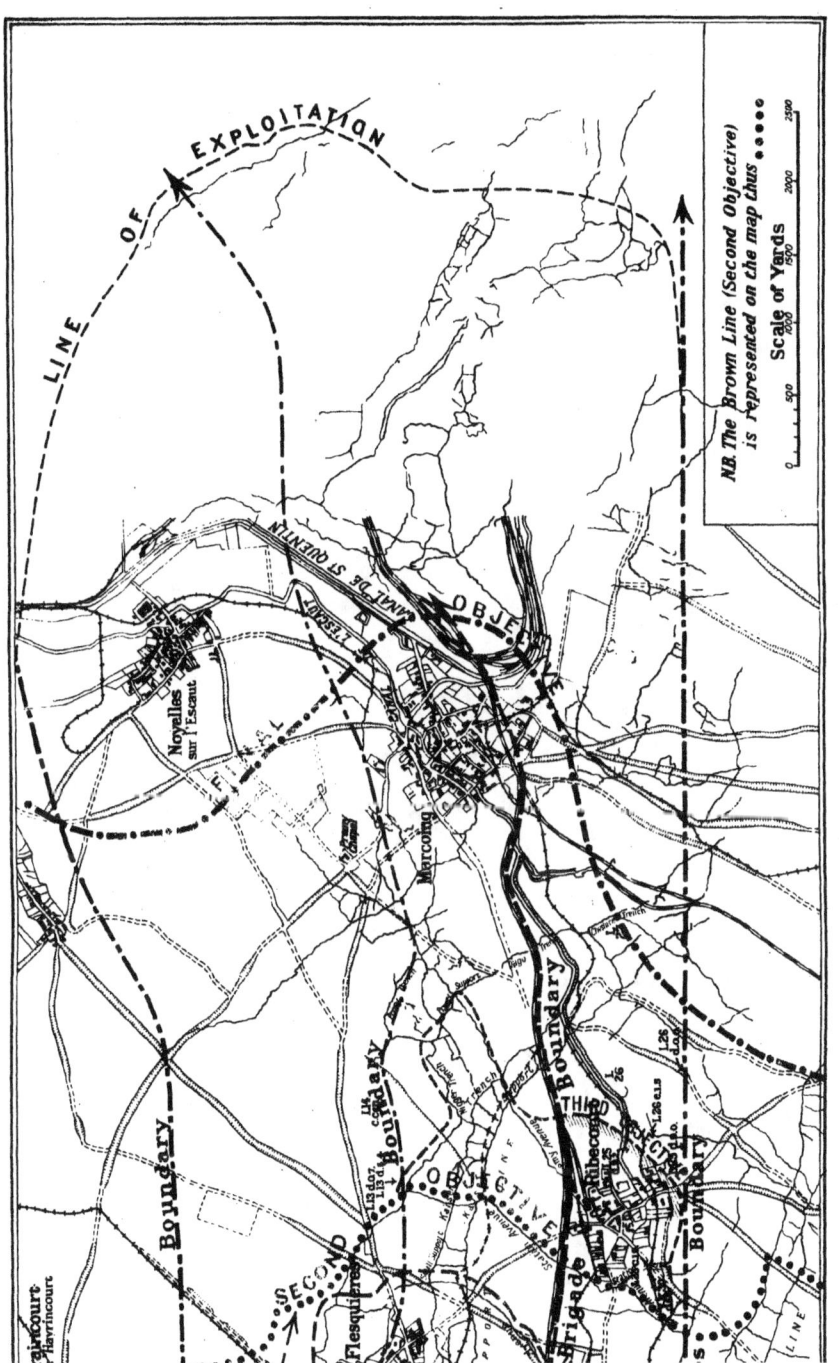

THE BATTLE OF THE CANAL DU NORD AND BREAKING OF THE HINDENBURG LINE.

Chapter V. 1918.

THE BATTLE OF THE CANAL DU NORD AND BREAKING OF THE HINDENBURG LINE
27th Sept.—1st Oct., 1918

I.—Operations of 27th September

THE Battles of Havrincourt and Epéhy closed the first stage of the British offensive. In these two battles fifteen British Divisions had defeated twenty German Divisions, the latter losing nearly 12,000 prisoners and 100 guns. These German Divisions were not inferior troops, neither were they of less strength than the British Divisions opposing them. The enemy's Orders of Battle for this period show that practically all the best fighting divisions of the German Army were massed against the First, Third and Fourth British and First French Armies and were contained in three German Armies Eighteenth (von Hutier), Second (von der Marwitz) and the Seventeenth (von Below), the Hindenburg Line on the front St. Quentin—Cambrai being literally "stiff" with hostile troops. The German front, south of the St. Quentin-Cambrai line to the Swiss frontier and north to the Belgian coast, respectively, were comparatively thinly held. The reason is obvious, the line Douai—Cambrai—St. Quentin was the most vital sector of the whole of the Battle front in France and Flanders. If this line gave way nothing could prevent the Allies advancing to the line Hirson—Maubeuge—Mons, cutting the enemy's communications south and north and inflicting on him an overwhelming defeat. Ludendorff was too good a soldier not to see this and too wise a general not to mass his best troops where the need was greatest. It is, therefore, clear, that in the operations which began on 27th September (the opening of the Battle of the Canal du Nord) the three British Armies, First, Third and Fourth and the First French Army were given the momentous task not only of breaking through that great defence system—the Hindenburg Line—but of fighting a battle fraught with the greatest of possibilities, that of a decisive action.

To the glory of the British Army it should never be forgotten that just as that small Expeditionary Force in August, 1914, stood

15TH/16TH SEPTEMBER

15TH/16TH SEPTEMBER

between Paris and the advance of overwhelming enemies, so to that Army in September, 1918, belongs the honour of dealing the enemy the hardest blow he had received throughout the war. Controversy has raged (and will probably continue to rage) about this point, but Lord Haig himself stated in his despatch : "*I am convinced that the British attack was the essential part of the general scheme.*"

And what was the general scheme?

On the same day (12th Sept.), as the Battle of Havrincourt was being fought, the First American Army, assisted by several French divisions, fought and drove the enemy from the St. Mihiel Salient. The results of these two battles determined the development of the Allied plans, whereby four convergent and simultaneous offensives were to be launched by the Allies :—

By the Americans west of the Meuse in the direction of Mezières ;

By the French west of the Argonne, in close co-operation with the American attack and with the same final objectives ;

By the British on the St. Quentin—Cambrai front, in the general direction of Maubeuge ;

By Belgian and Allied forces in Flanders, in the direction of Ghent.

By these attacks it was expected........ " that the important German forces opposite the French and Americans would be pressed back upon the difficult country of the Ardennes, while the British thrust struck on their principal lines of communication. In Flanders, it was intended to take advantage of the weakening of the German forces on this front to clear the Belgian coast by a surprise attack. Success in any one of these offensives might compel the enemy to withdraw to the line of the Meuse."[1]

But it is clearly obvious that the results obtained in the first, second and fourth offensives would depend very largely on that obtained by the third offensive, *i.e.*, by the British on the St. Quentin —Cambrai front. What also will be obvious, is the serious nature of the results if failure met the attack on the Hindenburg Line. For the British Armies had been fighting hard practically since the 8th August, " Germany's Black Day." Little rest could be given the tired troops. Compared with the number of prisoners taken from the enemy, the British losses had been small, but Sir Douglas Haig said " In the aggregate, however, they were considerable and in face of them an attack upon so formidably organized a position as that which now confronted us could not be lightly undertaken."

[1] Official Despatches.

Failure would give an enormous fillip to the moral not only of the German Army but of the German people.

15TH/16TH SEPTEMBER

The strength of the Hindenburg Line has been referred to many times, but what was of considerable importance was the use the enemy had made and would make of the Canal du Nord and the Scheldt Canal, both of which cut the line at various points, the former north of Havrincourt Wood and the latter at Banteaux, running thence along practically the whole length of the Hindenburg Line as far as St. Quentin. The Hindenburg Line with the Scheldt Canal south of Banteaux was a position of enormous strength. The Canal, so the despatches said, " does not appear to have been organized as the enemy's main line of resistance, but rather as an integral part of a deep defensive system, the outstanding characteristic of which was the skill with which it was sited so as to deny us effective artillery positions from which to attack it. The chief rôle of the Canal was that of affording cover to resting troops and to the garrisons of the main defence trench lines during a bombardment. To this end the Canal lent itself admirably and the fullest use was made by the enemy of its possibilities."

Sufficient has been said to suggest the strength of the Line facing the southern front of the British attack, *i.e.*, that front allotted to the Fourth British Army (between Holnon and Vendhuille) and that of the IV. Corps of the Third Army between Vendhuille and Marcoing. On the northern front of the Third Army the Canal du Nord had already been partly won (in the Battle of Havrincourt) by the 62nd and 2nd Divisions, the northern portion, however, had yet to be crossed.

The line occupied by the Fourth, Third and First British Armies (in the order named from right to left) when the Battle opened ran from the village of Salmez (west of St. Quentin) to Gricourt and Pontreut, thence east of Villeret and Lempire to Villers Guislan and Gouzeaucourt (both exclusive), thence northwards to Havrincourt, just north of which the line crossed the Canal du Nord, thence along the western banks of the Canal du Nord to Moeuvres and the floods of the Sensée River at Ecourt St. Quentin.

The scheme of operations adopted by the British Commander-in-Chief was for the Third and First Armies to attack the enemy on the morning of the 27th September, after a very heavy preliminary bombardment, carried out during the night 26th/27th. But the principal attack was to take place from along the front held by the Fourth Army which, after the Third and First Armies had gained

15TH/16TH SEPTEMBER

ground nearer to their final objective, would launch the main offensive on a front of 12 miles between Holnon and Vendhuille.

17TH SEPT.

On September 17th, instructions were received from the VIth Corps, that further operations were intended on the Third Army front.

The VIth Corps was to capture the Hindenburg Support Line together with the villages of Ribecourt and Flesquieres, and to establish a bridge head across the Canal de St. Quentin, east of Marcoing.

The first stage of the attack of the VIth Corps was to be carried out by the 3rd Division on the right and the Guards Division on the left. These two Divisions were to capture the first two objectives, the Red and Brown Line.

The 62nd and 2nd Divisions were to close up on the day previous to the attack and were to move forward to the assembly positions behind the 3rd and Guards Divisions respectively, so as to be in a position :—

(1) To complete the capture of the Hindenburg Support Line should the leading Divisions not succeed in doing so ;

(2) To continue the advance east of the Line when the leading Divisions came to a standstill.

After careful consideration by the G.O.C.'s 3rd and 62nd Divisions, it was decided that the best means of ensuring that the successive attacks of the two Divisions were pushed with the greatest possible vigour and of avoiding delay in the commencement of the attack of the rear Division, was to fix a definite line on which the 62nd Division should pass through the 3rd Division.

The line selected by the two Divisional Commanders was the Brown Line and the village of Ribecourt.

25TH SEPT.

On September 25th, Divisional Orders for the attack were issued, briefly they were as follows :—

1. The 187th Infantry Brigade on the right was to advance in rear of the 9th Brigade (3rd Division) and was to be prepared either,

(a) by advancing round the Northern and Southern sides of Ribecourt, pass through the 9th Brigade beyond the Eastern Edge of that village and exploit the success gained as far as the Southern portion of Masnieres (inclusive) ;

(b) or, to capture Ribecourt in the event of the 9th Brigade being unable to do so, and then to continue the advance on Masnieres.

2. The 185th Infantry Brigade on the left was to follow closely in rear of the 76th Brigade (3rd Division) and passing through that Brigade on the capture of the Brown Line west of Flesquieres, was to advance on Marcoing and secure the crossing over the Canal de St. Quentin.

3. The 186th Infantry Brigade, in Divisional Reserve, was to be assembled between Havrincourt and the Canal du Nord at zero+300 minutes in readiness to exploit success beyond Marcoing by the capture of Rumilly.

4. Of the 62nd Battalion, Machine Gun Corps, one Company was allotted to each Infantry Brigade, the remaining Company to be in Divisional Reserve.

5. The 9th Durham Light Infantry and the 457th Company R.E. were detailed to work with VIth Corps on improving the crossings over the Canal.

6. The 460th Field Coy., R.E., with pack transport only, was to follow as closely as possible, the advance of the 185th Brigade. The 461st Field Coy., R.E., with its wheel transport, was to be assembled off the road running east and west at the south-west corner of Havrincourt Village, ready to move forward on receipt of orders.

7. The advance of the Division at zero plus 270, the time at which the 62nd was to pass through the 3rd Division, was to be covered by a creeping barrage by two groups of Field Artillery Brigades: Sherlock Group (310th, 312th, 76th Brigades R.F.A.), covering 187th Infantry Brigade. Mair Group (40th, 42nd and 34th Brigades R.F.A.), covering the 185th Infantry Brigade.

The 54th Battery, R.G.A., was also affiliated to the 62nd Division.

On receipt of these orders the Brigadiers set to work to draw up their own instructions for the attack and settle the many necessary details before the operations could take place. Throughout the war there was much idle and foolish criticism of the amount of work done (or not done) by Staff officers. These criticisms were usually indulged in by those who had never had to work out the details of a big operation or make vital decisions at short notice.

The orders issued by Brigadier-Generals Reddie and Viscount Hampden to their respective Brigades, *i.e.*, 187th and 185th, and by Lieut.-Colonel J. Walker, temporarily commanding the 186th Infantry Brigade (Brig.-General Burnett being then on leave) may be summarized as follows :—

25TH SEPT. The 187th Brigade would attack on a one-battalion front, units leap-frogging on successive objectives as the advance continued; the 185th Brigade, with two battalions in the front line, the remaining battalions leap-frogging the two front battalions.

Of the 187th Brigade, the order of advance of battalions would be—2/4th K.O.Y.L.I., 2/4th York and Lancs. Regt. (Hallamshire), 5th K.O.Y.L.I.

Of the 185th Brigade the 1/5th Devons. would be on the right and the 2/20th London Regt. on the left; the 8th West Yorks. was the "leap-frogging" battalion.

One Company of the 62nd B.M.G.C. was to be attached to each attacking Brigade.

The orders issued to units of the 186th Infantry Brigade were for the Brigade to assemble west of Havrincourt and east of the Canal du Nord by zero plus 300 minutes and be prepared to exploit success beyond Marcoing by the capture of Rumily.

Zero hour was fixed for 5-20 a.m. 27th September.

All ranks were warned that the success of the operations depended upon the greatest secrecy being observed; movement in the front areas before dusk was to be confined to a minimum; no fires or light were to be shown in the assembly areas. Contact aeroplanes which would call for flares at various intervals during the attack, a counter-attack machine and machines for dropping small arms ammunition to the forward troops as required were to co-operate. Two Companies of Tanks were to move with the 3rd and Guards Divisions.

At dusk on September 25th the Division moved forward to a staging area :—

    185th Infantry Brigade Group to Beugny area.
    187th   ,,   ,,   ,,   ,, Fremicourt area.
    186th   ,,   ,,   ,,   ,, Vaulx area.

Most elaborate arrangements had to be made for the move forward from these areas to the assembly position as no bridge existed over the Canal du Nord from Yorkshire Bank northwards, and all troops moving south of the Canal had to pass through the bottle neck at Yorkshire Bank.

The following routes were allotted :—

    (*a*) 185th Infantry Brigade to cross the Canal by ladders and ramps in K.20.

    (*b*) 187th Infantry Brigade by a plank bridge at J.36 a.

Scene in the Canal du Nord: Clearing away the Debris of a Destroyed Bridge.

Face p. 72

(c) 186th Infantry Brigade and all wheeled transport to cross by bridge at P.4.a.8 8 and proceed thence *via* Matheson Road—Clayton Cross—to Yorkshire Bank.

When darkness had fallen and during the night 26th/27th, the attacking Brigades moved forward to their assembly positions.

26/27TH SEPT.

At 7-20 p.m., the 2/4th Battalion K.O.Y.L.I. set out from Fremicourt, following the route—La Bucquière, south of Hermies—Canal du Nord crossing at J.36.c.0.9 and by 1-30 a.m. was in position —A and B Companies in Shropshire Trench and C and D Companies in Cheetham Switch, Battalion Headquarters at K.32.c.2.5. The Hallamshires (2/4th York and Lancs. Regt.) following the 2/4th K.O.Y.L.I. assembled in Jargon Trench, west of Hermies, whilst the 2/5th K.O.Y.L.I. were just north in Hermies Switch. 187th Infantry Brigade Headquarters were some hundred yards south of the Hallamshires.

Similarly, at dusk, the 1/5th Devons. and 2/20th Londoners of the 185th Infantry Brigade, moved forward to positions between Hermies and the Canal du Nord and the 8th West Yorks. to south of Hermies. Brigade Headquarters were established on the Slag Heap west of the Canal.[1]

The 186th Infantry Brigade was assembled immediately east of Beaumetz.

The night of the 26th/27th was wet and the ground muddy and slippery. One of those wretched nights in fact, which, if men are prone to depression, very soon affects their spirits. But where was the British soldier in all France or Flanders who was depressed at that momentous period? Where the British officer or man, who did not know that the Germans in front of him were fighting desperately with their backs against the wall? That splendid spirit of readiness and willingness to seize every opportunity, which all along had been so integral a part of the 62nd Division, was at no time more keen than on that night in September, 1918; that spirit indeed, which was to shine so brightly during the operations of the next few days, when again and again a critical situation was saved by the quick decision of the commanders of small units, sections, platoons and battalions.

The 2/4th K.O.Y.L.I. assembled in Shropshire Trench and Cheetham Switch without any incident happening worth recording. The 185th Brigade, however, while assembling between Hermies and

[1] The Diaries do not contain precise information of the exact assembly positions of the three battalions of the 185th Infantry Brigade.

26TH/27TH SEPT.

the Canal du Nord were caught in desultory hostile shell-fire and although several casualties were suffered, the troops continued to move close up to the Canal, carrying the ladders with which to cross early next morning and making whatever final preparations were necessary.

Throughout the night the guns of all three Armies (Fourth, Third and First) poured shell on to the enemy's trenches and positions to be assaulted. The terrible effect of this bombardment was afterwards confirmed by prisoners who stated that it drove them to their dug-outs and tunnnels, and in many places completely severed communication with their supports and reserves, preventing even the ration parties from supplying them with food.

27TH SEPT.

At 5-20 a.m., on 27th September, the Third and First Armies attacked with the IVth, VIth, XVIIth and Canadian Corps in the direction of Cambrai, on a front of thirteen miles from Gouzeaucourt to the neighbourhood of Sauchy Lestrée. The vital point of attack was the Canal line immediately east and in the neighbourhood of Mœuvres, which was commanded from Bourlon Wood and the high ground about it.

With great gallantry, troops of the Naval Division, and 4th Canadian Division, stormed the Canal, debouching on the eastern bank (according to plan) south-east and north-east, forcing the enemy back in an easterly direction.

Of the IVth Corps (the right of the attack) the 5th Division took Beaucamp, the 42nd Division advancing on the left of the 5th, between that village and Ribecourt.

Of the VIth Corps, the 3rd and Guards Divisions, in the face of fierce opposition from machine-gun nests, which poured a terrific fire upon the troops as they advanced over the Canal crossings, and from forward field guns, forced their way forward though losing heavily.

General Whigham had established his Headquarters just north of Hermies, along with 3rd Divisional Headquarters, and the earliest information of progress of the attack to reach him was received at 7-15 a.m., when the 3rd Division reported the capture of the first objective with 238 prisoners.

News of progress of the attack of the 9th Infantry Brigade (3rd Division) through which the 187th Infantry Brigade was to pass when the former reached the Brown Line, was difficult to obtain, but Brigadier-General Reddie (187th Infantry Brigade) stated in his report that it " seemed to be satisfactory owing firstly to the large number of prisoners being sent down and, secondly, to the cessation of hostile artillery fire, indicating a withdrawal of the enemy's guns."

27TH SEPT.

The action of the 187th Infantry Brigade will be narrated first. The 2/4th K.O.Y.L.I. in accordance with orders moved forward at 8 a.m., following as close as possible on the heels of the reserve battalion of the 9th Infantry Brigade (the 4th Royal Fusiliers) detailed to capture Ribecourt. C Company of the K.O.Y.L.I., with D Company in support, advanced with the intention of passing south of Ribecourt, whilst A Company with B in support, set out with the idea of moving round the northern outskirts of the village. The objectives allotted to the battalions were (1) if the 4th Royal Fusiliers succeeded in capturing Ribecourt, to pass through the left of the 9th Infantry Brigade and capture the Hindenburg Support system between the southern divisional boundary and the Havrincourt—Marcoing railway (exclusive) and then to exploit success by pushing forward to the Cheshire—Dago trenches (within the same boundaries) and the spur running north-east from the latter trench towards Marcoing; (2) if the 4th Royal Fusiliers failed to take and consolidate east of Ribecourt the 2/4th York and Lancs. (Hallamshires) were to pass through and take the objective (Hindenburg Support system) allotted to the 2/4th K.O.Y.L.I.

The advance of the 2/4th K.O.Y.L.I. was made under extremely difficult circumstances. A great amount of wire had to be crossed; a number of batteries were in action along the battalion front; and Havrincourt Chateau Wood was full of obstacles. Nevertheless all went well until the battalion arrived just north of Ribecourt. Here, however, the further advance of C Company on the right was stopped by a company of the Royal Fusiliers held up in the west part of Station Avenue, whilst on the left the commanding officer of another company of Fusiliers (held up by machine-gun fire) asked the officer commanding A Company of the K.O.Y.L.I. to lend assistance in clearing the northern portion of the village.

Immediately Captain Spencer, commanding A Company, 2/4th K.O.Y.L.I., moved his Lewis gun team forward into the northern portion of Station Avenue, and very soon knocked out three German machine-gun posts. The Royal Fusiliers then moved forward.

Meanwhile, on the right, C Company had forced its way into the eastern portion of Station Avenue, and on clearing up the trench captured two officers (one a battalion commander) and about thirty men. Neither C nor D Companies had, as yet, succeeded in gaining touch on the right with the 42nd Division, but they advanced round the south of the village. From the direction of Highland Ridge very heavy machine-gun fire swept this line of advance whilst two hostile field guns firing over open sights from Kaiser Support plentifully besprinkled the ranks of the K.O.Y.L.I. with shrapnel. The two companies then took up positions, C on the road-junction at L.26 d.o.o., in the trench running north from L.26.c.1.5., D Company in support some 200 yards in rear from L.25.d.9.o. to L.25.d.9.9. Every effort to gain touch with troops on the flanks failed, until eventually a party of 4th Royal Fusiliers was found in a ravine just north of the trench running from L.26.c.1.5, and a company of the same Regiment was found consolidating in the southeast corner of Ribecourt. A little later, touch was also established with some men of the Hallamshires (2/4th York and Lancs. Regt.) who had moved forward north of the village.

A and B Companies, who as a result of moving north of Ribecourt, had lost touch with C and D Companies, had reached the line of Station Avenue. On making a reconnaissance of the area east of the village, the Officer Commanding, A Company, reported the ground swept by very heavy machine-gun fire, both from northeast and south-east, and that in his opinion any further advance would entail heavy loss. Some of the Hallamshires were, however, seen along the railway in front of the village, but the whole situation was obscure. The two Companies were, therefore, ordered to remain in Station Avenue. Patrols pushed north along Station Avenue found machine gunners and men of the King's Own Regt. and Leinster Regt. of the 3rd Division, whilst in the road running north of the village and in front of Station Avenue, more men of the Hallamshires were discovered. Another patrol was sent up Premy Avenue but the officer in charge was killed and all five men wounded by shell-fire. Subsequent patrols found Premy Avenue unoccupied and pushing on gained touch with men of the Devonshire Regt. in Kaiser Support.

The 2/4th York and Lancs. Regt. (Hallamshires), less fortunate than the 2/4th K.O.Y.L.I., had early suffered casualties from shell fire. The Battalion left Jargon Trench, west of Hermies, at 7-10 a.m. and crossing the Canal du Nord, south of the village, marched to that now-familiar stronghold, Boggart's Hole. The "going" was very heavy and, although no difficulty was experienced in crossing the Canal, the route forward to Havrincourt and Chateau Wood was difficult. The Lewis guns were carried on pack mules, but on reaching the Wood they were off-loaded. The trouble began as soon as the battalion debouched from the Wood, the enemy opening very heavy and accurate shell-fire immediately the four Companies—D on the right, supported by C, and B on the left, supported by A, with Battalion Headquarters in rear—advanced close on the heels of the 2/4th K.O.Y.L.I., then going towards Ribecourt. The Companies were deployed in platoons in artillery formation, those on the right advancing south, and those on the left north of Ribecourt.

27TH SEPT.

Heavy machine-gun fire from both flanks now met the Hallamshires, hostile machine guns on Welsh Ridge from which observation was good, taking full advantage of their position. But, in spite of losses, the Companies pushed gallantly forward taking some prisoners. The two right Companies, having reached the sunken roads just west of Ribecourt and having attempted to move through the eastern exits of the village were, however, forced to halt and take cover.

The left Companies were in a similar position.

The enemy was then discovered, about 300 yards in front of the left Companies, massing for a counter-attack, which was delivered immediately with great vigour. He was, however, repulsed by the Hallamshires, who with fine determination flung him back, capturing thirty-five prisoners. The right-half of the Battalion now gained touch with the 2/4th K.O.Y.L.I. in a sunken road just south of Ribecourt, the K.O.Y.L.I.'s advance being held up by the enemy's violent machine-gun fire.

As a further advance for the time being was impossible the two right Companies of the Hallamshires took up positions in the southern portion of Station Avenue. The two left Companies in pushing along through the northern part of Ribecourt came upon a large house in which the enemy had mounted some machine guns. For a time this house held up the advance, but presently it was rushed and the German garrison of twenty men were overpowered. The Hallamshires then proceeded through the village, clearing it of the enemy as they went. Touch was not yet obtained on the right, but on the left communication with the 1/5th Devons. of the 185th Infantry Brigade had been maintained. At dusk the two right companies moved north, i.e., further up Station Avenue, changing places with the 2/4th K.O.Y.L.I.

The 5th K.O.Y.L.I. was not actually engaged with the enemy, though the Battalion moved up close behind the two forward Battalions of the 187th Infantry Brigade and by 2 p.m. was located in Station Avenue and the trench immediately west of it, with a

27TH SEPT. defensive flank thrown out between L.25 c.1.9 and K.30 d.5.4. The Battalion was withdrawn soon after 4 p.m. and disposed in depth between Wood Switch and Bilhem Trench and Ribecourt.

Thus the attacks of the 9th and 187th Infantry Brigades had resulted in the capture of Ribecourt and the consolidation of a line on the eastern outskirts of the village, no mean success considering the strength of the opposition put up by the enemy.

Meanwhile on the northern flank of the attack, Flesquières had already fallen to the 76th Infantry Brigade of the 3rd Division and the 1/5th Devons. and 2/20th London Regt. were in their assembly positions.

It will be remembered that the 76th Infantry Brigade was to capture the Brown Line (second objective), units of the 185th Infantry Brigade passing through towards Marcoing.

The Diary of the 1/5th Devon Regt. records the day's operations very briefly in the following words : " Battalion moved at 6 a.m. across Canal to assembly positions—Station Avenue and Kaiser Support, east of Flesquières, and attacked Premy Avenue, Kaiser Support and a portion of Kaiser Trench. At 9-50 a.m. attack complete success. All objectives gained with slight casualties. Prisoners taken 350, machine guns thirty, trench mortars three, field guns 11. Total casualties 7 Officers, 85 O.R. killed and wounded.[1] On reaching their objectives the Devons. sent out bombing parties to clear Kaiser Support and Kaiser Trench as far south as the railway."

At 5-50 a.m., half an hour after zero, the 2/20th London Regt. advanced from assembly positions (between Hermies and the Canal du Nord) in the following order of Companies—D, C, B, A and Battalion Headquarters. The enemy's 5.9 shells were falling plentifully on the ground over which the Battalion had to pass, but there were no casualties. The descent into the Canal by ladders and the ascent on the far side was a slow process, but the Companies, crossing by platoons, reached the eastern bank without incident. From this point they moved forward in artillery formation to Knightsbridge and London Trenches. D and C Companies then passed along Clarges Avenue and A and B Companies along George Street to the Sunken Road immediately east of Flesquières, and by 9-30, were formed up thus :—D Company in Scull Support ; A and C Companies in Ravine Avenue (immediately east of the Sunken Road

[1] Premy Avenue from the railway L.25.b to its junction with Kaiser Trench.

east of Flesquières); B Company in the Sunken Road west of Ravine Avenue; Battalion Headquarters were in a dug-out in Smile Trench. The Battalion advanced at 9-50 a.m. through the leading troops of the 76th Infantry Brigade (3rd Division), but between that hour and 11-30 a.m. when the next entry occurs in the Battalion Diary, nothing is recorded. From a private account,[1] written by an officer of the London Battalion it appears that: " The Brown Line was captured with a rush and companies pushed some distance down ' Scull Trench ' and along the ridge running east of Flesquières to Premy Support Trench, where it was necessary to halt. The 1st Battalion Grenadier Guards was held up on the left, and 'A' Company on the left flank of the Battalion was heavily enfiladed from Premy Chapel and Nine Wood, on the Guards front. The advance of the Battalion had been wonderfully successful, and 520 prisoners, six field guns, thirty-four machine guns and six Trench Mortars had been captured. Capt. Bacon and his men could see German guns unlimbering and coming into action at Premy Chapel. Though exposed to deadly enfilade fire, and in spite of heavy casualties, all companies maintained their advanced and isolated position."

Then occurred one of those acts of treachery by which the enemy placed himself beyond the pale of all right-minded soldiers : " Two platoons of C Company, under Lieut. Slaughter, went forward and actually reached their final objective—the Blue Line, but they became heavily engaged, and few survivors got back. One section came across a party of the enemy with machine guns. The enemy raised their hands in token that they surrendered, and when Lieutenant Slaughter and his men advanced towards them to take them prisoner, they opened fire with a machine gun. As a result Lieutenant Slaughter was killed and there were several other casualties. Private T. L. M. Haynes then at once worked to a flank and rushed the enemy by himself, capturing the entire party and their two machine guns. For this very gallant and resourceful act he received the D.C.M."

The action of Private Haynes is a very good instance of the initiative displayed throughout the Battle by small unit commanders, due to the splendid training they had received in the handling of sections and platoons. There were many other instances.

Heavy artillery and enfilade machine-gun fire from the direction of Premy Chapel and Nine Wood was still sweeping the ranks of "A" Company, 2/20th Londoners, when the 8th West Yorks. passed

[1] " The Second Twentieth," Capt. W. R. Elliot, M.C.

27TH SEPT. through the line of the former battalion. The hour was about 10-30 a.m.

At 6-15 a.m. the 8th West Yorks., moving by platoons at 100 yards interval had advanced from their assembly positions south of Hermies to the Canal du Nord. Crossings had been put up during the night and the Battalion got across just north of the Spoil Heap without incident. The whole Battalion was located on the eastern bank of the Canal by 7-30 a.m., and touch was obtained with the 1/5th Devons. and 2/20th London Regt. For three-quarters-of-an-hour the West Yorkshiremen halted, awaiting orders to continue their forward movement. Fierce fighting was going on in front and on both flanks, for to the roar of field and heavy guns was added the ever-continuous barking of machine guns, accompanied by the loud crackle of rifle-fire, leaving no doubt that the infantry in the front line was closely engaged with the enemy.

At about 8-15 a.m., just as the West Yorkshiremen were about to move forward again, the enemy's guns began to shell the area east and west of the crossings by which the Battalion had passed over the Canal and for a while the ground was swept by shrapnel and "H.E." Twenty casualties were suffered by the Battalion ere a start was made but presently the Companies moved forward, finally reaching Scull Trench, east of Flesquières. From Scull Trench the Battalion, though fired on by hostile machine guns from the direction of Beet Trench and a bank north of Kaiser Trench, pushed along the northern edge of Kaiser Trench until Premy Support Trench, held by the 2/20th London Regt., was reached. It was here that the West Yorkshiremen passed through the line held by the Londoners. Then followed a brilliant attempt to capture Marcoing, an exploit ultimately to rank with the most gallant actions of the 8th Battalion West Yorks. Regt.

Clear of Premy Support Trench, the Battalion began to advance due east on Marcoing. A Company led the way but the others were, unfortunately, drawn off in the direction of Premy Chapel and Nine Wood, whence hostile machine guns firing in enfilade blazed away without cessation at the advancing West Yorkshiremen. These Companies became heavily involved in hard fighting round Premy Chapel and were unable to assist A Company, which, unaided, still pressed gallantly on towards Marcoing. North-west and north of (and leading into) the village were two sunken roads, and here A Company took cover. Machine-gun fire swept the roads, whilst hostile field guns, firing over open sights, plastered the roads with shell. Only eighteen other ranks of A Company now survived and reluctantly these were withdrawn. The situation of B and C Companies was now obscure. The three Companies had lost all their officers, but the N.C.O.s (the small unit commanders again) splendidly maintained the discipline of the Battalion, inspiring their men by their fine fortitude under desperate circumstances.

27TH SEPT.

The enemy had by now worked round the left flanks of B and C Companies, and having cut them off in rear, inflicted heavy casualties upon them, capturing the survivors.

D Company, which had remained in reserve, was ordered to consolidate Beet Trench as far as L.13 d.o.7 (just east of the Beetroot Factory) where touch was gained with the Welsh Guards. Touch with the 1st Grenadier Guards was also obtained at L.20.d.5.4. In front of this line at about L.14.c.central, a strong point, garrisoned by one officer and thirty other ranks, was established and later in the evening another point, about 40 yards off Nigger Trench.

At 5 p.m. the line of the 62nd Division ran from L.25 c.1.3 to L.25.d.3.0, thence east of Ribecourt along Premy Avenue to Premy Support, through Dago Trench, L.14.d., Nigger Trench and Beet Trench.

All day long the 186th Infantry Brigade had not been engaged, being held in Divisional Reserve, though following the advance in rear of the two attacking Brigades. Shortly after zero hour, the Brigade began to move south from Beaumetz and crossing the Canal du Nord, marched *via* Long Valley—Matheson Road—Clayton Cross —to Pioneer Valley. Units marched in the following order :— 2/4th Duke of Wellington's, 5th Duke of Wellington's, 2/4th Hants. Regt. They were accompanied by Lewis Gun Carts and Ammunition Pack animals. One section of D Company, 62nd Battalion M.G. Company was attached to each unit, moving forward in rear of each Battalion. Two guns of the 186th Trench Mortar Battery were carried on a Supply Tank and two on the Battery Limber.

During this approach march, hostile shell-fire was negligible, and by 10 a.m. the three Battalions had occupied positions about Pioneer Valley, south-west of Havrincourt Village. Here they remained until the 187th Infantry Brigade moved forward. As the advance of the latter Brigade progressed, the 186th took up fresh positions immediately west of Havrincourt, the movement being completed by 11 a.m.

About 3 p.m., the G.O.C. Division visited 186th Brigade Headquarters and orders were issued to all three Battalions to advance,

27TH SEPT. the 2/4th Duke of Wellington's Regt. to a position north of Flesquières on the Havrincourt—Graincourt Road (Squares K.16.d and 17.c), the 5th Duke of Wellington's Regt. to K.16.b and there await further instructions, the 2/4th Hants. to K.16 a. As Havrincourt Village and the neighbourhood was being heavily shelled when these orders reached the three Battalions, movement was delayed, but eventually all units reached their allotted positions, awaiting fresh orders which the Battalion Commanders had been called to Brigade Headquarters (then situated in a dug-out in Smile Trench, north-west of the Cemetery, west of Flesquières) to receive.

" At 5-30 p.m., a telegram was received from the 42nd Division that they were renewing their attack on Highland Ridge at 6-30 p.m. Orders were then sent to 187th Infantry Brigade that the Brigade was to co-operate with the 42nd Division by pushing forward and gaining the Hindenburg Support Line in L.26 and L.27 as soon as arrangements for their attack could be made. At 6-55 p.m., the 42nd Division telephoned that their attack on Highland Ridge was postponed until 1-30 a.m., 28th September. G.O.C. 187th Brigade was consequently instructed to postpone his operations against the Hindenburg Support Line until that hour."

Meanwhile, about 7-45 p.m., the enemy began to shell Ribecourt heavily, and shortly after launched a counter-attack on the village, which was successfully beaten off by the 187th Brigade.

The situation then (at 8 p.m.) along the front of the 62nd Division was as follows :—"The 187th Infantry Brigade (right) with an exposed right flank was holding Ribecourt, facing south-east. The 185th Infantry Brigade held Kaiser Trench as far south as the Railway and Beet Trench ; elements of the 8th West Yorks. were in the neighbourhood of Marcoing."

At 8-40 p.m., instructions were received from the VIth Corps that the advance was to be continued on the morning of September 28th, with the object of securing the crossings over the Canal de L'Escaut, and that the 2nd Division was relieving the Guards Division on the left of the 62nd Division.

Orders were issued to the 186th Infantry Brigade to attack at 6-30 a.m. through the 185th Infantry Brigade and capture Marcoing, secure the crossings east of the village and then prepare to exploit success by the capture of Rumilly.

The 187th Infantry Brigade was ordered, after co-operating with the 42nd Division at 2-30 a.m. to continue the attack on the right of the 186th Infantry Brigade and advance on Masnieres.

The 185th Infantry Brigade, after the 186th Brigade had passed through, was to re-organize in depth and hold Kaiser Trench. Arrangements were made with the 42nd Division to smoke and shell Welsh Ridge until such time as the ridge was captured by the 11th Corps.

Two Troops, Oxfordshire Hussars were transferred from the 185th to the 186th Infantry Brigade.

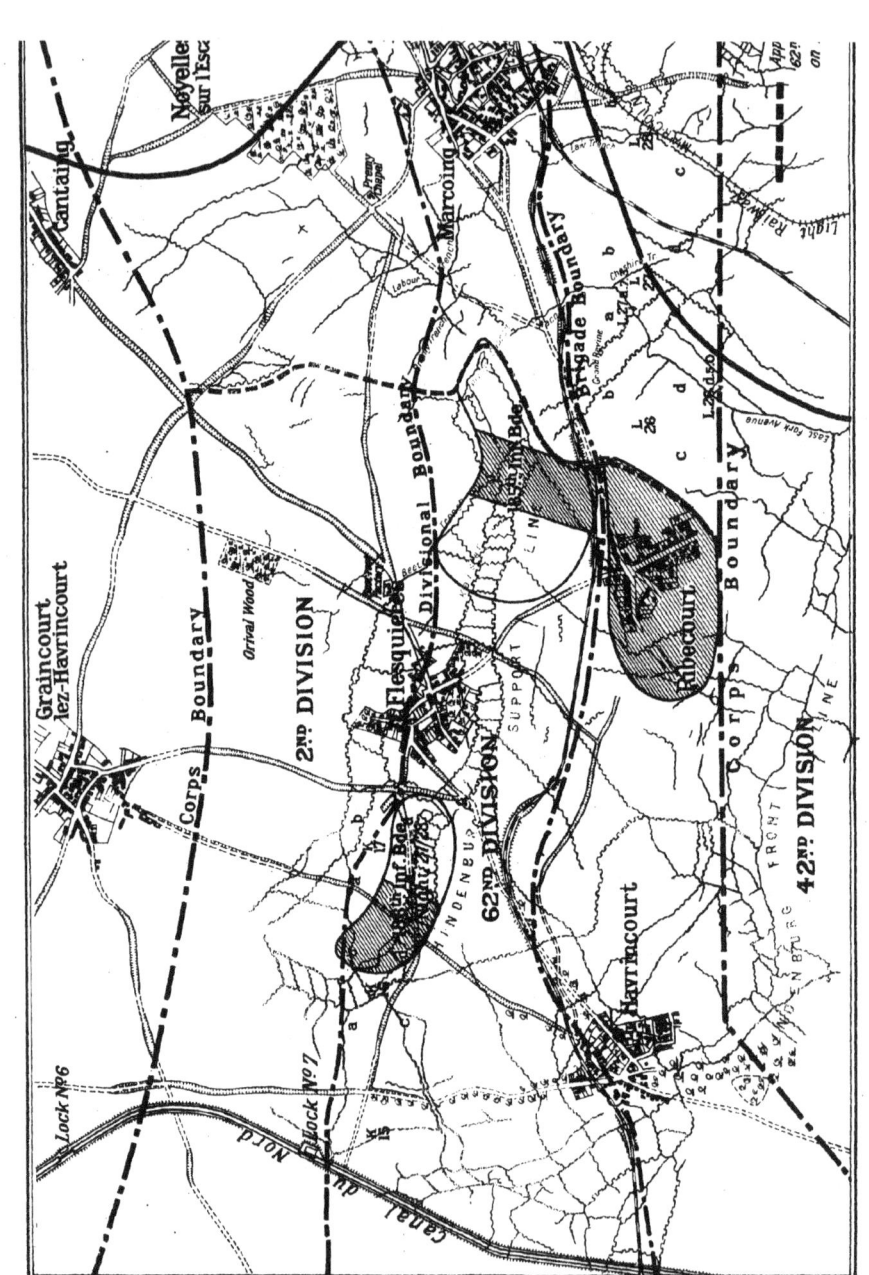

MARCOING AND MASNIÈRES.

Chapter VI.
II.—MARCOING AND MASNIERES 1918.
The Battle of the Canal du Nord and Breaking of the Hindenburg Line

OF all the hotly contested and fierce battles and actions in which the 62nd Division took part in France, none demonstrated more clearly the initiative and courage of the platoon commanders, N.C.O.s and men, than the capture of Marcoing. Neither was there any operation in which the spirit of close co-operation, the willingness of one unit to assist another and that fine feeling of brotherhood, so essentially an attribute of this West Riding Division, shone more brightly than in the hard fighting which took place between the 27th September and the 1st October, 1918. It had, indeed, become a point of honour with these Yorkshiremen and units of other county regiments which had recently joined them, that whenever a comrade or a unit of the Division was in need of assistance, such assistance must be given unquestionably and whole-heartedly *at once*, and as will be seen later, the success of the operations which took place on the 28th September, was the result largely of the readiness with which one Battalion took upon its own shoulders the tasks allotted to another, for owing to a series of accidents the original plans went astray.

27th Sept.

The operations are described in the order in which they took place, *i.e.*, from right (187th Infantry Brigade) to left (186th Infantry Brigade).

In detail the plan of attack, issued by Brigadier-General Reddie to his Battalion commanders, was as follows :—Two attacks were to be made by the 187th Infantry Brigade, the first in conjunction with the 42nd Division on the right, at 4-35 a.m. and the second in conjunction with the 42nd Division on the right and the 186th Infantry Brigade on the left at 6-30 a.m. The objectives allotted to General Reddie in the first attack were the Hindenburg Support system in L.27 a and L.26 b, and the line of the Sunken Road and trench running from L.26 d.5.0 to L.27 a 7.3.

The first attack was to be carried out by the 2/4th K.O.Y.L.I. (Lieut.-Col. C. A. Chaytor) on the right, and the 2/4th York and

27TH SEPT. Lancs. Regt. (The Hallamshires, under Lieut.-Col. L. H. P. Hart), on the left; the 5th K.O.Y.L.I. (Lieut.-Col. F. H. Peter) was to support the attacking Battalions. On reaching the line of their objectives the 2/4th K.O.Y.L.I. and the Hallamshires were to halt for seventy minutes and re-organize and wait until 6-30 a.m. (Zero hour for the second attack) at which hour both Battalions were again to go forward, attacking as far as the light railway running through L.28 c and b,[1] but halting on this line. On the latter the supporting Battalion (the 5th K.O.Y.L.I.) was to pass through and push forward along the southern edge of the Canal de St. Quentin, and secure the crossings on its front. The Divisional Artillery was to co-operate with creeping and protecting barrages.

28TH SEPT. The night of the 27th/28th was pitch black, but all was comparatively quiet and only desultory firing disturbed the battlefield. At 2-30 a.m. the 42nd Division, on the right of the 187th Infantry Brigade, launched its attack, for the Division was some distance in right rear of the 2/4th K.O.Y.L.I. This attack was completely successful, and by first Zero (4-35 a.m.) the 42nd Division was abreast the 187th Infantry Brigade, and both went forward together.

To C and D Companies of the 2/4th K.O.Y.L.I., the capture of the Hindenburg Support Line had been allotted; A and B Companies to pass through and take the further objective; C and D Companies moving up in support. These were the original orders. But Company Headquarters of both C and D Companies were in shell holes and it is not surprising that the unfortunate orderly who had to carry the orders experienced great difficulty in reaching the two Companies, with the result that A and B in moving up to support the attack found that C and D were not ready and could not be ready to attack at Zero. Moreover, in the inky blackness, it was almost impossible to read the orders, let alone read maps. With fine initiative, however, Captain Spencer, commanding A Company, realising the necessity for quick decision, decided to move his Company forward with B Company, taking over the objectives allotted to C and D and leaving the two latter Companies to follow on and pass through to the objectives which he had originally been ordered to capture.

Sending back a message to Battalion Headquarters stating what he had done, he led A and B Companies forward to the attack. These two Companies reached East Fork Avenue, where touch on the right was obtained with the Manchesters (of the 42nd Division).

[1] (L.28 a and L.27 d. ?)

They then worked forward towards Dago and Cheshire Trenches, and on the barrage lifting, touch on the left was obtained with the Hallamshires. But by this time the right flank of the 2/4th K.O.Y.L.I. had got beyond the left of the 42nd Division, the Manchesters apparently having been held up in their advance beyond East Fork Avenue. The Battalion had, however, reached its first objective—the Hindenburg Support Line.

Meanwhile on the left of the 2/4th K.O.Y.L.I., the 2/4th York and Lancs. Regt. (Hallamshires), following close on the heels of the creeping barrage had quickly gained the line of its first objective without opposition. Considering the intensity of the darkness and lack of previous reconnaissance (which owing to the late issue of orders had been impossible), this was a very creditable performance. The Battalion had also advanced on a two-company front—B on the right, A on the left, C and D following.

Thus the 187th Infantry Brigade having gained the first objective allotted to it, set to work to re-organize for its next phase of the operations, timed to begin at 6-30 a.m. Many prisoners were taken during the first phase, numbers of them expressing surprise at the early hour of the attack, which found them quite unprepared. The second phase, however, was to be much more difficult.

At 6-30 a.m. the creeping barrage fell just east of Dago and Cheshire Trenches, and the two attacking Battalions of General Reddie's Brigade again advanced, the 5th K.O.Y.L.I. also moving forward in rear of the 2/4th K.O.Y.L.I. and Hallamshires " ready to go through." Strong opposition now met the advance. Hostile guns firing over open sights poured shrapnel and H.E. on to the gallant " Pelicans " as they swept on, over the open ground, towards Marcoing. Machine guns searched their ranks, but still they pressed forward.

From the top of a railway cutting at the fork of the railway line just south-west of Marcoing, two German field guns opposed the advance of the left Company of the 2/4th K.O.Y.L.I. They were quickly silenced by the rifle and Lewis gun fire of B Company. Four more guns, also firing over open sights, from the sunken roads east of Cheshire Trench, engaged the right Companies of the K.O.Y.L.I. Again the Battalion Lewis guns put the hostile guns out of action, killing or wounding the German gunners. All these guns were taken later.

By noon, the 2/4th K.O.Y.L.I. had advanced to the first of the two sunken roads in L.28 c. A, with C in support on the right, and

28TH SEPT. B, with D in support on the left. Apparently the right of the Hallamshires had not yet won as far forward as the left of the 2/4th K.O.Y.L.I. for a German officer having about fifteen men was seen waving to the latter to turn the left flank of the K.O.Y.L.I. Rapid fire was opened on the German officer and he fell dead; his men then dispersed. B Company, which as this small counter-attack opened, had fallen back slightly, with the object of forming a defensive flank, again advanced to the sunken road.

On the left of the 2/4th K.O.Y.L.I., the Hallamshires (2/4th York and Lancs.) had encountered strong opposition east of Dago and Cheshire Trenches. In the line of their advance were two German 4.2 in. Howitzers and an H.V. gun, protected by the point-blank fire of two 77 mm. guns about the cross roads, north-east of the sunken road captured by the 2/4th K.O.Y.L.I. Two hostile anti-tank guns immediately west of the railway also endeavoured to stop the advance of the Hallamshires. But the latter were not to be stayed; they beat down opposition and captured the Howitzers and H.V. guns. They next dashed into the Grand Ravine—which the men forded successfully—the two left Companies advancing up the eastern slopes of the Ravine by rushes under covering fire from Lewis guns and rifles, towards the two 77 mm. guns in the cross roads. These guns, aided by the enemy's machine guns, poured a murderous point-blank fire on to the gallant Hallamshires, but in vain. The field guns were rushed and the gun crews, or rather the survivors, captured, for all had by now been either killed or wounded and taken prisoner.

Heavy machine-gun fire from Law Trench now met the Hallamshires, but nothing could stay their advance and beating down opposition, the trench was captured together with thirteen machine guns and several prisoners. The Battalion's Lewis gunners then found targets in four hostile guns firing from positions between the cross roads and Marcoing Copse. The gun-crews fled.

The 2/4th K.O.Y.L.I. and the Hallamshires had just reached Law Trench, their final objective, when a strong hostile counter-attack was launched from the direction of Marcoing Copse, and the south-east corner of Marcoing. This attack was immediately repulsed, many dead being left on the field by the enemy.

At this stage the 5th K.O.Y.L.I., according to pre-arranged plans should have passed through the two leading battalions of the 187th Brigade. But the enemy held with grim tenacity to the western edge of Marcoing Copse, whilst hostile machine guns,

The Guns Moving Up Through the Canal du Nord.

well-posted in the south-east corner of the village, frustrated every attempt of the Battalion to advance and secure the Canal crossings. In face of this stubborn resistance nothing could be done without further artillery co-operation. An attack, with the object of establishing a line along the southern edge of the Canal from L.23 c.6.9 to L.23 d.8.2, thence along the eastern edge of Marcoing Copse, and the sunken road immediately south of the Copse, was arranged ; Zero hour for this attack (which was to be carried out by the 5th K.O.Y.L.I.) was 6-30 p.m. The Battalion was then collected in position from which to carry out this attack, *i.e.*, the sunken road running north and south, just east of Law Trench.

This attack was eventually carried out and was completely successful, and the line of the objective established.

Meanwhile, what had happened to General Burnett's Brigade, the 186th, on the left flank of the attack?

In order to understand and appreciate the difficulties with which the Brigade had to contend it is necessary to go back to the Conference which had taken place at 185th Brigade Headquarters on the evening of the 27th September. The orders issued by General Burnett to his three Battalion commanders were :— The 5th Duke of Wellington's Regt. (Lieut.-Col. J. Walker) was to form up for the attack in rear of Kaiser Trench and Beet Trench prior to Zero hour, and at the latter, advance under the barrage and secure the village of Marcoing with the line of the Canal east of it. The 2/4th Hants. Regt. (Lieut.-Col. F. Brook) was then to pass through the 5th Duke's and form a bridge-head extending from the Lock in L.17 d through G.13 d to the bridge in L.18 a. The 2/4th Duke of Wellington's Regt. (Lieut.-Col. P. P. Wilson) was to be in Brigade Reserve prepared to exploit success by the capture of Rumilly.

The Conference over, Colonel Brook and Colonel Wilson set out with their guides for their own Battalion Headquarters. But Colonel Walker's guides had been held up by shell-fire, and after waiting in vain until 11 p.m., he set out without them in order to give his Battalion its orders.

The three Battalions of the 186th Infantry Brigade were at this period located as follows :—2/4th Duke of Wellington's Regt. in K.17 a and d : 5th Duke of Wellington's Regt. in K.16 b : 2/4th Hants. Regt. in K.16 b, *i.e.*, in the Hindenburg Support Line, west and north-west of Flesquières. But in the darkness and the maze of newly-captured trenches forming the Hindenburg Line, Colonel Walker missed his way, and at 4 a.m. on the 28th a message reached

28TH SEPT. Divisional Headquarters that he had not reached his Battalion, but was returning to the attacking point. Meanwhile, the delayed guides had reached 186th Infantry Brigade Headquarters, and having received written orders returned to their Battalions, arriving, as may be expected, very late. As a result the Brigade plan of attack had to be modified, for a message reached General Burnett from the 5th Duke's that owing to the late arrival of their orders it was doubtful whether they would reach Kaiser Trench in time to advance under the barrage. Verbal instructions were therefore issued to Colonel Brook that, should the 5th Duke's be late, the 2/4th Hants. were to attack the first objective (Marcoing) and the 5th Duke's would go through them and force the bridge-head, which task had originally been allotted to the Hampshiremen.

Zero hour was 6-30 a.m.

A difficult and dangerous task now confronted Colonel Brook's Battalion. The assembly position was about a mile and a half in rear of the line on which the barrage was to fall, which meant that their advance would be unprotected and at the full mercy of the enemy's machine-gunners and artillery, which were well placed in order to resist attack. Moreover, the Hampshiremen only knew that they were to attack the objective allotted to the 5th Duke's a few minutes before Zero. " There was time for nothing, a few hasty orders and away the Battalion went."

And how well it succeeded! Before reaching their forming-up position on the Flesquières road the men had already had a trying march of over two hours along an intricate and difficult trench system. The majority of them were dog-tired, having had little or no rest, during the preceding night. But with almost superhuman efforts the Battalion pushed on with all speed and caught the barrage up on a line a little short of Dago Trench; it was an altogether remarkable performance.

Colonel Brook had organized each of the Companies of his Battalion into three platoons. The leading Companies—A on the right and C on the left—went forward on a two platoon frontage, with one platoon in support. The two leading Companies were followed by B on the right and D on the left, on a one platoon frontage, with orders to " leap-frog " A and C and fight their way through the village.

The enemy's counter-barrage was fortunately light and very few casualties were suffered as the Hampshiremen swept forward;

THE RUINED CHURCH, MARCOING.

the two leading Companies making straight for their objective— 28TH SEPT. the system of trenches immediately west of Marcoing.

A Company was well in line with the left flank of the 187th Infantry Brigade (the Hallamshires). Near Dago Trench an enemy battery of three guns, for which the horses were just being brought up, was discovered. Without waiting to dispute possession of these guns the Germans made off, leaving the horses also in the hands of the Hampshiremen. Long-range machine-gun fire from the right now swept the line of advance of A Company, but the Hallamshires dealt with this, and after capturing eleven prisoners, several trench mortars and machine guns, the Company reached its objective without much difficulty, though machine-gun fire from the western edge of Marcoing caused trouble.

On the left of A Company, C reached Premy Support without serious opposition. The enemy's trench mortars, firing from the Railway, were very active, but were gradually silenced by Lewis-gun fire. Near Premy Trench, a German field gun and ten prisoners were captured.

Thus both A and C Companies had reached their objectives, and at this stage B and D " leap-frogged " through.

B Company got a footing in the village, but on attempting to cross the Escaut River came under machine-gun fire from the eastern banks. Two Lewis guns of No. 5 Platoon, therefore, opened fire on the Germans, who quickly fled, leaving many dead on the ground. Another machine-gun nest was encountered by No. 7 Platoon, but here also the enemy abandoned the guns, and three wounded men who fell into the hands of the Platoon.

The enemy's resistance was, however, more determined as B Company approached the Canal. From along the railway east of the Canal, hostile machine-gun and rifle fire swept the line of advance, and was not overcome without considerable difficulty. Eventually the Company commander, with a small party, got across the Canal and established a post on the eastern bank. The supporting platoons of B were meanwhile engaged in " clearing up " the village, a small number of prisoners being captured. On the left of B, D Company had gone through very similar experiences, but also succeeded eventually in establishing posts along the banks of the Canal ; the Hampshiremen were assisted in this operation by men of the 5th Duke's whose task was (it will be remembered) to form bridge-heads over the Canal. Having reached their objectives all four Companies of the 2/4th Hants. Regt. set to work to re-organize; the Battalion finally forming a line on the western banks of the Canal.

Once more it is necessary to return to the early hours of the 28th in order to follow the fortunes of Colonel Walker's Battalion (5th Duke of Wellington's Regt.) which without its C.O. was stumbling along in pitch blackness, endeavouring to reach the forming-up line in time for Zero hour.

The 5th Duke's had set off from L.10 b at 4-30 a.m. A glance at the map will show the distance which had to be traversed ere the Battalion reached its forming-up place in rear of Kaiser and Beet Trenches. Heavily laden and very tired with their previous exertions, the Companies set out to cross the maze of trenches of the Hindenburg Support Line. The men literally had to feel their way forward, and to keep to a path was extremely difficult. It was not surprising, therefore, that the Battalion did not reach its jumping-off line until half-an-hour after Zero, *i.e.*, 7 a.m. By this time the men were almost exhausted. In 1918 it was no easy thing for a British soldier, with all his equipment, often augmented by extra ammunition, bombs, Lewis guns, etc., to carry out a two hours march in darkness across a maze of trenches and masses of barbed-wire entanglements.

Colonel Walker met his Battalion on the forming-up line and once more took command, as the Companies marched forward with the intention of "leap-frogging" through the 2/4th Hants. Regt. The Battalion went forward in two waves. C Company on the right and A (two platoons) on the left formed the first wave, and D Company on the right and B on the left the second wave. A Section (No. 1 of D Company) of the 62nd Battalion M.G.C. accompanied (in rear) D Company of the Duke's Only one platoon of A Company remained in reserve at Battalion Headquarters which were in the sunken road running between Flesquières and Ribecourt.

Little happened until the village of Marcoing was reached, where the 5th Duke's overtook the 2/4th Hants., and with the latter took part in a regular man-hunt for German machine-gunners, who having repaired to the attic rooms of some of the houses, opened fire from the windows whenever troops of either Battalion showed themselves. This work of cleaning up the village was not, however, allowed to delay the advance, and soon a move eastward was made towards the Canal de St. Quentin. The latter was reached just before 9 a.m., and at once it was obvious that to cross the eastern banks would be a very difficult and dangerous operation. For

PTE. HENRY TANDEY, V.C., D.C.M., M.M.,
5TH BN. DUKE OF WELLINGTON'S REGT.

Face p. 93.

hostile machine-gun and rifle fire—frontal and enfilade—swept all approaches to the Canal. The bridges had been destroyed, and the Canal bank was very deep, which made the crossing all the more hazardous. But these Yorkshiremen were not to be denied. Lewis gunners were sent off to take up positions in the attics of houses along the western bank of the Canal. These gunners opened a furious fire on the enemy, which somewhat reduced the intensity of the latter's machine-gun fire. Then by means of planks the commanders of B and D Companies of the 5th Duke's succeeded in dribbling their men across to the eastern bank just before 11 a.m. It was here that No. 34506 Pte. Henry Tandey, D.C.M., M.M., of the 5th Duke of Wellington's Regt. (T.F.) won the Victoria Cross, " for most conspicuous bravery and initiative during the capture of the village[1] and the crossings at Marcoing."

Later, A Company (less one platoon at Battalion Headquarters) and C Company (less one platoon and Company Headquarters) crossed the Canal. About this period the 2/4th Hants. were establishing themselves along the western banks.

Once across the Canal the Duke's quickly pressed forward, but came immediately under very heavy machine-gun fire from Marcoing Switch, strongly held by the enemy. Companies had become somewhat mixed during the crossing, but all platoons maintained themselves as separate organized units. Under furious frontal and enfilade fire to which they were now subjected the gallant Duke's could make no headway, and all that could be done, for the time being, was to consolidate their position along the line of the railway from about L.17 d.8.2 to L.23 d.o.3.

The Canal crossings had, however, been won, though the Division as a whole had yet to pass over to the eastern bank, and before this could be done the bridges must be repaired. For this purpose the 460th Field Company, R.E., had been detailed to follow on behind the 186th Infantry Brigade, and get to work on the bridges once the crossings had been won. Two parties of Sappers, each twenty strong, under the command of Lieut. McGlashan and Lieut. Eyre, advanced in open order about 300 yards in rear of the first wave of the 186th Brigade and reached Marcoing without mishap. On reaching the village one of these parties set to work and rebuilt the bridges over the River Escaut. The other party pushed on to the Canal bank to carry out similar work on the destroyed 20 ft. span bridge. But this was impossible. The enemy had placed a

[1] London Gazette, 14/12/1918

28TH SEPT. heavy barrage on the line of the Canal, and a murderous machine-gun fire swept all approaches to the ruined structure, and although gallant attempts were made by the Sappers to get to work with the material they had collected, it was found impossible to carry out any repairs in daylight. The attempt was therefore temporarily abandoned, and the party marched back to Flesquières. The 461st Company, R.E. also carried out work on the bridge over the River Escaut.[1]

As the day wore on the position of the 5th Duke of Wellington's Regt. was becoming precarious. The Battalion was the only unit of the Division east of the Canal, and it was evident the enemy was making all preparations to launch a heavy counter-attack on Colonel Walker's troops. Observers posted in the attics of houses along the eastern bank of the Canal reported the arrival in Rumilly of enemy reinforcements, brought up in buses. Marcoing Trench also contained large numbers of Germans.

The G.O.C. who visited the 186th Infantry Brigade Headquarters during the forenoon, therefore decided that the 5th Duke's must gain more ground east of the Canal lest they should be driven back into it. General Burnett ordered the 5th Duke's to attack under a creeping artillery barrage and capture Marcoing Switch and Marcoing Support.

The attack was originally ordered for 2-30 p.m., but Colonel Walker asked to have it postponed till 6-15 p.m.

Finally all arrangements for the attack, including the artillery barrage, being ready by 6-0 p.m., Colonel Walker then launched his attack, forestalling a German counter-attack by ten minutes only.

At 6 p.m., the artillery barrage opened on Marcoing Switch, pounding the enemy's positions with every available gun. Five minutes later the barrage lifted to Marcoing Support, the Duke's following close behind. By sheer good fortune the barrage had fallen on the enemy's trenches, only a few minutes before he had timed his own attack on the Duke's, and as the latter, pressing their advance, stormed Marcoing Switch they found the Germans thrown into great confusion by the bombardment to which they had just been subjected, but still in very superior numbers.

Then ensued a regular soldier's battle, a hand-to-hand struggle, in which the 5th Duke's, though considerably outnumbered, never showed to greater advantage. All four Companies of Colonel

[1] The Divisional Engineers were at this period commanded by Lieut.-Col. Trench (R.E.).

Walker's Battalion were weak in numbers, they had also been unable to reorganize since their attack of the early morning. In consequence, each Company advanced on a one platoon frontage, with another platoon in support, and the remaining (two) platoons in reserve.

The right Company (D) all told, numbered just under ninety officers, N.C.O.s and men, but even so the attacking force of this Company (forty strong) captured its objective with 300 prisoners and nine machine guns, *and held on*, having been reinforced by the remaining platoons.

On the left (A Company) the leading platoon (strength eighteen only) reached its objective, Marcoing Switch. But the platoons in support were in Battalion Reserve on the west side of the Canal, and did not reach the attacking platoon up to time. Nevertheless, this gallant little band, keeping close on the heels of the barrage, headed straight for a hostile machine gun, which the platoon commander, 2nd Lieut. W. J. Lloyd, discovered firing from Marcoing Switch. The gun was quickly captured, with one German officer and eight other ranks, hidden in a dug-out close by. Continuing its advance, the platoon next reached Marcoing Support, in which were many enemy dug-outs. But now Lieut. Lloyd began to look about him, for he could see none of his Battalion on either flank. A man sent off down the trench to the right returned and reported no British troops on that flank, and the Germans only 100 yards away preparing to counter-attack. Another man sent up the trench to the left, had to beat a hasty retreat owing to heavy machine-gun fire ; he also reported the enemy close at hand. Marcoing Switch, behind the platoon, was likewise seen to be full of Germans. The platoon was surrounded and the situation desperate. So desperate, in fact, that there was only one way out of the difficulty ; for the platoon to fight its way through, or die in the attempt. And to the honour of the regiment, the brave young subaltern decided to fight it out. Ordering his men to get out of the trench, an order which they obeyed rapidly, Lieut. Lloyd next gave them the order to charge the enemy holding the trench in rear. With vigorous shouts this tiny band rushed upon the Germans, many of whom, terrified by the sight of the furious Yorkshiremen, began taking off their equipment and throwing up their hands in token of surrender. Others of the enemy fled from the trench back towards the Canal, where they were either killed or captured. Finally, after the platoon had extricated itself from its precarious position, it was found that thirty-eight prisoners had been taken and many other Germans killed or wounded. The spirit and élan of this single platoon was truly wonderful. One man being wounded, being shot through the leg and through the arm, stoutly refused to have his wounds dressed until the action was over. Meanwhile the centre Companies (B and C) had reached their objective, Marcoing Support. Here, however, they found themselves isolated, with the enemy on both flanks, who immediately counter-attacking from the north-east, forced the left of the line back to the railway siding at about L.23 b.4.8. And now occurred another instance of that treachery which even four years of warfare had not induced the Germans to abandon. The 5th Duke's had lost heavily in their attack, and had not been able to provide adequate escort for the large number of prisoners taken. Seeing the temporary success of the counter-attack on B and C Companies of the 5th Duke's, these prisoners picked up rifles and opened fire upon the backs of Colonel Walker's men, causing considerable (though only momentary) confusion. The reserve platoons of the 5th Duke's on the line of the railway, however, came to the rescue and restored the situation. The treacherous prisoners were adequately dealt with. The line in Marcoing Support was then established.

In all twenty-five machine guns and 500 prisoners, including six German officers, were captured by the 5th Duke of Wellington's Regt. Considering that the Battalion was only able to attack with small numbers of men, all ranks had shown the greatest courage and resolution.[1] Once again the small units by their élan and initiative had triumphed over extraordinary difficulties.

Fighting in the front line now died down, though the enemy's guns still continued to shell the bridges over the Canal, the line of the railway and Marcoing village.

At 11-22 p.m., General Whigham reported to VIth Corps Headquarters that the results of the attack at 6 p.m. by the 186th Brigade was the capture of Marcoing Switch and Marcoing Support.

Throughout the day, the 185th Infantry Brigade had remained in Divisional Reserve, consolidating its position in depth.

Just after 9 p.m., orders were issued from Divisional Headquarters containing instructions to the 186th and 187th Brigades to continue the advance on the following morning, and capture the villages of Masniéres and Rumilly; the 185th Brigade was to be p repared (on receipt of orders from Divisional Headquarters) to

---

[1] The casualties of the 5th Duke of Wellington's Regt during the 28th were five officers (two killed) and 110 other ranks.

advance through the 186th and 187th Brigades should the enemy's line give way.   28TH SEPT.

Before a further advance could take place, the repair of the bridges over the Canal was absolutely essential. As already described, the Sappers had attempted to do this during the day, but the enemy's guns poured an almost continuous tornado of shells upon the crossings and this, combined with intense machine-gun and rifle fire had stopped repair of the bridges during daylight. But when darkness had fallen on 28th, the C.R.E. was ordered to construct, during the night, at least two foot bridges over the Canal east of Marcoing, and as soon as possible after Zero on 29th to complete a bridge for wheeled traffic.

Throughout the night 28th/29th the enemy continued to shell the Canal crossings heavily, but the three Field Companies—457th, 460th and 461st—stuck devotedly to their work and when dawn broke on the latter date the bridges had been repaired and one, at least, prepared for heavy wheeled traffic.   28TH/29TH SEPT.

Zero hour for the attack on Masniéres and Rumilly had been fixed for 7-30 a.m., the troops to go forward under a creeping barrage.

The right objective—Masniéres—was allotted to the 187th Brigade, and Rumilly on the left, to the 186th. The two villages were on the line of the final objective—Green Dotted Line—as laid down in orders for the first day of the operations.

On the 187th Infantry Brigade front the attack was carried out by the 2/4th K.O.Y.L.I. on the right, and the 5th K.O.Y.L.I. plus one Company of the 2/4th York and Lancs. Regt. (Hallamshires) on the left; the three remaining Companies of Hallamshires were in Brigade Reserve.

The 2/4th Duke of Wellington's Regt. (who, on the capture of Marcoing, had moved up to Dago and Labour Trenches) carried out the attack on Rumilly from the 186th Brigade front.

The dividing line between the two Brigades was the Canal in L.24 and G.19 (inc. to 187th) railway line in G.20.c. and b, Cambrai Road at G.20.b.7.4 thence due east.

At an early hour troops of the New Zealand Division were to pass through the 42nd Division on the right of the 187th Brigade with Crévecoeur as their final objective, but just about Zero the New Zealanders were checked in their advance by a heavy hostile counter-attack, and for a little while there was trouble on the right of the 62nd.

A dense fog hung over the battlefield when dawn broke on the   29TH SEPT

29TH SEPT. 29th, and it was very evident that to maintain direction would be difficult. The assembling of the attacking troops was another serious question. But both of these difficulties were skilfully overcome. The 2/4th K.O.Y.L.I. had decided to attack on a two-company frontage, B and D, with C Company in support, and to picquet the bridges, and A Company with machine guns and T.M.B. sections in reserve, in case of trouble on the right flank. At 7 a.m. hostile machine-gun fire was still coming from the right of the 2/4th, and A Company was held back until the situation cleared. A little later, however, the New Zealanders were reported in advance of the right flank of the 62nd, and at 7-30 a.m. the 2/4th K.O.Y.L.I. advanced.

The mist was now gradually rising and soon word was passed back to Battalion Headquarters that les Rue Vertes had been cleared of the enemy, and that touch had been established on the right with the New Zealanders, at the bend of the Canal, and on the left with the 5th K.O.Y.L.I. also on the Canal. During the advance a party of about fifty Germans made an attempt to get round the right flank of B Company of the 2/4th. A platoon was promptly sent off to deal with this threat, and on seeing the K.O.Y.L.I. advancing towards them, the Germans threw down their arms and surrendered. B Company also captured another twenty-nine prisoners as well as three field guns with their barrels still hot from firing, twenty-one men of the battery being taken as they were having breakfast. D Company took fifty-two prisoners in les Rue Vertes, as well as a number of machine guns. The Battalion then pressed on and established itself on the Green Dotted Line.

On the left of the 2/4th K.O.Y.L.I., the 5th Battalion of the same regiment had assembled in the bend of the Canal, north of Marcoing Copse; a few casualties were incurred during this operation, including one officer killed. In this area the fog was very thick, and it was thought that loss of direction must occur. But at Zero hour, the Battalion, two Companies in the front line and two in rear with instructions to clear Masnières of any enemy troops left there, followed close on the heels of the barrage, and with fine dash reached their objective and took up a line along Rumilly Support. By 12 noon the whole of the village of Masinéres had been cleared of the enemy, and a line definitely established along Rumilly Support. Over 300 prisoners had been captured, but that number was considered small for rumour had been busy, and a haul of 3,000 Germans (said to be hidden in the Catacombs in the village) was expected, and in consequence

Troops Moving up on the Morning of 29th September, 1918.

the men had worked themselves up to a state of intense excitement. One Company of the 2/4th York and Lancs. Regt. (Hallamshires) had been detailed to assist the 5th K.O.Y.L.I. in clearing Masniéres, with the ultimate object of filling the gap between the two leading Companies of the K.O.Y.L.I., which it was felt would occur as the Companies advanced on their objective. This Company of Hallamshires did its work well.

By 1 p.m. the 187th Infantry Brigade had captured all its objectives, including Masniéres and les Rue Vertes, together with the trench system immediately east of the two villages.

Meanwhile, on the left of the 187th, General Burnett's Brigade —186th— had not been as fortunate as the former. The mist had enabled the 2/4th Duke of Wellington's Regt. (Lieut.-Col. P. P. Wilson) to cross the Canal unobserved by the enemy. Owing to the 5th Duke's having been driven back from Marcoing Switch and Marcoing Support, the original forming-up place (in the neighbourhood of Marcoing Support) had to be changed, and the 2/4th Duke's formed up for the attack west of the Canal (in L.23.a and b), the barrage being supplemented by an additional three and a half minutes barrage on Marcoing Switch and Marcoing Support.

Colonel Wilson's Battalion had been ordered to attack the trench system Rumilly Trench and Rumilly Support, and then move forward to the road running from Masniéres to Cambrai; Rumilly village was the final objective.

At 7-30 a.m. the barrage fell, and the Battalion on a two-company frontage, with three platoons in front and one in support, moved forward to the attack.

The attack went forward with the barrage until it reached Marcoing Support. On this line the guns halted for fifteen minutes, when it again crept forward. No serious opposition was met with until the Battalion drew near to Rumilly Trench, when machine-gun fire became very heavy. Nevertheless, in face of fierce opposition, the 2/4th Duke's captured Rumilly Trench, taking a number of prisoners. The advance on Rumilly Support was then begun. But again very severe opposition was met with. On the right of the Battalion, hostile trench mortars and machine guns poured a deadly fire on to the flanking Company of the 2/4th Duke's. But again, with fine dash, the enemy's resistance was broken down and the position, together with trench mortars and machine guns, was captured.

The left Company reached Rumilly Support without serious opposition, but on crossing this trench, further advance was

29TH SEPT. impossible owing to heavy machine-gun and rifle fire coming from Flet Farm and Mont sur l'Oeuvre. The latter place was a veritable hornet's nest, which had already held up the 2nd Division on the left of the 2/4th Duke of Wellington's Regt. In spite of the gallantry of two platoons, who went forward and captured three machine guns, the opposition was too severe, and as its left flank was now exposed the Battalion had, for the moment, to be content with having gained Rumilly Support.

By this time the right of the Battalion had, however, pushed forward to the Masniéres—Cambrai Road, a patrol entering the southern end of the village.

At 1-30 p.m. a counter-attack of considerable force drove the two flanks of the 2/4th Duke's back to the line of Rumilly Support. The latter was not a continuous line, but a series of posts connected by half-dug trenches. During this counter-attack the enemy established himself in the gap between the right and left Companies and cut off one platoon of C Company. The Germans had brought forward several machine guns, and two attempts by bombing to turn them out were unsuccessful.

During the late afternoon (about 5 p.m.) verbal instructions were given to the O.C., 2/4th Hants. Regt. (Lieut.-Col. F. Brook) to advance his Battalion across the Canal with the object of attacking Rumilly. The Hants. at once began to move forward, and in spite of heavy shelling, had crossed the Canal by 6 p.m. Darkness was now falling. On coming up with the 2/4th Duke's, the Hants. experienced very heavy machine-gun fire from Mont sur l'Oeuver, which in this part of the battlefield was the key to the enemy's position, and a further advance was impossible. Touch on the left had, nevertheless, been established with troops of the 2nd Division. The right Company of the Battalion, however, could not gain touch with troops on either flank, and took up a position in depth in Rumilly Trench.

Meanwhile, during the day, two Battalions of the 185th Infantry Brigade (Brigadier-General Viscount Hampden), 1/5th Devon Regt. (Lieut.-Col. H. V. Bastow) and 2/20th London Regt. (Lieut.-Col. W. St. A. Warde-Aldam) were concentrated west of Marcoing. At 5-30 p.m. verbal orders (subsequently confirmed in writing at 9-30 p.m.) were issued that on the morning of 30th September the 185th Brigade would pass through the 187th and 186th Brigades, and advance on Seranvillers and Wambaix.

Zero hour for the attack would not be later than 6-30 a.m. The New Zealanders on the right and the 2nd Division on the

left, were to co-operate in this attack, and would capture Wambaix
Copse and Esnes respectively. If the village of Rumilly had not
been captured by the 186th Brigade during the evening of 29th
September, the village was to be cleared by the 185th Brigade by
turning it on the eastern side before the advance was made on Seran-
villers and Wambaix. One Battalion of the 187th Brigade (2/4th
York and Lancs. Regt—Hallamshires) was placed at the disposal of
Lord Hampden for the operations.

Throughout the night the situation in the Divisional front line
(along the front of the 187th and 186th Infantry Brigades) remained
practically unchanged. The enemy continued to shell the Canal
crossings and the railway line very heavily.

A patrol sent out by the 2/4th Duke's in an endeavour to gain
touch with the isolated platoon of C Company was severely handled,
only a few survivors returning, and it was not until after the advance
on 1st October that the bodies of the platoon commander and some
of his men were found.

About 3-30 a.m. on 30th September the 185th Infantry Brigade
moved off, led by the 2/20th London Regt.; the 1/5th Devon Regt.
and the 8th West York Regt. following in the order given. The
three Battalions crossed the Canal and concentrated in the area east
of Masniéres and in that portion of Rumilly Support east of the village.
The leading Companies of the 2/20th arrived in Rumilly Support
at daybreak, having been shelled heavily on the way up from the
Canal. Again the enemy's machine guns, from the western edge of
Rumilly and Mont sur l'Oeuvre, swept the line of advance and the
shallow trenches held by the Londoners, and further advance was
impossible.

Meanwhile the 1/5th Devons, on the right, moving forward in
advanced guard formation, found the enemy still in possession of
Plaisir Trench and Plaisir Support, and although the Devon men
were met by a heavy rifle and machine-gun fire they charged the
trenches and cleared the enemy from them and pushed on as far as
the sunken road, running directly north of Crevecoeur.

The 8th West Yorks. (Lieut.-Col. N. A. England), advancing in
rear of the Devons, now covered the left flank of the latter Battalion
which had suffered heavy casualties. The enemy then tried to
outflank the Devons, but the West Yorkshiremen again covered their
flank and, facing north-east, took up a position along the road from
Crevecoeur to Rumilly. By this time 2nd Lieut. A. Foster was the
only officer left of the leading Company of West Yorkshiremen.

30TH SEPT. With fine initiative, this officer personally supervised the re-adjustment of his line, and established posts in front of his main line of resistance. The positions gained were held throughout the day, though the Devons and West Yorks. were withdrawn during the night of 30th September-1st October in order that the barrage for an attack by the New Zealanders ordered for 1st October could come down on the Crevecoeur-Rumilly Road.

The frontal attack of Rumilly by the 2/20th Londoners was a mistake, as the advance from this direction was swept by machine-gun fire from the village and from the commanding ground at Mont sur l'Oeuvre. The intention of the Divisional Commander had been to turn Rumilly and attack it from the east, and if the success of the 8th West Yorks. had been exploited by pushing through the 2/20th Londoners,[1] Rumilly would in all probability have been captured *this day*.

Meanwhile, at about 10 a.m., a bombardment of Rumilly was carried out, and as the guns ceased fire, the 2/20th Londoners pushed forward patrols with orders to penetrate into the village. But again a murderous machine-gun fire swept the line of advance, and the patrols were unable to make headway.

To return to early morning !

When dawn broke on the 30th September, the enemy was found, still in possession of the central portion of Rumilly Support Trench, part of which was also held by the 2/4th Duke's and 2/4th Hants. Colonel Brooke of the Hants. went out on a reconnaissance and on his return decided to clear the enemy from the centre of the trench.

At 11-45 a.m., under cover of smoke bombs and rifle grenades, a platoon of C Company of the Hampshires, under 2nd Lieut. Turner, made a dash across the open from Rumilly Trench. The gallant fellows at once came under a galling fire from machine guns and rifles, and although they succeeded in getting within thirty yards of the enemy's position, success was impossible, and the young officer, with the majority of his platoon, became casualties. Another platoon attacking up the trench, found it so shallow that no cover could be obtained from the enemy's machine guns which enfiladed it. Capt. Cottam was killed and the remainder withdrew across the trench-barrier with great difficulty.

At 2-30 p.m. another attempt was made, this time under 2nd Lieut. Shorland, and, although pressed with the greatest determination, was also unsuccessful.

[1] Only two Companies, under Lt. Col. St. A. Warde Aldam, attacked ; the other two were in Divisional Reserve.

"This was a small affair, but it enabled heroism, which has not been excelled in either this war or any other war, to be brought out. The charge of the Light Brigade was no finer than the mad dash of these twenty Hampshire men. Sergeant Hamilton can be recalled. He was an old veteran of the South African War; he was calm and cool, and had not that wild 'happy-go-lucky' carriage which many younger men possessed, but on this occasion, as on many others, he proved himself absolutely without fear. Then there was Sergeant Jarvis, a jockey in size, but a giant in grit. Along the trench he led his men in a daring attack, and although most of his men became casualties, and the remainder were exposed to enfilade machine-gun fire, he would not retire until the commanding officer gave the word to withdraw."[1]

30TH SEPT.

After the unsuccessful attack of the Hampshiremen, it was decided not to make any further efforts to clear the trench that day. The enemy was, however, given no respite, the Stokes mortars subjecting his positions to a heavy bombardment.

At 4-30 p.m. orders were issued from Divisional Headquarters for the line then held to be reorganized in three Brigade sectors. These orders were followed later, at 9 p.m., by others stating that the 3rd Division would pass through the 62nd Division on the following morning (1st October), and after capturing the village of Rumilly would continue the advance on Seranvillers.

At 6 a.m. on the morning of the 1st October, the 3rd Division attacked Rumilly, at which hour command of the right sector VIth Corps front passed from General Whigham to the G.O.C., 3rd Division.

1ST OCT.

The final act in the Battle of the Canal du Nord (so far as the 62nd Division was concerned) was the successful "consolidation" carried out by the 2/4th Hants. Colonel Brooke (the O.C.), suspecting that the Germans still in Rumilly Trench were in occupation of dug-outs, detailed two Companies to follow up the attack of the 76th Infantry Brigade (3rd Division). The left Company found eight Germans just emerging from a dug-out, who were promptly dealt with. The officer commanding this Company found no less than twenty-two German machine guns in the trench and twenty-five dead Germans, including three officers; the place was a shambles. The right Company found a large dug-out which concealed a considerable party of the enemy, seventy-five Germans being taken together with five machine guns. These captures undoubtedly

[1] "The 2/4th Battalion, Hampshire Regiment, 1914-1919."

1ST OCT. saved the 76th Infantry Brigade from being taken in rear by hostile machine-gun fire.

Thus ended the strenuous operations through which the Division had passed since the morning of the 27th September. Many splendid and gallant deeds had been done—
" and there was much glory,"
but many brave men, had alas ! joined the " Great Battalion."[1]

Every unit of the Division had been in some way or other *actively* engaged in the operations, and the gunners, the sappers, the medical units, the Army Service Corps, the T.M.B.s and the machine-gunners were not less gallant than the hard-worked infantry in the front line. Apart from the latter, if any unit is deserving of special mention, it is the Field Companies of Royal Engineers, who at this period and until the beaten enemy sued for peace, were truly magnificent in the way they repaired the bridges and built up the broken roads, often under galling shell and machine-gun fire, undaunted and with a devotion to duty never surpassed in the whole history of the Corps.

During the operations between the 27th September and 1st October, the Division had captured twenty-four German officers and 1,495 other ranks, sixty-five guns (including four 5-9 Howitzers, one naval gun and one H.V. gun) ; 358 machine guns, twenty-five trench mortars, two anti-Tank rifles and two automatic rifles.

The 62nd Division, on relief, withdrew to areas about Havrincourt. The village had almost become " home " to the Division, so often and so strenuously had the gallant " Pelicans " fought for it and held it.[2]

[1] The casualties suffered by the Division were :—Twenty officers and 243 other ranks killed, forty-two officers and 1,135 other ranks wounded, three officers and 262 other ranks missing. Total, sixty-five officers and 1,640 other ranks.

The 62nd Division had captured twenty-four German officers and 1,495 other ranks, and much war material.

[2] On the 1st October two special messages were issued to all units of the Division : One from General Whigham, in which, after detailing the Division's recent successes, the G.O.C. said : " I have to-day been visited by the Field Marshal Commanding-in-Chief, who has desired me to convey to all ranks of the Division his congratulations and high appreciation of their splendid courage and endurance. For myself I give you all my warmest thanks for the unfailing cheerfulness with which you have carried out the most arduous tasks, often in conditions of great hardship and discomfort." The second message was from General Braithwaite, who at this period commanded the IXth Corps : " Just heard of your great success at Ribecourt and Marcoing. It is all splendid and just like 62nd. Will you allow me to congratulate you and the Division and to say how very proud I am to have commanded so splendid a Division."

The 62nd Division took no further part in the battle which continued till October 5th, but at the end of the operations taking place between September 27th and October 5th, the Hindenburg Line had been broken, thus closing the first phase of the British offensive. " The enemy's defence in the last and strongest of his prepared positions had been shattered. The whole of the Hindenburg defences had passed into our possession, and a wide gap had been driven through such rear trench systems as had existed behind them. The effect of the victory upon the subsequent course of the campaign was decisive. The threat to the enemy's communications was now direct and instant, for nothing but the natural obstacles of a wooded and well-watered country-side lay between our armies and Maubeuge."[1]

[1] Official Despatches.

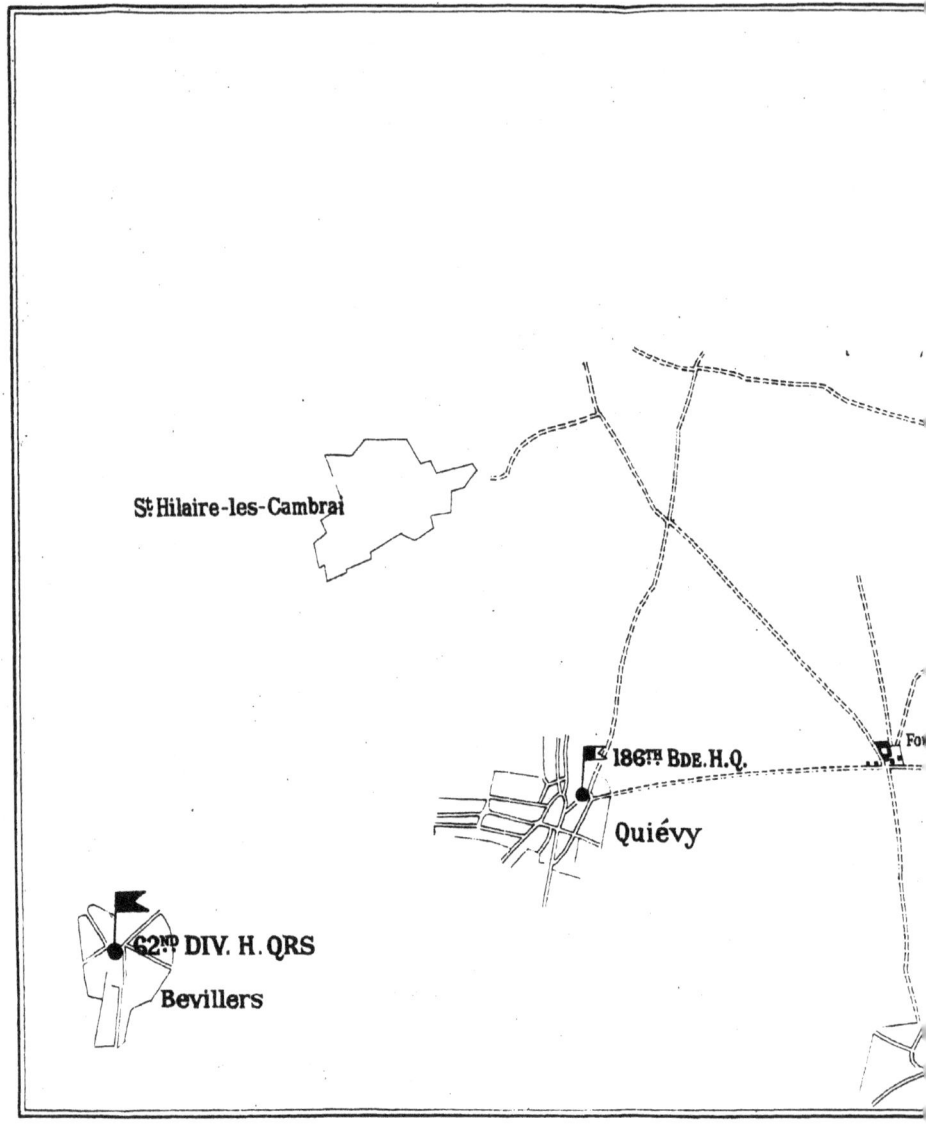

THE CAPTURE

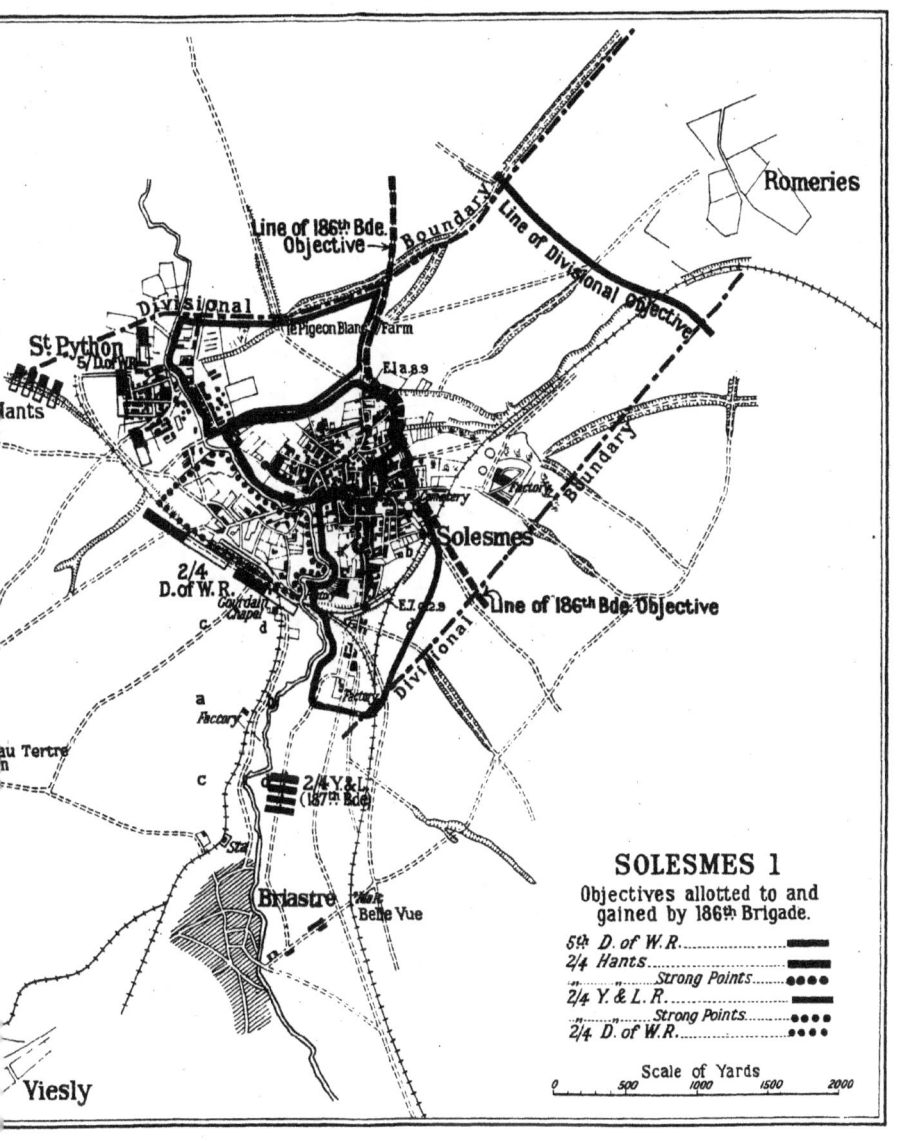

Chapter VII.   1918.

SOLESMES. I.

NO words can give an adequate picture of the tense situation along the Western Front during the early days of October, 1918; nor is it possible for mortal man to describe the wave of expectancy, the anxious feelings, that wonderful consciousness of great happenings close at hand, which held the peoples of the Entente Powers almost breathless in the Autumn of the final year of the Great War. In a last effort to save themselves from the consequence of their crime against humanity in forcing war in 1914, the German and Austro-Hungarian Governments had appealed to President Wilson of the United States of America, proposing an Armistice. Of the Allies of the Central Powers, Bulgaria had been beaten to her knees and had sued for Peace, and Turkey was on the eve of surrendering.

But pending the arrival of President Wilson's reply settling the conditions under which an Armistice could be granted, the German Armies in the west still made great efforts to stave off the defeat which had by now become a nightmare at German General Headquarters. It is impossible to read Ludendorff without receiving an impression that despair had gripped the Chief of the German General Staff : " Now we were weaker and one Division failed after another. The men who fought in the front line were heroes, but there were not enough of them for the long line. They felt themselves isolated ...... We may be proud of the men who fought those heroic fights. Our losses, however, were heavy. Our best men lay on the bloody battlefield."

Nemesis was indeed drawing nigh !

On 8th October, " The Battle of Cambrai, 1918 " opened, and again the Fourth and Third British Armies, attacking on a front of 17 miles from Sequehart to just south of Cambrai, penetrated the enemy's positions to a depth of between 3 and 4 miles ; whilst on the right the First French Army continued the attack as far south
               8TH OCT.

8TH OCT. as St. Quentin, advancing to the east of that town. By the night of 10th the British line ran from east of Bohain, northward through Audigny, St. Souplet, just west of Le Cateau, thence in a north-westerly direction past Neuvilly and east of St. Hilaire and Rieux to Estrun : and the pursuit to the Selle River had begun.

In these operations, however, the 62nd Division did not take part. But it is of interest to note that one Division of the VIth Corps—the 3rd—was probably the first of the Old Army Divisions to reach the scene of its early trials of August, 1914. For at the Battle of Le Cateau, on 26th August of that year, the 3rd Division held Caudry Village, just south of the Le Cateau—Cambrai road. The constitution of the VIth Corps at this period was indeed historic. It was formed of the Guards,[1] 2nd, 3rd and 62nd Divisions, two Old Army Divisions and one—62nd—the very embodiment of the New Army.[2] From the 2nd and 3rd to the 62nd was a far cry, but whilst the former, typifying the old professional soldier, were imbued with the traditions of past generations, the latter was a splendid example of the national fighting force, that product of the war, which will go down in the Military History of Great Britain as the finest body of men ever raised and trained in a state of emergency.

15TH OCT. As the front line of the VIth Corps advanced, so the Divisions in Corps Reserve moved forward also, and the 15th October found the 62nd resting in the area round Estourmel, a village about 4 miles south-east of Cambrai, and just south of the Le Cateau—Cambrai road. Here, on the above date, General Whigham received instructions from VIth Corps Headquarters that the Corps, in conjunction with the Corps on its flanks was to be prepared to capture the high ground east of the Selle River on or about the 20th October. The object of this operation was to drive the enemy from a line he had established east of the Selle and thereby secure passages over that river, which would facilitate the advance of the Third Army on Le Quesnoy. The 62nd Division, on the right, and the Guards Division on the left (both Divisions supported by ten Brigades of Field Artillery and all available Heavy Artillery) were to carry out the attack by the VIth Corps.

The capture of the town of Solesmes and the high ground 1 mile east of it, overlooking the village of Romeries, had been

---

[1]The Guards Division was formed in August, 1915, but consisted largely of old army troops.

[2]The term " New " is used in its comparative sense, and does not refer to the New (Kitchener) Army.

allotted to the 62nd Division. It was a formidable position to assault. The River Selle running along the front is some 20 feet from bank to bank, with an average depth of from 4 to 6 feet, the bottom is muddy and the banks steep and slippery—all the bridges had been destroyed by the enemy, and, on the Divisional front there was only one ford, namely, at St. Python. The destruction of the railway bridge over the river in the south-western corner of the town on October 18th had practically dammed the stream, and had caused an inundation for about 1,000 yards south of this point, making bridging operations impossible. In front of Solesmes, on the western bank, the enemy was holding the railway sidings and railway station strongly with machine guns, and also the eastern bank of the river at the suburb of St. Python. North and south of Solesmes, the 42nd Division had secured Infantry crossing over the river at Briastre, and the Guards had been able to push patrols across between Solesmes and Haussy by means of extemporized foot bridges.

After a thorough personal reconnaissance by the Divisional Commander, the 186th Brigade Commander, and their Staffs, the plan of attack was decided upon.

The governing idea of this plan was to outflank and overlap the town before any attempt to clear it was made. The success of the operation has since made it a typical illustration of the principle on which the capture of a village (or medium-sized woods) should be undertaken. Other factors that complicated the operation, and at the same time made it of particular interest, were that a river had to be crossed, that the operation was to be carried out during the hours of darkness, and that owing to the number of French inhabitants living in the village, bombardment had to be dispensed with.

The operation was divided into two phases, the first phase, the crossing of the River Selle and capture of Solesmes and St. Python was entrusted to the 186th Infantry Brigade—part of the Brigade was to cross the river at St. Python by foot bridges, capture that suburb and the strong point of Le Pigeon Blanc, and then turn southward to clear the northern part of Solesmes, whilst another Battalion crossed the river south of the inundation in the 42nd Divisional area, captured the factory and railway triangle south of Solesmes and were then to clear the southern half of Solesmes.

The second phase of the attack, the capture of the high ground overlooking Romeries, entailing a further advance of about a mile from the eastern edge of Solesmes, was entrusted to the 185th

15TH OCT. Infantry Brigade. It was decided to carry it out by passing one Battalion north and one Battalion south of Solesmes.

The 187th Infantry Brigade was in Divisional Reserve.

Although the presence of French inhabitants in Solesmes and St. Python precluded a bombardment of these places it was decided to cover the attack with a shrapnel and machine-gun barrage, as the inhabitants would certainly take refuge in the cellars on the firing commencing.

Zero hour was fixed for 2 a.m. and, as the whole of the first phase would take place during the hours of darkness, the troops of the 186th Brigade were to wear a distinguishing mark, a white band on the right arm, and were given a pass-word " Pelican." Electric torches were provided for all Company and Platoon Commanders.

By means of a local directory containing a map which gave the names of the streets of Solesmes, and an aeroplane mosaic photograph, it was possible to issue to each platoon commander a map with exact instructions as to the portion of the town he was to clear. This saved the confusion that often arises during fighting in an unknown town.

17/18TH OCT. On the night of 17th/18th October the 186th Infantry Brigade moved forward from Carnières and Boussières and relieved the 1st Guards Brigade (Guards Division) in the Sector west of Solesmes, the 2/4th Duke's taking over the right sub-sector and the 5th Duke's the left : the 2/4th Hants. were in reserve in Quievy.

Command of the Sector passed to General Whigham, whose Headquarters were then at Estourmel (but opened on the following day at Bevillers) at 11-40 p.m.

18/19TH OCT. In accordance with the plan of attack the 2/4th Duke's took over the whole of the Brigade front on the night of 18th/19th, enabling the 5th Duke's to withdraw to Quievy (where Brigade Headquarters were established) and prepare for the coming operations.

" Zero " had been fixed for 2 a.m. on the 20th October, at which hour the 2/4th Duke's, holding the front line, were to attack and capture the line of the railway in D.12 a. and b. and then clear the ground east of it as far as the Selle River. The 5th Duke's were to assemble amongst the houses of the western portion of St. Python ; they were then to cross by the northern bridges on the Selle and, with one Company, capture the eastern portion of that village, and the road running north and south through Le Pigeon Blanc Farm with two other Companies; the remaining Company was to form a defensive flank facing south towards Solesmes.¹

18/19TH OCT.

The Hallamshires (2/4th York and Lancs. Regt.) at Zero minus 30 minutes, were to cross by the bridges over the river, in the southern Divisional Area and form up on the eastern banks of the river. At Zero they were to go forward, one company attacking the Factory immediately south of the Railway Triangle, a second company the northern area of the Railway Triangle and the southern portion of Solesmes, the remaining two Companies to advance along the railway as far as the crossings south-east of Solesmes and then turn inwards and attack the town from that direction.²

The 2/4th Hants. were to assemble in the railway cutting (west of St. Python) about the Northern Divisional boundary, and cross the bridges over the Selle on this front as soon as they were cleared by the 5th Duke's. The Hampshiremen were then to attack Solesmes from the north and join hands with the Hallamshires, who should be advancing from the south-east.³

A Company of the 62nd Battalion M.G.C. had also been detailed to assist in the capture and consolidation of the Brigade objectives, and for this purpose two sections were to cross the northern bridges in rear of 2/4th Hants. Regt. and move to positions near the cross roads south of Le Pigeon Blanc Farm and the Farm respectively, whilst two sections were to cross by the southern bridges in rear of 2/4th York and Lancs. Regt. and take up positions on the railway in the south-east corner of Solesmes in order to protect the right flank of the 186th Brigade.

Eight-foot bridges were to be constructed by the Divisional Royal Engineers at the northern end of St. Python, for the passage of the 5th Duke's and the Hampshiremen; 4-foot bridges to supplement two already built by the 42nd Division were to be thrown across the Selle, south of Briastre, prior to Zero hour, for the Hallamshires, and two pontoon bridges to carry field guns, and a trestle bridge to carry 60-pounders were to be constructed at the most suitable points as soon as the situation permitted.⁴

¹The outflanking and overlapping movement in the north.
²The enveloping movement in the south.
³The operation of clearing the town.
⁴As no account of the capture of Solesmes would be complete without adequate mention of the devoted efforts of the Divisional Royal Engineers, the full Report by the C.R.E. is given as an Appendix.

19/20TH OCT.

The night of the 19th/20th was very wet, and when at 10-30 p.m. the Hallamshires (Lieut.-Colonel L. H. P. Hart) left their billets in Quievy and marched to the Selle River in D.18.d rain was falling steadily. The western bank was reached at about 12-30 a.m., but the river was found much swollen and Colonel Hart decided to move his troops across to the eastern bank earlier than Zero minus 30 minutes. The crossing was successfully accomplished, mainly across the bridges constructed earlier in the night by the Sappers, though in some instances the men had to wade through water up to their waists. Nevertheless, at Zero minus 30, the Battalion was formed up on the road in D.18 b.c.d., facing north-east.

The 5th Duke's (Lieut.-Colonel J. Walker) moved off from Quievy by platoons at 8 p.m., and by 11 p.m. had assembled amongst the houses of St. Python, west of the Selle. The river at this point was a formidable obstacle, being about 25 feet wide, with a depth of from 1 to 6 feet, the bed of thick slimy mud. It was fordable at only one point—V.30.c.5.0. The crossing was well defended by enemy machine guns, which kept up intermittent fire during the crossing and bridging operations which were carried out notwithstanding.

Only one Company (A) of the 5th Duke's crossed by the ford, the men carrying five light ladders with which to scale the eastern banks of the river, which were steep and muddy. This Company got across in 15 minutes and formed up 100 yards east of the river. With marvellous rapidity, though fired at by a persistent enemy sniper and hostile machine guns, the 461st Company, R.E., in a very little while had constructed no less than eight foot bridges of cork floats and trestles, and the remaining three Companies of the Duke's, also carrying ladders to help them up the opposite banks, crossed over, reaching their assembly positions about 2 minutes before Zero hour (2 a.m.). The Companies then lay down in orchards.

20TH OCT.

The 2/4th Hants. (Major G. E. C. Cockburn, temporarily commanding) reached their preliminary assembly position, a cutting in the St. Vaast—St. Python railway, about half a mile from St. Python, at about 11-30 p.m. At 12-50 a.m. on the 20th, the Battalion moved up to its final assembly position (in rear of the 5th Duke's)—the western edge of St. Python.

Finally, at 1 a.m., the two Companies of 2/4th Duke's (Lieut.-Colonel P. P. Wilson) formed up about 150 yards west of the railway.

The enemy does not appear to have been very observant. Perhaps the falling rain and wretched conditions generally persuaded him that no attack would be made before dawn, or else his one-time cat-like vigilance had deserted him.

At 2 a.m. the barrage (which was most effective) opened on the railway in front of the 2/4th Duke's and the leading Company of that Battalion captured the first objective, practically without opposition. On the barrage lifting the second Company passed quickly through the first and gained its objective on the west bank of the Selle. Both positions were then consolidated, though the enemy shelled the position heavily, inflicting some twenty casualties on the two Companies.

One officer and seventeen other ranks, with one machine gun, were captured by the 2/4th Duke's.

The 5th Duke's,[1] having crossed the river, were able to keep close on the heels of the barrage which fell on that front of St. Python, which lay east of the Selle. At Zero, plus 3 minutes, the barrage lifted and A Company, following close on the barrage, rushed the village, but at once met with fierce opposition from the block of houses which overlooked the river, where the crossings had taken place, and from each flank. This resistance was, however, speedily overcome and, splitting up into sections, the Company began to advance through the village. At two points in the main street the roadway was blocked by barricades and held by the enemy. At the first barricade some sharp hand-to-hand fighting took place but presently the Germans gave way and A Company passed on to the second obstacle. Here machine-gun opposition was met with, but again the Duke's broke down the enemy's resistance and passed on to take up a line of defence, running north from the south-east outskirts of St. Python. At the latter point a hostile machine-gun post had to be rushed and the gun and team captured before a halt was called. This Company had had quite a formidable task in "clearing" the village, and in the stiff street-fighting which had taken place the men used their bayonets freely, killing and wounding large numbers of the enemy who resisted capture. On the barrage lifting to the eastern outskirts of the village, C Company immediately moved forward behind A from the position of assembly. On moving to its forming-up position at the south-east corner of St. Python, "C" experienced opposition along the main road through the village. This was effectively dealt with and the Company pushed

---

[1]Colonel Walker and his Intelligence Officer (Lt. Todd) had previously reconnoitred the river, and on testing its depth, the latter officer suddenly found himself up to his middle in water.

20TH OCT. on in an easterly direction, still fighting, but dropping posts on the way until the road junction at E.I.a.8.9 their objective was reached, thus completing the defensive flank covering the northern exits of Solesmes. Touch was obtained on the left with B Company which, with D Company (on the left of B), had passed through A Company and was on the line of the objective.

B Company (right) and D Company (left) had formed up in rear of A and C Companies and had pushed forward behind the barrage to the eastern side of St. Python where, after a certain amount of " clearing " which had to be done, the advance was continued to the line of the final objective. At Le Pigeon Farm (allotted to D Company) the enemy made a stand, but his machine guns having been put out of action by Lewis-gun fire, the buildings were captured after 15 minutes and many prisoners were taken. Touch by these two Companies was gained with C Company on the right and the Guards Division on the left. The two Companies then dug in and consolidated. " By 4 a.m. the whole of the Battalion objectives had been taken. The men attacked with a will and dash beyond all praise, tackling each little opposition with great initiative and resource."[1] Over 300 prisoners, fifteen machine guns and four trench mortars and much equipment was taken by the 5th Duke's.

In the meantime the 2/4th Hants. Regt., which, after marching from Quievy, had reached its assembly position in the railway cutting, moved forward to St. Python, in rear of the 5th Duke's, and began crossing the river at Zero hour (2 a.m.). Half an hour later the three leading Companies (A, B and D) had reformed on the eastern bank, without the loss of a single man. The rear Company (C), which was to clear the centre portion of Solesmes, did not begin to cross the river until 3 a.m.

A Company, after reforming on the eastern bank, moved off along the St. Python—Solesmes Road, but met with heavy rifle and machine-gun fire from houses in St. Python, which had not been cleared of the enemy. This opposition was eventually overcome and the Company passed on, the leading platoons establishing the first post at about 4-20 a.m. Up to that hour A Company had captured two machine guns and thirty prisoners. The second platoon on passing through the first, though meeting with considerable opposition, established another post at 5-15 a.m., capturing two more machine guns and twenty prisoners ; the third platoon then cleared the area allotted to it.

[1]Battalion Diary, 5th Duke of Wellington's Regiment.

D Company, skirting St. Python, passed through the flank company of the 5th Duke's and advanced on its objective. From a brick wall along its front this Company was met by heavy machine gun fire, and enfilade fire was also opened from the right flank. Progress was, therefore, delayed until an outflanking movement was put in motion and the resistance broken down. Here, one machine gun was captured and another driven off into the town, where it was subsequently captured by the Hallamshires. Two posts were now established by D Company and a platoon at once began " clearing " operations between them.

B Company, close behind D, passed through the 5th Duke's and established a post, without encountering serious opposition, at E.I.c.8.8, at about 5-30 a.m. The second platoon met with serious resistance from machine-gun and trench mortar fire and it was not until the hostile post was rushed, the machine gun captured and the crew either killed or taken prisoner, that a second strong point was established by this Company. The remaining platoons then cleared the area and gained touch with the Hallamshires on the first objective.

Finally C Company, which had crossed the Selle just after 3 a.m., advanced through A Company's posts and cleared the area allotted to it, capturing altogether five machine guns and two trench mortars without incurring a single casualty.

By 7-15 a.m. the 2/4th Hants. had captured all its objectives with a total loss of only one officer and twenty-three other ranks, killed and wounded.

Thus so far, the 2/4th Duke of Wellington's Regt. had captured the railway station and the suburbs of Solesmes up to the western bank of the Selle River, the 5th Duke of Wellington's Regt. had taken St. Python, Le Pigeon Blanc Farm and the area north of Solesmes, and the 2/4th Hants. Regt. the northern half of the town ; the southern half of Solesmes and the important railway triangle had been allotted to the 2/4th York and Lancs. Regt. (Hallamshires).

Half-an-hour before Zero, the Hallamshires, though many of them were wet to the skin, having waded through the Selle, stood shivering with cold in their assembly positions between the river and the road in D.18 b. and c. facing north-east. The Battalion was in the following formation :—A Company on a two-platoon frontage, B Company similarly, with C and D Companies in rear on a one-platoon frontage in depth. At Zero plus 15 minutes (2-15 a.m.) Nos. 1 and 2 platoons of A Company advanced in a

20TH OCT. north-east direction on the Factory, north of the Railway Triangle. Heavy machine-gun fire from the Factory and the houses on the Neuvilly—Solesmes road and from a sunken road on the top of a ridge east of the Factory met the gallant Hallamshires as they went forward. The ground over which they advanced was intersected by a number of barbed wire apron fences and thick hedges running in different directions, but on many occasions they had met with worse obstacles and were not to be denied. The barrage which, as on other parts of the front attacked had been splendid, lifted off the Factory at 2-30 a.m. and men dashed through a breach which had been made in the southern wall, having captured en route their first machine gun which had been in action in the Factory grounds. Simultaneously, one section of No. 2 platoon on the left, and two sections of No. 1 platoon, on the right, enveloped the Factory, cutting off the enemy's retirement, whilst the remainder cleared the Factory buildings, which were much larger than had been anticipated. In this operation twelve prisoners and two machine guns were captured.

Nos. 3 and 4 Platoons now passed through, heading for the railway line. More barbed wire obstructions and heavy machine-gun fire was met with, but advancing by rushes these two Platoons reached the foot of the railway embankment, where a machine-gun post was encountered; three of the gunners were killed and the remainder captured. From the railway line the enemy now began to hurl bombs on the Hallamshires and hostile machine guns searched their ranks but, after some stiff hand-to-hand fighting, in which the bayonet was used freely, two more machine guns were captured with six prisoners and the Platoons established posts on the embankment. The latter was, however, under fire which came from a chateau north of the railway. A patrol was therefore sent off to clear the chateau and presently returned driving thirty-eight more prisoners before it.

B Company now passed through A, the two leading Platoons capturing the railway line from E.7.c.1.8 to E.7.d.2.9. Two more Platoons then passed through the former and, after forming strong points at E.7.c.8.8 and E.7.a.7.9, cleared the buildings in E.7.a between the strong points and the Selle. The darkness and heavy rain made control of the men extremely difficult, and the very thick hedges and barbed wire fences tended to throw the Company off direction.

A little later occurred another of those outstanding deeds of

SERGT. J. B. DAYKINS, V.C., 2/4TH BN. YORK AND LANCASTER REGT.

Face p. 117.

gallantry which earned for the Division the greatest reward a soldier can obtain—the Victoria Cross.

No. 7 Platoon of B Company of the 2/4th York and Lancs. Regt., under Sergeant John Daykins, had met with heavy machine-gun fire from the railway embankment, but the gun was rushed by the Hallamshires and the Platoon then proceeded up the main street of Solesmes towards the church. By this time the Platoon numbered only twelve men, but they were under a skilful leader who, picking his way carefully along the street and taking advantage of whatever cover presented itself, was an inspiring example to his comrades. About half-way up the street Sergeant Daykins came upon a machine gun, the German gunner just about to open fire on the Platoon. Daykins promptly shot the man and the gun was rushed. Again the advance was continued up the main thoroughfare and again, about 50 yards from the church, the enemy's opposition became very strong. Heavy machine-gun fire was now turned upon Daykins and his gallant comrades, bombs were thrown at them, and from the cellars of houses on all sides the enemy emerged, surrounding the intrepid Hallamshires. A hand-to-hand fight now ensued, in which Daykins personally accounted for seven Germans. This (to use a phrase common during the war) put " the wind up " the remainder, who fled, and the Sergeant then led his men to their objective, where a strong point was formed. The astounding thing was that up to this point the party (only thirteen strong be it remembered) had captured thirty prisoners and had killed about twenty-five of the enemy, besides wounding many more, after having been isolated in the town for half-an-hour.

The climax, however, was still to come.

From one of the prisoners Daykins learned the position of a machine gun which had been holding up another portion of B Company and, although other of his men begged to be allowed to go with him, after urging on them the absolute necessity of still maintaining the important post already established, and of keeping a close guard over the prisoners, he set off alone to capture, or put out of action, the hostile machine gun and its crew. Exactly what happened it is impossible to say, but it appears that, although under heavy machine-gun fire all the while, Sergeant Daykins worked his way from house to house until he came to the post. The next his comrades saw, shortly afterwards, was this very gallant man returning, carrying the machine gun on his shoulders and driving before him twenty-five more prisoners. He then mounted the

20TH OCT. captured machine gun in his own post. Little wonder that the Victoria Cross was bestowed on him for, as the *London Gazette* stated : " his magnificent fighting spirit and example inspired his men, who would follow him anywhere. He was the outstanding figure in the success of the attack."[1] The tactical effect of this astounding deed was considerable. " This action of Sergeant Daykins, although it appeared, owing to the previous strenuous opposition, almost certain death, undoubtedly saved many casualties to the remainder of his Company, and enabled the village to be carried at an earlier hour of the operations."

Simultaneously with the action of No. 7 Platoon, No. 8 had cleared the Factory in E.7.a and the houses round about; this was completed by 3-30 a.m. Nos. 5 and 6 Platoons then passed through, working up the main street and establishing another post at E.7.a.7.9. No. 5 Platoon assisted by a Platoon of A Company, then cleared the remainder of the area allotted to B Company and, although opposition was encountered, the 2/4th Hants. Regt., arriving on the scene (from the north-west) joined hands with the Hallamshires, and the enemy in the neighbourhood then surrendered. All was quiet in B Company sector by 9 a.m., many civilians being released.

C Company, having passed through B Company, was temporarily checked by machine-gun fire, but owing to the initiative of two sub-sections and the platoon commanders, strong points were eventually established at E.7.b.7.7 and E.1.d.4.2, and that area of Solesmes, west and south-west of B Company's area was cleared. Another N.C.O.—Sergeant Orwin (Platoon commander)—showed exceptional initiative and gallantry in the capture of an enemy point, situated in the sunken road at E.7.d.6.2. Another Platoon took three machine guns and about thirty prisoners near the chateau on the east side of the road in E.7.a.7.7., where heavy fighting was experienced. About 5-30 a.m. connection was established with the 2/4th Hants. C Company was subjected to heavy shelling all day and sustained casualties.

D Company, which had " leap-frogged " A and B Companies, had come upon C Company when temporarily held up by machine-gun fire from the church. This Company (D), which was to join hands with the Hampshiremen at the eastern edge of Solesmes, successfully formed strong points at E.1.d.7.4 and E.1.d.2.9, the attacking platoons working in sections along the various streets. About 150 prisoners, three machine guns and a field kitchen had been

[1]*London Gazette*, dated 6th January, 1919.

captured by the time this Company had cleared the area allotted to it. 20TH OCT.
At about 5 a.m. the success signal was fired from the cemetery in E.1.d. Solesmes had fallen!

The Hallamshires, during their gallant attack, had escaped with extraordinarily light casualties, *i.e.*, one officer wounded, five other ranks killed, forty-five wounded and four missing. The total number of prisoners captured by the Battalion was 250, with twenty machine guns.

The way was now clear for the second phase of the operations, *i.e.*, the capture of the high ground overlooking Romeries.

THE CAPTURE OF SOLESMES—II.

Chapter VIII. 1918.
SOLESMES. II.

DURING the attack on St. Python and Solesmes, the 20TH OCT. 185th Infantry Brigade (Brigadier-General Viscount Hampden) had marched out of billets in Bevillers to Quievy, the head of the column reaching the latter village just as the last Battalion of the 186th Infantry Brigade left it. Before the Brigade reached Quievy heavy rain had begun to fall and by the time the Battalions arrived in the village all ranks were drenched through. There was, however, a fairly long wait before the Brigade was timed to go forward again (Zero plus 6¼ hours) and carry out the second phase of the operations. So, having got the troops under cover the Battalion Commanders were able to give their men a short sleep, after which a hot meal was served out from the cookers, before the advance to assembly positions was begun.

The attack on the high ground overlooking Romeries was carried out by the 8th West Yorks. (Lieut.-Colonel N. A. England) on the right and the 2/20th London Regt. (Major W. M. Craddock, temporarily commanding) on the left; the 1/5th Devon Regt. (Lieut.-Colonel H. Bastow) was in Brigade Reserve.

At 3-50 a.m., the 8th West Yorks. resumed their march towards Solesmes by way of Fontaine au Tertre Farm and Briastre Station. When the Battalion reached the Selle it was found that the bridges constructed by the Sappers had, owing to the rise of the river, become flooded. On the road up from Quievy hostile shelling caused the Battalion five casualties—one officer and four other ranks wounded—but eventually the river was crossed in good order and, without further loss the assembly position on the eastern outskirts of Solesmes was reached.

The 2/20th London Regt. left Quievy at 4 a.m. and, passing through St. Python, crossed the Selle River without casualties, by 6-20 a.m., successfully reaching its assembly positions along the Solesmes—Valenciennes Road.

During the first phase of the operations the Divisional Artillery

20TH OCT. kept up a standing barrage for over an hour beyond Solesmes, whilst the town was being "cleared." At 4-20 a.m. the guns ceased firing, and some of the more distant batteries moved up to closer range. At 7 a.m. the barrage for the second phase of the attack fell heavily in front of the 185th Infantry Brigade, and the West Yorkshiremen and Londoners advanced to the attack.

The 8th West Yorks., advancing on a two-company front (A right and D left), almost immediately encountered opposition, from a Factory on the right front of the Battalion, but on the right Company carrying out a turning movement from the south, the ground east of the Factory was captured after some opposition together with two 77 mm. field guns, two trench mortars, four light machine guns and 130 prisoners. The successful attack of A Company cleared the way for D Company, whose objective was the Factory. This Company then advanced and captured the buildings, pushing forward a further 200 yards and establishing a line of posts. A Company then advanced to the road running north-east from the Factory, and together the two Companies established a line of posts from E. 2. d. 5.6. and E. 8. b. 1.9., with platoons in support. B Company, allotted the task of clearing the ground to the west of the railway, suffered heavily from shell fire while crossing the railway, and during the work of clearing the ground, met with very stiff opposition from hostile machine-gun fire from the Quarry. The advance of the Londoners, however, on the left of B Company, relieved the opposition in front of the latter and enabled the Company to push on and capture the post with forty prisoners. C Company, well in touch with the situation, kept close up to the leading Companies.

By about 10 a.m. the 8th West Yorks. had captured the final objective and a line of posts was established from W.27. c.7.9. to W.27. d. 5.0., *i.e.*, the high ground west of Romeries. Touch was gained with the 2/20th London Regt. on the left, but as there were no signs of troops of the 42nd Division on the right, a defensive flank was formed and a patrol sent out to gain touch on that flank.

Meanwhile, the 2/20th London Regt., meeting with only slight opposition, had captured the final objective (from the railway in W.27. a. to the Le Pigeon Blanc—Vertain Road—W.20 central) in the first bound. Touch on the right with the 8th West Yorks. and on the left with the Guards Division was then gained. The line gained was organized for defence and platoon posts were established some 300 yards in front of the main line of resistance. Patrols sent forward to ascertain if the line of the River Harpies and the village of Romeries

were held by the enemy, were fired on from west of the village. 20TH OCT.
Shortly afterwards, the enemy's guns opened fire on the line of the objective gained by the Londoners and inflicted a number of casualties on the forward Companies which were then " digging in."

Thus the whole of the objectives allotted to the 62nd Division had been captured, captured in its own inimitable style, with that " dash " and " go " which had won for it a place amongst the first-class fighting divisions in France and Flanders. The enemy, however, made one attempt to regain a portion of what he had lost. About 4-15 p.m., after heavily bombarding the new forward positions gained by the 62nd, he delivered a counter-attack on the left of the 2/20th London Regt. His troops followed close on a barrage, advancing from Romeries in extended order. But in answer to the S.O.S., the Divisional Artillery put down a very heavy barrage which, combined with rifle and Lewis gun fire from the forward positions, completely broke up this counter-attack, and the enemy retired in disorder. This incident closed the operations and the troops continued with their work of consolidating and organizing the positions gained.

Throughout both phases of the Battle the devoted gunners had splendidly supported the infantry in the front line and the following note from Brigadier-General J. C. Burnett (commanding 186th Infantry Brigade) to Brigadier-General A. T. Anderson, the C.R.A., shows how greatly the attacking Battalions appreciated the splendid shooting of their comrades serving the guns : " As I know that your people like to know what the infantry who attacked thought of the barrage, both the left attacking Battalions and those that took the railway station, wish me to say that it was the most accurate barrage which they have yet advanced under. Would you please convey our thanks to the men behind the guns, who so largely contributed towards the success."[1]

The Divisional narrative concludes with this paragraph : " From 11.00 hours (11 a.m.) onwards and throughout the night of 20th/21st, 20TH/21ST hostile shelling of the back areas was considerable, really heavy OCT. concentrations being fired at intervals on Solesmes, St. Python and the river crossings. Little damage was done, however, and all

---

[1] During the operation the 62nd Division captured in prisoners : twelve officers and 687 other ranks ; in war material, seventy-one machine guns, thirteen trench mortars and five guns. Total casualties in the Division were : ten officers wounded (one died of wounds—Lieut. A. Clarkson, 8th West Yorks.), fifty-seven other ranks killed, 370 wounded and fifteen missing. Total : ten officers, 442 other ranks.

20TH/21ST OCT.

23RD OCT.

arrangements for a further attack by the 3rd Division were completed by the early morning of the 23rd October, when that Division passed through (the 62nd) and continued the advance."

The 185th and 186th Infantry Brigades moved back to the area Quievy—Bevillers during the night 22nd/23rd; the 187th Brigade being already at Cattenières, where the 2/4th York and Lancs. (Hallamshires) rejoined.

In Quievy, the " Pelicans "—the famous Divisional Troupe—" commandeered " the local cinema theatre and played nightly to crowded houses, whilst during the day " Soccer " and " Rugger " matches between the various units took place to the huge delight of all ranks; the hard fighter is usually a hard player.

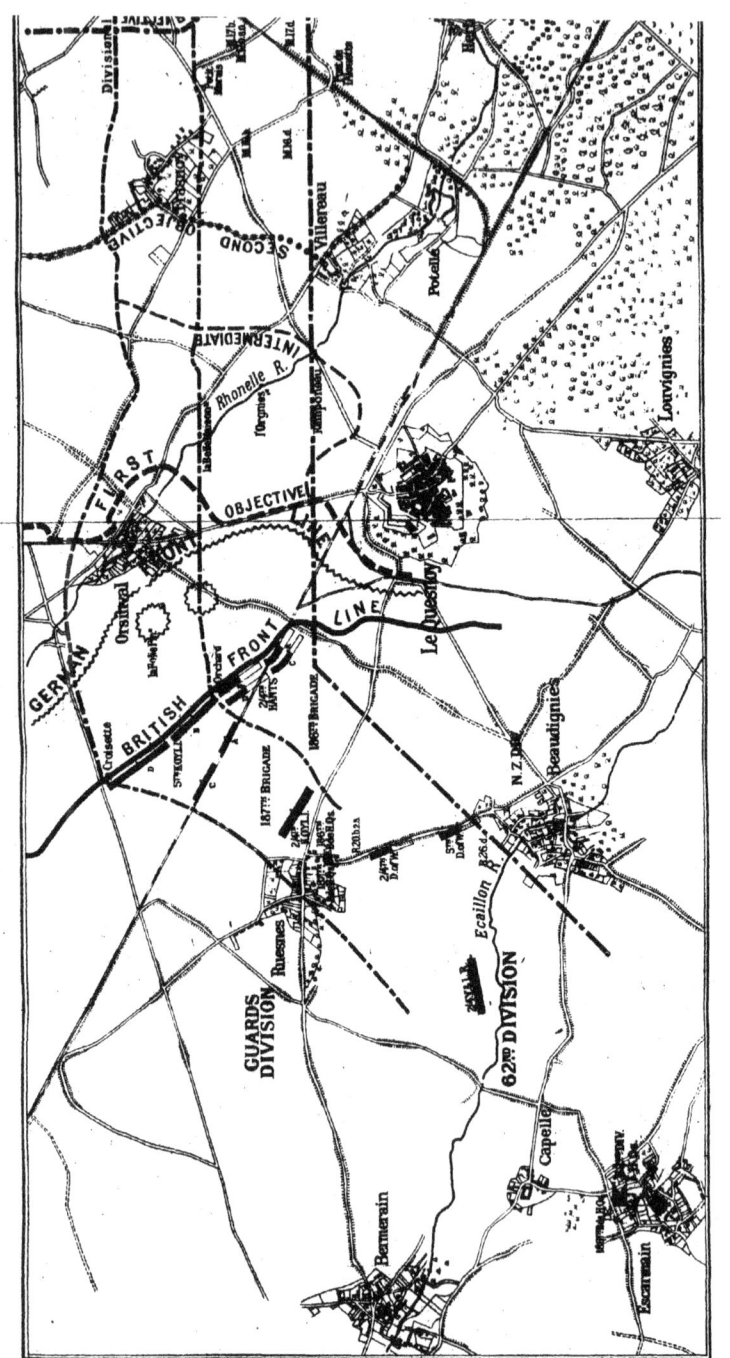

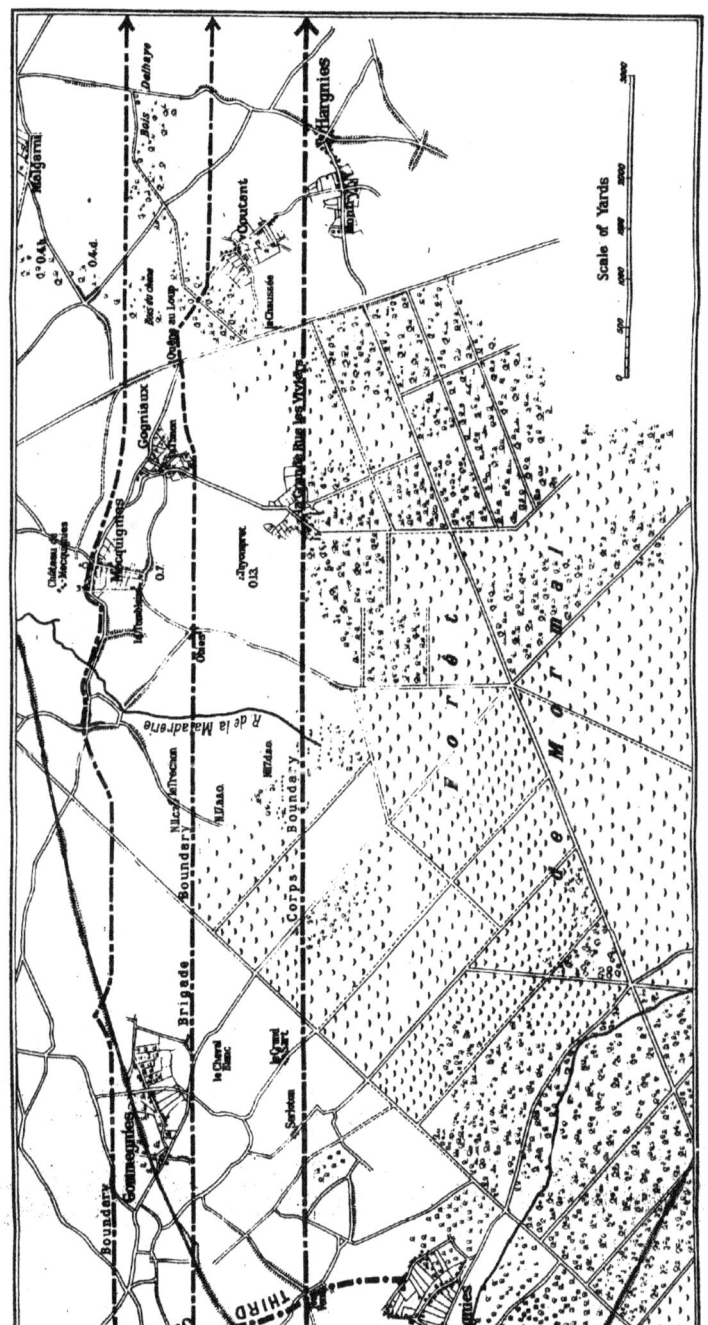

ORSINVAL AND FRASNOY.

Chapter IX. 1918.

ORSINVAL AND FRASNOY.

" By this time the rapid succession of heavy blows dealt by the British forces had had a cumulative effect, both moral and material upon the German Armies."
Official Despatches.

THE Battle of the Selle yielded a further 20,000 prisoners and 475 guns, captured by twenty-four British and two American divisions from thirty-one German divisions. Demoralization, which had slowly penetrated the Armies of the Central Powers, although evident amongst the German infantry and machine-gunners along the Western front, was nevertheless not general, neither was the enemy finally beaten to his knees. Turkey and Bulgaria had capitulated and Austria was on the very brink of collapse. In France and Belgium the German Armies could not be allowed to withdraw to shorter lines and prolong the struggle through the winter of 1918-1919. To prevent this, and in order to anticipate the enemy's withdrawal and force an immediate conclusion, an attack upon a vital centre (from the Sambre, north of Oisy, to Valenciennes) was to take place at the beginning of November.

On 30th October, General Whigham received notification from 30TH OCT. VIth Corps Headquarters that on 4th November the advance was to be continued. To the First French and the Fourth, Third, and First British Armies, in the order given from right to left, belongs the honour of dealing the enemy the final blow from which he never recovered.

The lines selected for the final thrust ran from Avesnes, through Maubeuge to Mons. The British Army was to end the war upon the very ground on which the terrible struggle had begun. Two divisions at least, of the VIth Corps—2nd and 3rd—were soon to tread the very soil over which, in 1914, tired and worn and hungry they had begun

30TH OCT. the famous Retreat from Mons[1]; but now their steps were directed eastwards and not towards the south, east to the German frontier with the enemy hard put to it, his back against the wall in a despairing and, as it will be proved, a vain effort to ward off utter defeat. The towns and villages through which the VIth Corps was to pass, the very roads which were to echo their tramping feet, were they not patrolled by the ghosts of that glorious Old Army of 1914 now passed away; and the two divisions—the Guards and the 62nd—New Divisions detailed to make this attack, may they not be likened to the New Guard marching to relieve the Old Guard—the silent dead—who, in the quiet night kept watch, turn and turn about, waiting for the " relief " that came at last—in November, 1918.

For the attack of the VIth Corps was to be directed on Maubeuge and carried out by the 62nd Division on the right and the Guards Division on the left, the 3rd and 2nd Divisions in Corps Reserve, were to complete the task if required. The first objective of the Third Army was the line Locquignol-Herpignies-Frasnoy. On the capture of this line the advance was to be pressed energetically to the line of the St. Remy-Pont-sur-Sambre-Bavai-Montignies-sur-Roc Road. On attaining the latter line the first stage of the operations would be completed, after which the attack was to be continued towards the line Avesnes-Maubeuge-Mons.

The New Zealand Division, on the right of the 62nd, was attacking Le Quesnoy. " Zero " hour for all Armies was 5.30 a.m. on the 4th November.

The plan of attack by the 62nd Division was comparatively simple. At " Zero " hour the 186th Brigade, on the right, and the 187th Brigade, on the left, were to advance under a creeping barrage to the Red Line. On the latter they were to halt, when the advance was to be continued by the 185th Brigade which, at " Zero " hour, was to move forward from Escarmin in readiness to pass through the leading Brigades. When the 185th Brigade had passed through the 186th and 187th Brigades the latter were to reorganize and be ready to continue the advance at " Zero " plus 1 day.

The attack was to be supported by five brigades of Field Artillery and one brigade of " Heavies." A creeping barrage was to cover the advance as far as the Green Line. One brigade of R.F.A. was to be held in Mobile Reserve to move forward on the capture of the

[1] And at least one German Division (6th of the Seventeenth German Army) which, flushed by success at Mons in 1914, pursued the B.E.F. to the Marne with the remainder of Von Kluck's First German Army, was now engaged in a precipitous retreat, beaten and demoralized, back to Germany.

Blue Line, the remaining brigades of Artillery were to move forward under the orders of the C.R.A. as they dropped out of effective range. One company of the 62nd M.G.C. was to be attached to each of the 186th and 187th Infantry Brigades, whilst two companies were to occupy positions from which, by overhead fire, they could cover the advance of the two brigades. On the Blue Line being captured one of these two latter Companies was to move forward to cover the advance of the infantry to the Green Line. The remaining Company was to reorganize and go forward with the 185th Brigade. Two sections of Sappers were to accompany the attacks of the 186th and 187th Brigades and prepare crossing places for guns and limbered G. S. wagons over the Rhonelle River. A bridge was also to be constructed at Petit Marais (M.11.c.7.5.) to take lorries. The remainder of the Divisional R.E. and the Pioneers (9th Durham Light Infantry) were to repair and maintain the roads east of the line of departure.

On the night of 2/3rd November the 187th Infantry Brigade moved up and took over the front held by the right Brigade (6th) of the 2nd Division near Ruesnes at the same time extending its right, taking over two posts from the New Zealand Division. On completion of the relief the 5th K.O.Y.L.I. held the front line, the 2/4th K.O.Y.L.I. was in support and the 2/4th York and Lancs. Regt. (Hallamshires) in reserve. Headquarters, 187th Brigade, were at R.20.b.2.5. The 186th Infantry Brigade on the same night moved up from Solesmes to Escarmin, whilst the 185th Brigade moved two battalions from Quievy to Romeries (1/5th Devons and 2/20th London R.) and one (8th West Yorks.) to Solesmes.

On the 3rd November the 185th Brigade moved forward to Escarmin, the leading battalion arriving just before midnight (3rd/4th) as the rear battalion of the 186th Brigade (then marching out to take up its assembly positions for the attack) cleared the village. The Artillery, to cover the attack on the following morning, also moved into position when darkness had fallen. The C.R.A., 62nd Division (Brig.-General A. T. Anderson) had his Headquarters in Escarmin; both the 310th and 312th Brigades, R.F.A., came into action N. of Ruesnes, the two Brigades having been "grouped" together, forming the "Johnson" Group, under the command of Lieut.-Colonel Johnson. One Battery (B/312) of the 312th Brigade had unfortunately suffered the loss of 48 horses, the result of a concentration of "H.V." guns put down on Escarmin on the night of 2nd, where the Battery was billeted.

3RD/4TH
Nov.

As gas concentrations had been fired on Ruesnes nightly, and it was possible the village would be shelled heavily during the operations, it was necessary to avoid passing the 186th Brigade and the reserve battalions of the 187th Brigade through that place. A track was therefore marked out and picqueted, " from an artillery bridge in R.25.c. across country S.E. of the village to the Le Quesnoy-Ruesnes road." Also, the only way of getting transport forward, until Le Quesnoy was captured, was *via* Capelle and Pont de Buat. These two places were, however, in the area of the Guards Division, but arrangements were made with the latter to use the road for the purpose of moving forward the 185th Brigade and the fighting transport of the two leading Brigades from " Zero " (5.30 a.m.) minus 30 minutes to " Zero " plus 90 minutes.

At 11.30 p.m. on the night 3rd/4th November, all three Battalions of the 186th Infantry Brigade (Brig.-General J. C. Burnett) began the march out of Escarmin to their assembly positions. The 2/4th Hants. (Lieut.-Col. F. Brook) leading, took up a position along the railway in R.16.d. and along the road in R.16.a. to the S.E. corner of the Orchard (E. of Bellevue Farm), companies being drawn up in the following order :—" A " on the right, " B " on the left, " C " Right Support, " D " Left Support. Hostile shell and machine-gun fire, during the forming-up operations were severe, but there were no casualties.

In rear of the Hampshiremen, the 2/4th Duke of Wellington's Regt. (Lieut.-Col. P. P. Wilson) was in the Sunken Road running south from Ruesnes, whilst the 5th Duke of Wellington's Regt. (Lieut.-Col. J. Walker) was sheltering under the high bank of the Sunken Road in R.26.d., *i.e.*, north of the village of Beaudignies.

The attack of the 186th Brigade was to be on a one-battalion front, rear battalions passing through to the various objectives. To the 2/4th Hants. had been allotted the first objective—the Le Quesnoy-Orsinval road (Blue Line) ; to the 2/4th Duke of Wellington's Regt. the second objective—from the eastern edge of Villerau (exclusive) to the road-junction just W. of Frasnoy (Green Line) ; to the 5th Duke of Wellington's Regt. the third objective—from the road-junction at Tous Vents northwards to a point about 500 yards E. of Petit Marais (Red Line).

The 187th Brigade (Brig.-General A. J. Reddie), on the left of the 186th, disposed the 5th K.O.Y.L.I. (Lieut.-Col. F. W. Peter) in the front line, from the S.E. corner of the Orchard (E. of Bellevue Farm) to La Croisette, " B " and " D " Companies " on a line of our outpost line" (presumably the line as given) and "A" and "C" Companies on the line of the railway; the Battalion was to capture the Blue Line, which included the village of Orsinval. The 2/4th K.O.Y.L.I. (Lieut.-Col. C. A. Clayton) formed up just east of Reusnes, "D" Company on the right, "C" in the centre and "B" on the left, each Company with two platoons in the front and second lines. "A" Company was in support. The objective of the 2/4th Battalion was the Green Line, immediately west of Frasnoy. The 2/4th York and Lancs. Regt. (Hallamshires—Lieut.-Col. L. H. P. Hart commanding) formed up just north of the Ecaillon River (west of La Haute Borne) in the following order of Companies :—"C," "B," "A" and "D," Headquarters. The objective allotted to the Hallamshires was the Red Line between the villages of Frasnoy and Gommegnies.

3RD/4TH Nov.

Brigadier-Generals Burnett and Reddie had established " double Headquarters " at Reusnes.

The 185th Infantry Brigade (Brig.-General Viscount Hampden) which had been ordered to "leap-frog" the 186th and 187th Infantry Brigades on the latter gaining possession of the Red Line, was at Escarmin, with instructions to move forward from the village at "Zero" hour, and concentrate in the neighbourhood of Reusnes, where the Headquarters of this Brigade also were to be established.

All battalions of the 186th and 187th Infantry Brigades reached their assembly positions without incident.

Half-an-hour before "Zero" (5.30 a.m.) the enemy gave a brilliant firework display and flares of all colours went up everywhere along the front line and any moment the hostile barrage might fall.

4TH Nov.

In front of the 2/4th Hants. Regt. the railway embankment was only about 3 feet in height and gave little cover. Some 80 yards distant was a small copse, held by the enemy with numbers of machine guns, and the Hampshiremen were certain to receive a warm reception when they advanced. As it was, when "Zero" hour arrived, the Battalion had already suffered a good many casualties.

At 5.30 a.m. as the Divisional barrage fell, the 2/4th Hants. dashed forward towards the enemy's position. "A" Company, on the right, came immediately under heavy fire, and this opposition combined with the enemy's barrage which had just fallen caused many more casualties. But, in fine style, the Hampshiremen went forward and, beating down the enemy's resistance, captured the line of the steep wooded ravine. Three machine guns and 55 Germans had been taken, and many more of the enemy killed. "B" Company, on the left of "A," had no sooner left the railway embankment than the copse, 80 yards away, began to spit out tongues of flame and heavy machine-gun fire swept the front of the Company. With great determination, however, "B" dashed towards the copse and, though the enemy put up a stout resistance, and some sharp hand-to-hand fighting took place, during which the bayonet was used freely, this strong point was captured and the hostile machine-gun crews were either killed or taken prisoner. Several guns and about 80 prisoners were captured here. Both "A" and "B" Companies had reached the first objective allotted to the Battalion, and "C" and "D" were now to "leap-frog" through to the final objective.

The two Companies advanced up the slope of the ravine under heavy machine-gun fire, but their dash could not be stayed and, although the enemy held a strong position on the high ground and offered a stout resistance, by the skilful handling of platoons and gallantry of the men, the line of the Orsinval-Le Quesnoy road was captured together with a further seven machine guns and about 160 prisoners.

Thus, by 7 a.m. (just one hour and a half from "Zero" hour) the 2/4th Hants. had captured that portion of the Blue Line allotted to the Battalion (and 186th Brigade) and had taken an approximate total of 300 prisoners, 18 machine guns and trench mortars.

On the left of the 2/4th Hants., the 5th K.O.Y.L.I. of the 187th Brigade, at "Zero," experienced great difficulty in keeping direction. The enemy's counter-barrage was fortunately light, but the heavy ground mist, which clung to the Orchard, and smoke from the smoke screen put down by the New Zealanders on the right of the 62nd Division, which blew across the Battalion front, caused momentary hesitation, though the advance was not deflected. The first serious opposition offered by the enemy was at La Folie Farm, where stiff fighting took place before the buildings were captured (6 a.m.) Severe opposition next met the K.O.Y.L.I. as they reached the Mill, but here again it was beaten down. At the northern end of Orsinval village the Germans put up a hard fight, but the T.M.Bs. lent their assistance and by 9 a.m. the Blue Line, allotted to the 5th K.O.Y.L.I. was captured, together with numerous machine guns and many prisoners.

The time had now arrived for the advance to be continued to the Green Line, the 2/4th Duke of Wellington's Regt. (186th Brigade) on the right, and the 2/4th K.O.Y.L.I. (187th Birgade) on the left, passing through the 2/4th Hants. Regt. and the 5th K.O.Y.L.I., respectively, on the Blue Line.

The Advance to the Green Line

At 7.51 a.m. the leading companies of the 2/4th Duke's passed 4TH Nov. through the line held by the Hampshiremen. The right Company immediately came under heavy harassing fire from machine guns but, working gradually forward, captured several guns, killing or taking prisoner the gun crews. North of Remponeau the enemy tried hard to hold his positions, but the Duke's overcame his resistance and thirty more prisoners were added to the list of captures, the right Company finally reaching its objective on the Green Line well up behind the barrage. This position was now consolidated. Similarly, bitter opposition met the advance of the left Company of the 2/4th Duke's and, on reaching the Rhonelle River, the Germans were found in strong positions on the eastern bank. A frontal fire from Lewis guns was therefore opened upon the enemy, whilst two platoons outflanked his position, a third platoon clearing the ground. In this way resistance was overcome; the Company then advanced on La Belle Maison. Here the enemy was strongly posted. Heavy machine-gun and trench-mortar fire came from the buildings, whilst two hostile field guns, behind the house, were firing over open sights. The centre platoon of the Company, however, by working forward under cover of the walls, entered the house, capturing four machine guns and killing a number of the enemy. The advance was then continued, and a number of Germans were next captured in the Sunken Road, running S.E. from the house, whilst the two field guns in rear were taken by the left platoon.

The first objective allotted to the Battalion—the Blue Dotted Line—had been reached by the leading companies and the two support companies now passed through towards the final objective. The Right Support Company, meeting only slight machine-gun fire, advanced some distance before being held up at about M.15. c.6.6. The enemy's resistance was not immediately overcome though the Company had captured three officers, seventy-three other ranks and ten machine guns.[1] By about 10.15 a.m. the positions just west of the Green Line on the right had been reached and held by the 2/4th Duke's.

From a small enclosure, right in the line of advance, and from the western outskirts of Frasnoy, the 2/4th K.O.Y.L.I. on the left of the 2/4th Duke's, encountered considerable machine-gun fire, but the attack was pressed with vigour and by 9.25 a.m. the Battalion had reached its objective on the western exits of Frasnoy, *i.e.*, the Green Line.

[1] No mention is made in the Reports of the action of the Left Support Company

4TH Nov.

The third battalions of the 186th and 187th Infantry Brigades (5th Duke of Wellington's Regt., on the right, and 2/4th York and Lancs. Regt. [Hallamshires], on the left), then passed through the 2/4th Duke's and 2/4th K.O.Y.L.I. respectively.

The 5th Duke of Wellington's Regt. reorganized for the attack (after the march forward from the assembly positions) in the sunken road just west of the Blue Line. From this point, on receipt of information that the Green Line had been captured, the Battalion advanced in artillery formation of platoons—" B " Company on the right, " D " Company on the left, " C " Company supporting " B " and " A " Company supporting " D," the two latter Companies to leap-frog the former on the line of the first Battalion objective.

The Battalion advanced in a due easterly direction.

On reaching a north and south line, about 400 yards east of the Blue Dotted Line, the leading Companies of the 5th Duke's came under heavy machine-gun fire from orchards immediately S.W. of Frasnoy and just N. of Villereau and both Companies had to extend. It was found that the 2/4th Duke's had not quite reached the Green Line and several hostile machine-gun nests were witnessed in front of this line. After a consultation, both companies of 5th Duke's decided to leap-frog the 2/4th Duke's and continue the advance at once. The enemy's artillery was particularly active S.W. of Gommegnies, in the neighbourhood of the Red Line.

" D " Company first encountered opposition from machine guns firing from the orchard S.W. of Frasnoy. This was, however, soon overcome. A little later, the same Company was held up for some time by several machine-gun posts, east of the Green Line, in the sunken road between Frasnoy and Villereau. They were eventually overcome with the assistance of the Lewis gunners and two hostile machine guns were captured. " D " Company then pushed on and gained its objective, *i.e.*, the high ground S. of Petit Marais, after having captured 90 prisoners, eight 4·2 in. howitzers, three machine guns and a considerable amount of shells and other stores.

" B " Company on the right of " D " Company, on reaching the high ground just west of the Green Line, found two companies of the 2/4th Duke's held up by machine-gun fire from an orchard north of Villereau. The time was about 9.30 a.m. " B " at once extended and advanced, as already stated, in conjunction with " D " Company on the left.

The Commander of " B " Company sent one platoon round the left flank and advanced frontally with one platoon. On finding himself outflanked the enemy beat a retreat but not before " B " 4TH Nov. Company had captured twenty Germans in the sunken road from which most of the opposition had been experienced. Touch had been gained with " D " Company on the left and at 11.30 a.m. the advance was continued, " B " reaching its objective, the high ground south of Petit Marais (on the right of " D " Company) after encountering very little resistance. A liaison post was at once established with the New Zealand Division at Pont de L'Alouette. Two platoons of " B " Company had, however, during the fighting in front of the Green Line, somewhat lost direction, and after becoming involved with the enemy on the southern outskirts of Frasnoy (where some prisoners were taken) eventually fetched up on the left of " D " Company. During the advance " B " Company had taken thirty prisoners, two field guns, one howitzer and three machine guns.

" B " and " D " Companies having now captured the Battalion's intermediate objective, reorganized their line in depth, each with two platoons in front and two in support.

The right support Company—" C "—advancing to leap-frog " B," found troops of the 2/4th Duke's still held up by the enemy in the sunken road and orchards just north of Villereau; by an outflanking movement the enemy was forced to surrender. The Company then passed on, though touch with one of its leading platoons had been lost. All appears to have gone well until " C " crossed the railway between Gommegnies and Pont de L'Alouette. About 800 yards east of the railway was a house, very strongly held by the enemy. In the upper rooms machine guns had been mounted, covering all approaches, whilst both flanks were likewise protected. One platoon first attempted to rush this stronghold but, after losing its commander and several men, had to fall back. The O.C., Company, then decided to take up a line west of the sunken road running from Les Tous Vents to Petit Marais. The New Zealand Division then attacked the house, employing three platoons, but again the attempt failed.

The Left Support Company—" A "—passed through the leading Company (" D ") south of Petit Marais, but losing direction reached a position some hundreds of yards south of where it should have been (M.17. d. instead of M.17. b.). On finding that it was too far to the right the Company reorganized and endeavoured to work round on to its allotted frontage. Owing, however, to heavy machine-gun fire from the railway cutting, which caused several casualties including the Company Commander, the movement was

4TH NOV. not successful. Two attempts to capture the railway bridge and house at M.17.b.6.0 were unsuccessful and eventually a line was established some 200 yards west of the bridge astride the railway.

On the left of the 5th Duke of Wellington's Regt. the 2/4th York and Lancs. Regt., on passing through the 2/4th K.O.Y.L.I., captured Frasnoy. Considerable opposition met the Hallamshires as they worked through the village, but finally the enemy's resistance was broken and the advance was continued towards the Red Line. Beyond the eastern outskirts of the village, however, the Hallamshires were held up by very heavy machine-gun fire; the left company of the Battalion succeeded during the afternoon in reaching its objective, while the right company was thrown back in touch with the left of the 186th Brigade, east of Petit Marais.

The New Zealand Division, on the right, and the Guards, on the left of the 62nd Division, succeeded during the afternoon in reaching the Red Line. It is evident, on reading the records of the operations of 4th November, that the attack had gone with almost clock-work regularity. Splendidly covered by the guns, whose shooting was never more accurate, or their support more effective, the battalions of the attacking brigades moved forward and leap-frogged one another with fine élan, and when the Red Line was finally reached the 62nd Division had again made a victorious advance of 7,000 yards.[1] Two villages had also been captured and over 600 prisoners taken with much war material.

Behind the front line of advancing infantry the Divisional Artillery had had a strenuous day, the guns having to move forward as each objective was captured. Early in the battle the C.R.A.— General Anderson—advanced his Headquarters to a ruined chateau in Ruesnes. The "Mark of the Beast" was upon that house, for before he had evacuated it, the enemy had done a great deal of wanton damage to a large and valuable library contained in one of the rooms. The canker which the Germans left behind in France and Flanders will not be eradicated before many generations have come and gone.

Satisfaction at Divisional Headquarters and in all units over the day's fighting was further increased during the night of 4th November by the receipt of news that Austria had capitulated.

At 8.45 p.m. orders to continue the advance on the following morning (5th) were issued from 62nd Divisional Headquarters.

---

[1] It will be remembered that 7,000 yards was the distance advanced by the 62nd on the 20th November—the first day of the Battle of Cambrai, 1917.

The 185th Infantry Brigade was to pass through the 186th and 187th Infantry Brigades at 6 a.m. and press forward towards the Brown Line, gaining touch with the New Zealand Division on the right flank at each post formed by the New Zealanders,[1] and the Guards Division on the left. A troop of cavalry (Oxfordshire Hussars) and a platoon from the VIth Corps Cyclist Battalion were placed at the disposal of the G.O.C., 185th Brigade for the operations.

4TH Nov.

The 186th and 187th Brigades were to reorganize and be prepared to pass through the 185th Brigade. Each of the former Brigades were to detail one battalion to follow up the advance of the 185th Brigade, ready to pass through when required. The 62nd Battalion M.G.C. was to support the advance and a detachment of R.E. was to follow the attack and establish crossing places for wheeled traffic over the River Aunelle at the earliest possible moment.

The advance was to be covered by the 310th, 312th and 76th Brigades R.F.A. General Whigham's Headquarters were then S. of Ruesnes at R.20. b.1.6.

Of the 185th Brigade (Brigadier-General Viscount Hampden) the 1/5th Devon Regt. (Lieut.-Col. H. Bastow) on the right and the 2/20th London Regt. (Lieut.-Col. Wm. Craddock, commanding) on the left, were to carry out the attack; the 8th West Yorkshires and 5th K.O.Y.L.I. (of the 187th Infantry Brigade) were to follow as right and left support battalions, respectively.

During the night 4th/5th November the 185th Brigade moved forward to its assembly positions, the 1/5th Devons to the Sunken Road in M.16. b. and d.; the 2/20th London R. was on the left of the Devons.

4/5TH Nov.

An officer of the 8th West Yorkshire (the right support battalion in this attack) has given the following pen picture as the Divisional Artillery opened fire just before Zero hour :—" The guns have just commenced their barrage, and the horizon in the German lines has become a wonderful display of fireworks, red, green, yellow, white, golden rain and so on. In a few minutes the Hun is retaliating ; a few shells drop in our vicinity, one on the road just behind our Company, fortunately doing little damage. A 5·9 in. has dropped into a dump of Verey lights which are throwing out their balls of fire in every direction."

At 6 a.m. the attack began.

5TH Nov.

The Devons, who had been given Le Cheval Blanc as their

[1] These posts more closely defined were to be formed at N.13. c.1.0, N.20. a. 4.0, N.20. b. 9.8, N.15. d. 8.3, and N.17. d. 5.1.

K

5TH Nov. objective, attacked through the Sunken Road N.17 b. and d. and quickly captured Cheval Blanc, La Cavee, Le Grand Sart and Sarloton and, by 9 a.m., the line of the main road at N.8 and N.15 central along the edge of the Foret de Mormal was held. Touch had been gained with the New Zealand Division on the right.

The 2/20th London R., whose objective was the road from the cross roads N.8.c.7.3 to N.2.c.6.0. appear to have reached it without much difficulty.

The first objective of the 185th Brigade having been captured the 8th West Yorkshire and 5th K.O.Y.L.I. leap-frogged the Devons and Londoners.

As Le Cheval Blanc had been cleared by the 5th Devons, the West Yorkshiremen found it possible to march along the roads at the opening stage of their advance without deploying. But on reaching the eastern edge of the wood and southern portion of the village of Le Trechon, hostile machine guns in force were encountered. Patrols were then sent out towards the River de la Maladrerie, but it was found impossible to continue the advance without further artillery preparation. The Battalion therefore consolidated on the line N.11.c.7.0.—N.17.a.8.0—N.17.d.8.0. with " A " and " D " Companies in front and " C " and " B " in support.

The 5th K.O.Y.L.I. passed through the 2/20th London R. at 1 p.m. but was early held up by machine guns from Le Trechon. The O.C. the Battalion, therefore organized an attack on the high ground east of the village, which was well carried out and resulted in the K.O.Y.L.I. reaching the River de la Maladrerie. Here, however, considerable machine-gun fire was encountered and as the position was very much exposed a line was eventually established along the Sunken Road east of the village. At dusk the 8th West Yorkshire swung up their left flank to conform to the right of the K.O.Y.L.I., but no further advance was practicable owing to hostile machine-gun and artillery fire.

Interesting details of the day's fighting are not to be found in the official diaries—the records being mostly brief and dull. But from a private diary kept by an officer of one of the support companies of the 8th West Yorkshire, the following extract throws further light on the advance of his Battalion :

" After a stiff dose of rum which gladdened our hearts, and a nip of tea and biscuits we move on to the cross roads of Petit Marais where we wait until the dark has gone and longer. At 7.30 a.m. we are still waiting and news comes that the Bosche has gone, goodness knows where. We still wait. Motor lorries now keep coming 5TH Nov. up, a sure sign that something has happened. At last we move on a mile or so and stand on a ridge overlooking the village of Gommegnies, about three miles away. The plain is well wooded and away on our right lies the Forest of Mormal. Large columns of smoke are rising from various places behind the trees and there we can locate the homesteads of the poor French inhabitants. After some difficulty in getting across the railway (for the bridge has been mined) we push on in artillery formation, through several villages in which large German guns lie fast in the mud, or damaged by our shells. A few civilians, very shaken, wave us onward singing the ' Marseillaise ' and giving us apples ; my pockets are full..... These gifts cannot last for ever, the poor French peasant has had all her cows, etc., taken, and the only thing left is a little coffee and a little bread, and a few apples, and the Lord knows she gives these away generously enough as long as they last.

" Many improvised bridges have to be made for our limbers over streams where the road bridges had been blown in to impede our advance. We reach a little village called the Cheval Blanc, billet the men in a barn and then partake of food which the French people give us, just a bit of bread, brown and unsavoury, a little coffee and a few pears. We give them in exchange a little white bread, at the sight of which one old woman nearly had hysterics, and a little corned beef. We can't spare much as we don't know where we shall get our next rations.

" We are instructed to form up on the north-eastern edge of Mormal Forest and pass through ' A ' and ' D ' Companies, who are at present occupying the front posts. Our positions are gained at about 4.30 and the K.O.Y.L.I. on our left and also the Guards have been repulsed and machine-gun fire is extremely heavy..... We are to carry out the ' stunt ' at six in the morning, when the barrage will commence. The night is beastly ; we have a certain amount of fun in trying to find our picquets in the dark, and do not succeed in locating O.... until an hour before we move off. Machine-gun fire throughout the night (5th/6th) has been heavy, and the bullets have fortunately been mostly above our heads, though several men have been hit. It is an eerie feeling in the dark when ' Whu-ee ' and a bit of branch falls at your feet."

The " stunt " here mentioned, was the attack which the 185th Infantry Brigade had been ordered to carry out at 6 a.m. on 6th November. The Brigade, with the 5th K.O.Y.L.I. of the 187th

5TH Nov.

Infantry Brigade still attached, was to continue the advance as far as the high ground east of Obies in O.13 and O.7. Having attained this position, the 186th Brigade was to pass through the 185th and secure the Brown Line as its first objective and the line of the Hargnies-La Longueville Road as its second objective. The 187th Brigade was to leave the area about Gommegnies at " Zero " plus 90 minutes and after passing through the 185th Brigade was to advance in support of the 186th Brigade, holding its leading battalion in readiness to assist the 186th should the enemy counter-attack. These orders were given verbally to the G.Os.C., Brigades, at 5 p.m. and were confirmed at 9 p.m.

The general situation on 5th November was as follows :—" The Fourth Army realized a further advance of some four miles, penetrating beyond Prisches and Maroilles. On the Third Army front the 5th, 21st and 23rd Divisions pushed well forward to the east of Mormal Forest, while further north, by the evening, we were approaching Bavai. Only on the First Army front was the resistance encountered at all serious. Here, after regaining during the morning the ridge east of the Aunelle and capturing Roisin, Meaurain and Angreau, the divisions of the XXII. Corps were held up for a time in front of Angre and along the line of the Rhonelle River."

6TH Nov.

At 6 o'clock, on the morning of 6th, the 8th West Yorkshires on the right and the 2/20th London R. on the left, advanced to the attack. The former Battalion reached its objective without encountering serious opposition, and the Londoners captured the villages of La Tomblaine and Obies and the high ground east of these two places. On reaching this line the 2/20th sent one company to engage the high ground in O.1.b. and the Chateau de Mecquignies from which the Guards Division, on the left of the 62nd, was encountering heavy machine-gun fire.

Meanwhile the 185th was consolidating its position and at 12 noon, just as the Guards had captured the Chateau de Mecquignies, the 186th Brigade, which had left the area about Hitonsart at " Zero " hour, passed through the former Brigade. Of the 186th, the 2/4th Duke of Wellington's Regt. was on the right and the 2/4th Hants. Regt. on the left.

With little opposition the 2/4th Duke's had, by 12.30 p.m., reached the eastern bank of the Ravine de Mecquignies in O.4.b. and d. The supporting companies then passed through, but owing to the difficult nature of the enclosed country and the heavy condition of the ground, sodden by incessant rain, the advance was slow and the Pont-sur-Sambre-Bavai Road was not reached until just before dusk.

On the left the advance was more difficult. The 2/4th Hants. had to pass over ground swept by heavy shell fire, which covered the whole Battalion area. Little opposition was experienced from the front, but German machine guns were very active on the left flank and caused the Hampshiremen trouble. In spite of it, however, the village of Cognaux was captured after sharp fighting in the orchards where some Germans were killed and four captured with two machine guns. On emerging from the eastern exits of the village hostile machine guns on the left again opened heavy fire on the Hampshiremen. The leading platoon of the right company, under 2nd-Lieut. Willsher, reaching the road at Quene au Loup, drove the enemy towards the Bois du Chene, inflicting several casualties on the Germans. This platoon did great service. Although isolated and exposed to enfilade fire it held on to its position until the leading company had worked round on the right and had occupied the main road as far north as the Brigade Boundary, the enemy retiring towards La Longueville. At about 3.30 p.m. the 5th Duke of Wellington's Regt. moved up to Obies, but owing to the lateness of the hour and considerable machine-gun fire still coming from the left flank, it was decided not to continue the advance beyond the La Chaussée-Quene au Loup Road (*i.e.*, the Brown Line) until the following morning.

Soon after 7 p.m. the enemy delivered a heavy counter-attack on the right company of the 2/4th Duke's, but was driven off by rifle and machine-gun fire after losing very heavily.

The night of the 6th/7th November was wretched in the extreme. The Divisional front line (as already stated) ran along the main road and without shelter of any kind from the heavy rain which had fallen almost continuously for 24 hours, the troops remained in a state of great discomfort. Gone, however, was the time when having (as in this instance) won a position, they would probably have to spend days, weeks and months on the newly-won line. The discomforts were but temporary; the enemy was fast retiring, a beaten foe, and through the dark night of war men began to see light—a brighter dawn was near. How near no one knew exactly, but all were on the very tip-toe of expectation.

During the afternoon of 6th verbal instructions had been issued to the G.Os.C., 185th and 186th Brigades to continue the attack on 7th, the latter Brigade with two Battalions (5th Devons and 8th

6TH Nov.

7TH Nov.

West Yorkshires) of the 185th attached. The 185th Brigade, which had been halted about Le Cheval Blanc, was to move at 9 a.m. to the area Mecquignies-Le Timon-Tayompret, the 5th K.O.Y.L.I. rejoining the Brigade en route. At 7.30 p.m. these orders were confirmed by telegram.

In spite of an exceedingly dark night all battalions successfully formed up in their assembly positions and the attack was launched at 6 a.m. as arranged.

The 5th Duke of Wellington's Regt. was on the right, the 1/5th Devon Regt. in the centre and the 8th West Yorkshires on the left.

Three objectives were allotted to the 186th Brigade, the final objective being the line of the Hargnies-La Longueville Road. Each battalion was to employ one company for each objective, the remaining company to be in reserve, prepared to continue the advance if necessary

No opposition was experienced by the attacking battalions and by 10 a.m. the line of the Hargnies-La Longueville Road had been reached. Several casualties were suffered by the Brigade owing to an overlapping barrage put down by the Division on the right of the 62nd, " Zero " hour of the former division not being till 8 a.m. Thus the 186th Brigade was, at first, in advance of, and out of touch with, the flanking divisions. A patrol sent out by the 5th Duke's captured a few Germans in Hargnies.

At 10 a.m. General Burnet received a message from the G.O.C., 62nd Division, which stated that touch should not be lost with the enemy, and orders were immediately issued for the reserve companies of all three attacking brigades to continue the advance to the line Vieux-Mesnil (exclusive)—Eastern edge of the Bois Delhaye. Hostile machine-gun fire was encountered from Trimouton and Bois Hoyaux, but the advance was successfully carried out and touch with the flanking divisions was obtained at Hargnies and the northern edge of Bois Delhaye. Orders were again received to continue the advance at 4 p.m. as far as the general line running through Trimouton-Western edge of Bois Hoyaux. But the enemy's resistance had been gradually hardening and, no sooner had the advance begun than close-range artillery fire, combined with heavy machine-gun fire along the whole front, held up the attacking troops. As it was obvious that further ground could only be gained at the expense of heavy casualties, battalions consolidated on their previous objectives between Vieux-Mesnil and the eastern edge of the Bois Delhaye.

During the afternoon, Coutant and the Coutant-Quene au

Loup Road were very heavily shelled and the 310th Brigade, R.F.A., 7TH Nov. whilst moving forward, suffered severe casualties.

In four days the 62nd had driven the enemy back 20 miles, and all ranks were very tired, but the way the gunners followed up their infantry was truly wonderful. On the Divisional Ammunition Columns this advance entailed very heavy work. No sooner was a dump of ammunition formed in one place than the tide of battle had rolled on far beyond it, and another had to be begun further on. " Never," stated General Anderson, " during the whole war were the men and horses of the Brigades and D.A.C. worked to a greater state of exhaustion than in these closing days." It was the same with all units ; the Army Service Corps had strenuous work in going back for, and bringing up, supplies ; the Sappers were constantly at work on bridges and roads ; the Field Ambulances had all they could do to evacuate the wounded. But where the will exists, a way can always be found and it may be said, without undue boasting, that the " will to do " was always an integral part of this West Riding Division.

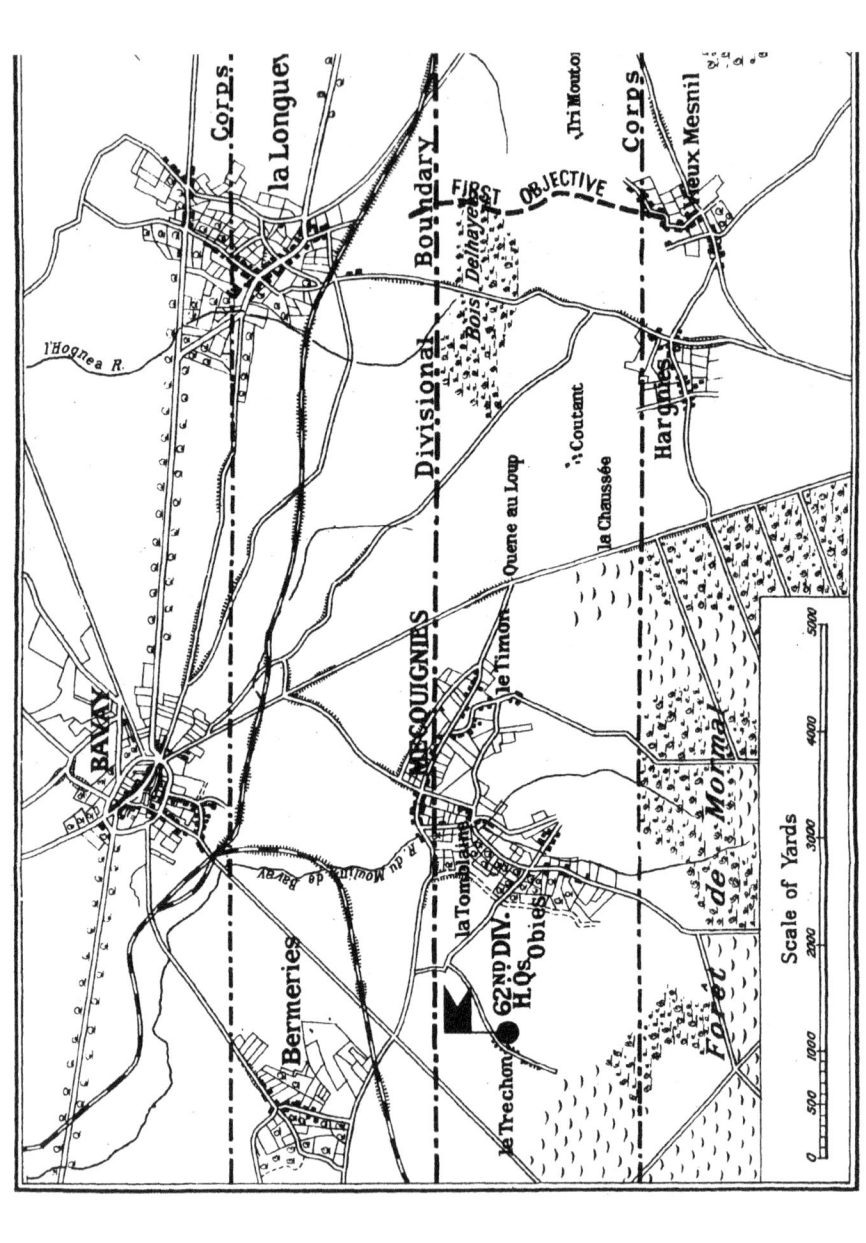

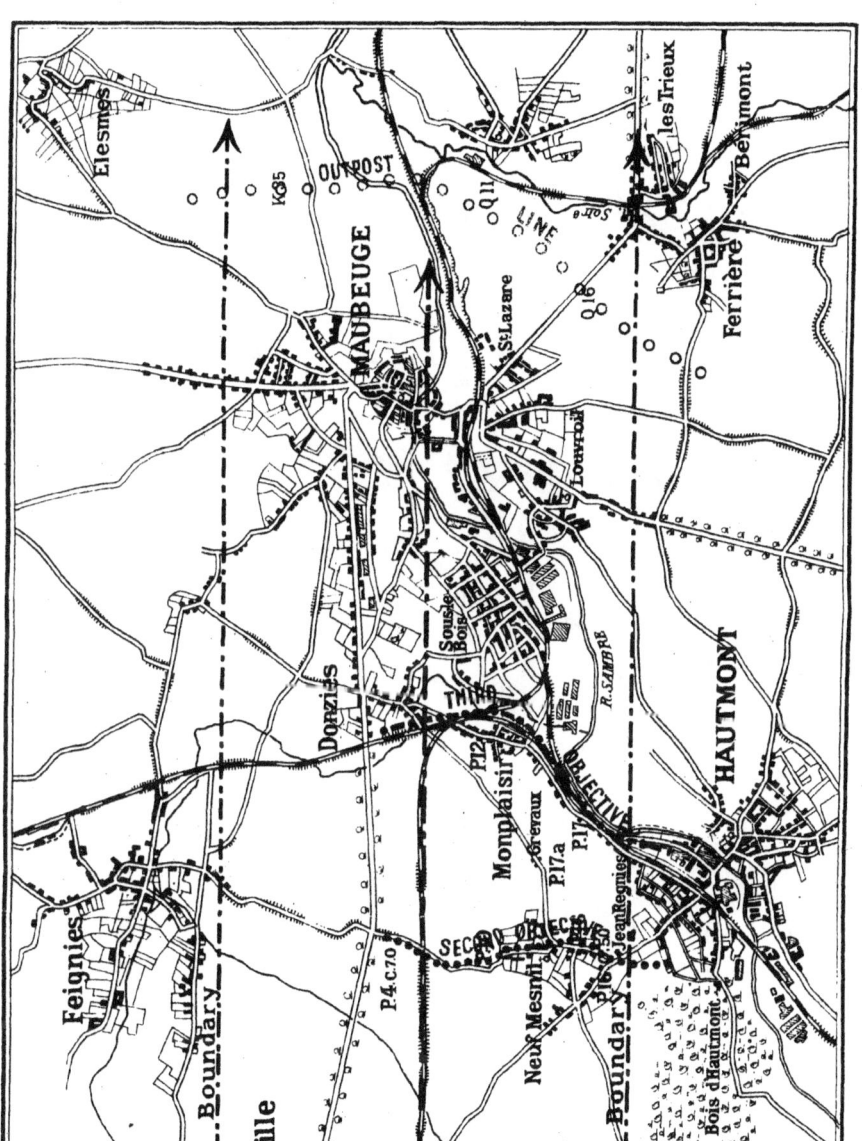

MAUBEUGE.

Chapter X.

1918.

MAUBEUGE

"On the 9th November the enemy was in general retreat on the whole front of the British Armies. The fortress of Maubeuge was entered by the Guards Division and the 62nd Division (Major-General Sir R. D. Whigham)"....
Official Despatches.

AT 12 noon on the 7th November General Whigham 7TH Nov. moved his Headquarters from Frasnoy to Le Trechon, and at the latter place, about 6 p.m., orders were received from VIth Corps Headquarters stating that as the enemy was retiring on the whole Army front the advance was to be continued on the following morning, the objective of the Third Army being the road Avesnes-Maubeuge-Mons, with outposts pushed out beyond.

On receipt of these orders at 62nd Divisional Headquarters instructions were issued outlining the operations of the 8th: "Advance will continue to-morrow to Army objective line of road Avesnes-Maubeuge-Mons with outposts on high ground in Q.16 central, Q.11 a (62nd Division), K.35 central (Guards Division) and touch being maintained with the enemy by mounted troops aaa. On 62nd Divisional front 187th Infantry Brigade will pass through 186th Infantry Brigade on line held by latter, maintaining touch with flank divisions aaa Zero 06.30 hours aaa Successive objectives will be First—line of road from P.16. c.5.0. to P.4 c.7.0; Second—line of railway in P.17, P.18 a and P.12; Third—Avesnes-Maubeuge road aaa Initial advance will be covered by 310th and 42nd Brigades R.F.A., latter Brigade providing Batteries to move with attacking battalions aaa. As advance progresses 310th Brigade R.F.A. will be replaced by 312th Brigade R.F.A. aaa 186th Infantry Brigade will reorganize in depth and be in support at one hour's notice in the area between the line now held and the Pont sur Sambre-Bavai road aaa 185th Infantry Brigade including 1/5th Devons and 8th West Yorks. will concentrate in area Mecquignes-Le Timon-Obies, in Divisional Reserve at two hours' notice aaa Divisional Headquarters remain at N.11 C.5.6." (Le Trechon). A Field Company of Royal

7TH Nov. Engineers was placed at the disposal of the G.O.C. 187th Brigade, to help the infantry cross the River Sambre, all bridges near which had been destroyed.

At this period (night of 7th November) the Divisional front line, held by the 186th Brigade, ran approximately from Vieux Mesnil to the eastern edge of the Bois Delhaye.[1] The 187th Brigade was in billets in the La Tomblaine area. Of the 185th Brigade the 8th West Yorks. and 1/5th Devons were still at the disposal of the G.O.C., 186th Brigade, the former Battalion at the eastern exits of Bois Delhaye, the latter on the right of the 8th West Yorks.; the 2/20th Londons were at Bavisiaux.

How near the total collapse of the enemy was no one knew, though the Higher Command were aware that his resistance had been definitely broken. But at any time a dramatic change in the situation might be announced for, at 11.30 p.m. that night, the Divisional Diary recorded : " A message in French was picked up by our wireless from the enemy stating that no firing would take place in a certain area E. of Guise up to midnight, in order to allow the German Parlementaires to pass through the lines." Three hours earlier the Brigadiers had been informed that German Parlementaires might be expected to pass through the lines and, although the wireless message at 11.30 p.m. disposed of the probability of the peace envoys passing through the 62nd Divisional area, the excitement occasioned by the news still held the troops almost breathless. Beaten and cowed, the enemy was at last to sue for peace. No one can picture what that meant to the troops holding the line in France and Flanders. Visions of those quiet years before the war, when everyone led a normal life and all the horrors of bloody battlefields were unknown began to take definite shape again. During the years of torture men had forgotten that there had ever been such a thing as peace. It seemed to them that all their lives had been passed in filthy trenches amidst the interminable boom of guns, the shrieks and cries of the maimed and wounded and dying. And now, wonder of wonders, " Jerry " was about to sue for Peace, almost it was beyond human understanding ! The final act in the great drama—the capture of Mons—was, however, yet to take place, meantime there was more fighting to be done. Death was still to claim many a gallant soul.

The 2/4th K.O.Y.L.I. and the 2/4th York and Lancs. Regt. (on the right and left respectively) had been ordered to carry out the attack of the 187th Brigade on the morning of the 8th November,

[1] The Divisional Diary gives the line as O.18. d. 3.0.—P.13 d. 0.6—P.1.0.0.

and during the night 7th/8th these two Battalions moved up to their assembly positions which followed the line of the Hargnies-La Longueville Road. " A " Company of the 62nd Battalion M.G.C. was attached to the Brigade for the attack. " B " Company of the machine gunners following the Brigade in support. One troop of Oxfordshire Hussars was placed under the orders of the G.O.C., 187th Brigade.

7/8TH Nov.

Zero hour was 6.30 a.m.

At 4.15 a.m. on the 8th the 2/4th K.O.Y.L.I. moved off from Mecquignies and assembled along the Hargnies-La Longueville Road, " A " Company on the right, " B " on the left, " C " as right support and " D " as left support—each Company on a two-platoon frontage. The forming-up operations were successfully accomplished without casualties.

8TH Nov.

On the left of the 2/4th K.O.Y.L.I. the Hallamshires (2/4th York and Lancs.), moving *via* Le Timon and Quene au Loup, had assembled along the roadway, the northern flank of the K.O.Y.L.I. being at Keeper's House in the Bois Delhaye. The Battalion was formed up on a two-company frontage, " B " and " C " Companies leading with " A " in support to " C," and " D " to " B."

The 5th K.O.Y.L.I. were in support of both attacking Battalions.

At Zero hour both the 2/4th K.O.Y.L.I. and the Hallamshires advanced to the attack. An early morning fog covered the ground and in the dim light it was impossible to see far ahead. The country over which the attacking troops advanced was much cut up, intersected by enclosed gardens and fields, with hedgerows and fences. Progress was therefore slow, but direction was well maintained, for only slight opposition was offered by the enemy who, by now, had lost much of his old stubbornness. The 2/4th K.O.Y.L.I. reached the first objective (a N. and S. line running through P.16 P.10) and, according to orders, halted and consolidated in depth; the time was about 8 a.m. Similarly the Hallamshires, without serious opposition, appear to have reached the eastern edge of Bois Hoyaux and the hamlet of Les Petites Mottes at the same hour.

Both Battalions then sent out fighting patrols to the high ground in front of their positions. At 8.45 a.m. and onwards the line held by the K.O.Y.L.I. and the Hallamshires was very heavily shelled which, combined with intense machine-gun fire from all along the front of both Battalions, prevented a further advance without an organized artillery barrage. On the right of the 62nd Division the 42nd Division had gained possession of Hautmont and had crossed

8TH Nov.
the Sambre without opposition, but on the left the Guards were held up by machine-gun fire.

Orders were then issued that a fresh attack was to be made, and the G.O.C., 187th Brigade (General Reddie), decided to employ the 5th K.O.Y.L.I. to carry out a turning movement from the right flank with the object of capturing Fort Grevaux, the village of Mont Plaisir and the railway line up to the north Divisional boundary. The 5th Battalion was to advance through the 2/4th K.O.Y.L.I. and turn the line of the railway. The right flank of the 5th was to be protected by the 2/4th as the former advanced to the attack. An 18-pounder barrage to fall at 2.30 p.m. in front of the 2/4th K.O.Y.L.I and 4·5 Howitzers to fire on selected localities, were the artillery arrangements.

The 5th K.O.Y.L.I. formed up on the line of the road running south-east from Tri Mouton (at the S.W. corner of Bois Hoyaux) to the cross roads, and at 1.58 p.m. advanced to the attack. By 2.30 p.m. the Battalion had reached the line of the road which runs north and south from Neuf Mesnil to Jean Regnies.

At this period, 2.30 p.m., the Divisional barrage had just fallen in front of the 2/4th K.O.Y.L.I. and on the first " lift," at 2.45 p.m. the 5th K.O.Y.L.I. continued their advance on the enemy's position. It is impossible, however, to give any details of the fighting, for the Diary of the 5th Battalion sums up the situation in the following brief and uninteresting words : " All objectives were reported gained at 16.15 hours (4.15 p.m.) and the high ground in our possession." The correctness of this statement is doubtful, for the Divisional narrative states that heavy machine-gun fire from Fort Grevaux and the houses along the railway prevented further advance and that the attack had reached the road between the railway and P.17 a 4.9 (about " Grattieres "). The 5th K.O.Y.L.I. were therefore ordered to continue the attack after dark, orders having been issued at 4 p.m. from Brigade Headquarters which stated that the attack was to be continued by the 187th Brigade until the final objective, the high ground east of the Avesnes-Maubeuge road, had been captured.[1]

[1] " The Divisional Commander was determined to reach his objectives as early as possible on the morning of 9th November before the enemy had time to consolidate, and so he issued orders at 4 p.m. that the attack of the 187th Brigade was to be continued with the utmost possible vigour. The 186th Brigade was placed at the disposal of 187th Brigade in case serious opposition was encountered. On receipt of these orders General Reddie ordered the 5th K.O.Y.L.I. to continue its attack after dark."

THE CANAL NEAR MAUBEUGE, NOVEMBER, 1918.

But Fort Grevaux formed a very formidable strong point; it 8TH Nov. was held in great strength by machine guns and the German machine gunners clung tenaciously to their positions. Two determined attempts during the early part of the night, to capture the Fort, proved unsuccessful, though good progress was made along the railway. At 4.30 on the morning of 9th November a third attack on Fort 9TH Nov. Grevaux was made by the 5th K.O.Y.L.I.; this attack was successful and the garrison was captured.

The Division was now on the very outskirts of Maubeuge and the next phase in the operations was the capture of the suburbs—Louvroil, St. Lazare and Sous le Bois.

The 2/4th K.O.Y.L.I. during the night of 8th/9th had received orders to attack and capture the road running N. and S. through Q.9.c. and Q.20 a. 7.7. (the Maubeuge-Avesnes road) and the village of Louvroil as far north as the railway, while the 2/4th York and Lancs. Regt., on the left, was to make a simultaneous attack on Sous le Bois.

At 6.30 a.m. the 2/4th K.O.Y.L.I. on a one-company frontage (" C " Company leading, followed in turn by " B," " D " and " A " Companies) advanced, crossed the Sambre, and without opposition gained the high ground in Q.16 and Q.11 (S.E. of Maubeuge) and there dug in, pushing patrols down to the River Solre to guard the crossings. The enemy had withdrawn during the night and, by 9.15 a.m., the Battalion had gained all its objectives, capturing a large amount of booty, without losing a man.

Similarly, the Hallamshires, on the left of the 2/4th K.O.Y.L.I., gained a bloodless victory: " The attack," records the Battalion Diary, " was duly carried out and no opposition whatsoever was encountered, the troops marching into the village (Sous le Bois) to receive a great welcome at the hands of the inhabitants. Large quantities of booty of every description were captured in the village." The Hallamshires, after reorganizing in Sous le Bois, moved to St. Lazare, establishing an outpost line S.W. of the village, thus filling the gap between the 2/4th K.O.Y.L.I. and the 42nd Division. In concluding his report of the operations of his Battalion the C.O. (Lieut.-Col. L. H. P. Hart) said of his officers and men: " Under the very trying conditions of wet weather and the fatigue of the long advance and incessant fighting, no troops could have conducted themselves with greater spirit or more splendid bravery. Well led by its officers and showing the fine fighting qualities with which its

9TH Nov. name is always associated, the Battalion achieved its usual performance of attaining all objectives."

But not only had the Hallamshires achieved their "usual performance of attaining all objectives," but the Division had once again carried out its task with that precision for which it had become famous. Maubeuge had fallen and the enemy was now in general retreat on the whole front of the British Armies. The word "Maubeuge" is not mentioned in the Divisional narrative for the last three days of the war, and only from the objectives given and reached by the Battalion is it clear that the great fortress-town had passed into the possession of the 62nd and Guards Divisions.[1]

Under the heading of "The Return to Mons," the official despatches, in a paragraph which will always remain of historic interest to those who served with the West Riding Division, stated : " The fortress of Maubeuge was entered by the Guards Division and the 62nd Division (Major-General Sir R. D. Whigham) while the Canadians were approaching Mons."

On the Hallamshires moving to St. Lazare the 5th K.O.Y.L.I. withdrew to Sous le Bois, in which place the Battalion was concentrated as Brigade Reserve.

General Burnett's Brigade (186th) had marched from the area Coutant-Quene au Loup-La Chausse at 6.30 a.m. to assembly positions west of the Bois d'Hautmont in readiness to take over the outpost line as originally intended. But as the 187th Brigade had secured all its objectives without opposition, the relief was postponed until 10 a.m. on the 10th November. One Battalion, however (5th Duke of Wellington's Regt.), of the 186th, was placed under the orders of the G.O.C., 187th, and moved up to Louvroil as support Battalion to the outpost line, the remaining Battalion of the Brigade moving to Sous le Bois.

The march to Sous le Bois is thus described by an officer of one of the battalions which were moved up to the village : "On the way, during one of the halts, we talk to an old man and his wife who

---

[1] Both the Guards and 62nd claimed that their patrols were the first to enter Maubeuge. It was not established which arrived first and so the two Division were allowed to share the honour. The real explanation is that the Guards and 62nd Divisional zones of attack were respectively north and south of the river Sambre. The Guards therefore, had not to cross this obstacle, but the 62nd had to do so, and while both Divisions had to overcome opposition from the outer and more modern perimeter of the fortress, the older works encircling the old town itself lay on the northern bank. Patrols of the 62nd Division entered the old town from the south to establish liaison with the Guards.

bring out chairs for the officers to sit on. The C.O. calls all Com- 9TH Nov. pany Commanders to pass down the news that the Kaiser has abdicated and that no signs of the enemy can be found in front of us. The old man calls out 'Vive les Anglais!' and the old woman bursts into tears of joy."

The Battalion then moved on : " We marched to the tune of 'Tipperary.' Strange that we should be covering the old ground of the Battle of Mons again, just as an Armistice is being declared." Strange, indeed, without equivalent in the world's history of war.

" In the doorway of a little cottage," stated this diarist, who for a brief moment tears aside the curtain of obscurity and describes something of what was happening all up and down the front line during that intensely interesting and dramatic period, " stands a bearded, aged man at the salute. On his breast are medals, and in his cap are feathers such as children put in their paper hats when playing at soldiers. The old fellow is singing at the top of his voice, and our men begin to laugh, when suddenly it strikes them that he is singing the ' Marseillaise.' The band carries on the strain and it is picked up by the men—and so we made our entry."

The 10th November was uneventful. The 186th Brigade re- 10TH Nov. lieved the 187th at 10 a.m. as ordered, the latter withdrawing to billets in Sous le Bois. Viscount Hampden's Brigade (185th) moved up to the area Mont Plaisir-Neuf Mesnil.[1] The Sappers, who during the night had been busily engaged constructing a pontoon bridge over the Sambre just west of Louvroil, for horse transport and field artillery, finished their task by 10 a.m. Patrols out everywhere along the Divisional front discovered large quantities of abandoned material. And, during the afternoon, desultory shelling broke out, the sullen enemy firing gas and other shells into Recquignies, Rousies and St. Lazare.

Early on the morning of 11th November the Divisional outpost 11TH Nov. line of resistance was advanced to the River Solre, and the Picquet line to east of the river, with observation posts east of Rousies and Bois des Bons Peres. Cyclist patrols were sent out as far as the line Cerfontaine-Recquignies without encountering the enemy But by 9 a.m. all ranks knew that at 11 a.m. hostilities were to cease,

---

[1] In Neuf Mesnil the British troops found ghastly evidence of a horrible incident which had happened before they reached the village. On a bed in one of the cottages the lifeless body of a young girl lay stretched out. This girl, when she heard that the British were advancing on the village, ran up from the cellar and shouted mockingly to the German rear-guard : " Run ! Here come the English." A German soldier turned and shot her dead.

11TH NOV.

THE ARMISTICE.

and that an armistice would be signed at that hour, which would force upon Germany an acceptance of the hardest terms ever offered a defeated nation.

Strange indeed was the comparative stillness of the battlefield on that last morning of the war, broken only by the sound of firing from the direction of Mons, where the Canadians were capturing the town and killing or taking prisoner the whole of the German defending force. But along the Divisional front all was quiet.[1]

A story was told of a German machine gunner who, at one minute to eleven o'clock, fired off his last remaining belt of ammunition then, as the hour struck, jumped upon the parapet, removed his steel helmet, bowed and disappeared. There was no cheering and very little outward excitement, only a great and wonderful calm settling down over the closing scene of the greatest struggle in the world's history. As yet men hardly realized what Peace meant, or would mean. They only remembered the years—terribly long years —of pain and torture and misery. Far away across the lines of dirty, muddy, trenches, beyond the blackened and disfigured villages and towns which lay between Mons and Maubeuge and the French coast, across the English Channel, in all the cities, towns and villages of England, Ireland, Scotland and Wales, men, women and children were acting as beings demented, as if black plague had been lifted from the country. But in the firing line in France and Flanders quietude reigned, it was the only way to signal the coming of a great end. For men remembered the price which had been paid ere they had come to where they then stood. *They* had come through but others had not, and it was as if the soldier (communing with himself in that momentous eleventh hour and remembering his fallen comrades) said in his heart :

". . . . . We've no price,
No utmost treasure of the seas or lands,
No words, no deeds, to pay their sacrifice.
Only while England stands,
Their pearl, their pride, their altar—not their grave—
Bid us remember in what hours they gave
All that mankind may give—
That we might live."[2]

[1] The total casualties suffered by the 62nd Division between the 4th and 11th November, 1918, were 2 officers killed and 26 wounded ; 117 other ranks killed, 693 wounded and 61 missing. Captures from the enemy during that period were : Prisoners—13 officers and 900 other ranks : Guns, 24, including two 8-in. howitzers, two 5·9-in. howitzers and one 10-cm. H.V., 115 machine guns and 11 trench mortars.

[2] Marjorie L. C. Pickthall.

CONCLUSION.   1918

ON Armistice Day, after General Whigham had moved his headquarters to Sous le Bois, he received notification from VIth Corps Headquarters that the 62nd Division was to form part of the force which, under the terms of the Armistice, was to occupy part of Germany and hold the Bridge Heads over the Rhine. No other Territorial Divisions had received orders to join the Army of Occupation and thus a great honour had fallen to the 62nd. And never was honour more richly deserved as this history shows. Looking back over the years 1917, 1918, it is possible to follow accurately the gradual evolution of the Division from its novitiate to its final stage—that of a well-seasoned and hardened fighting unit of the finest type. Profiting by its bitter experiences at Bullecourt early in 1917, the Division, with the true grit and determination of Yorkshiremen, never failed in any other task allotted to it; it was altogether an extraordinary record. Terrible and sanguinary were the battles and actions it passed through, and if blood be the price of victory, they paid in full for the triumphs they had won.

On 13th November, preliminary instructions for the march into Germany were issued. The advance, in two stages, the first taking the line to Charleroi where a short halt was to be made, and the second to the Meuse, was to begin on 17th. The roads forward to the Solre River were found, generally, in a good state. The bridges at Cousolre had been blown up, but the majority of those along the Solre, though prepared by the enemy for demolition, had been left undamaged.

At night on 16th, " owing to the difficulty with regard to supplies,"[1] the advance was put back twenty-four hours, though the Advanced Guard Troops, under the orders of the C.R.E., were ordered to move as originally laid down, so as to be available for road work. During the 17th a portion of the pontoon bridge at Louvroil, over which troops and transport of the 186th and the whole of the 187th Brigades were due to pass on the 18th, sank, but the sappers of the 3rd Division got to work at once and by 5 a.m. on

[1] *Vide* 62nd G.S. Diary, 16th Nov., 1918.

the latter date the bridge had been repaired and the advance began and was carried out without difficulty.

Through towns and villages hung with flags and peopled with a cheery, smiling populace, the great march into Germany proceeded. But as the troops tramped along the roads they met crowds of hungry and ragged released soldiers belonging to the Allied Armies, turned loose by the Germans when the Armistice had been signed. " The roads," said an officer of the 8th West Yorks., " are full of returning prisoners of all nationalities—Frenchmen with British caps and haversacks, British with French overcoats, Italians with all three, a ' fag ' or two picked up from passing troops, feet wrapped in puttees or old cloth where their boots had been worn out or taken by the Germans. Unfed, uncared for, but all with one intention—to get well through our lines."

On 28th November (Divisional Headquarters being then at Leignon)[1] notification was received that the 62nd had been transferred from VIth to the IXth Corps; the latter Corps was now commanded by Lieut.-General Sir W. P. Braithwaite. K.C.B.

In fair weather, in rain, in snow, sometimes short of rations, but in great cheeriness, the Division pushed on, crossing the Meuse at Yvoir, through Spontin, where practically every other house had been burnt in 1914 by the enemy. At last, on 23rd December, Divisional Headquarters reached the Schleiden area, the destination of the Division. The 185th and 187th Brigade Group completed their march on the following day, but it was Christmas Day before the remaining units reached their final area and completed their march.[2] Very bad weather was experienced during the final stages, for heavy rain fell almost without cessation from morning till night.

Thus, the march of the 62nd Division into Germany which had begun on 18th November from Sous le Bois, Maubeuge, had taken just over five weeks.

[1] " We halted at Leignon 27th November to 11th December, due both to difficulties of supply and to give the Germans more time. During this period extraordinary kindness was shown by the inhabitants to all ranks. Wine was dug up from gardens and lakes, and everything that the Belgians possessed was given to the troops. Dances and dinner parties were got up daily for the officers, and in the cottages even old people slept on the floor so that the soldier should have a bed."

[2] Turkeys which had been ordered from Paris for Xmas dinners got side-tracked on the way and when they arrived could only be buried, and so the troops had to wait for their Xmas dinners until arrangements could be made locally, which presented considerable difficulties, as the troops were not allowed to buy turkeys, chickens, eggs and butter from the inhabitants, owing to shortage of supply."

On 15th December, the day on which the Division crossed the frontier, General Whigham with his staff and the G.O.C., 185th Infantry Brigade, with his Brigade Staff, rode at the head of the main body and a " Ceremonial entry " into Germany was carried out in accordance with Army Orders.

For nearly three months the 62nd remained in Germany. In March, 1919, the Division was replaced in the Army of Occupation by a Highland Division.[1] It is not possible to follow the return of the units of the Division to their homes in England, but Sir Douglas Haig, in his despatches, thus pays a final tribute to those who served under him during the years of stress :

" The strain of those years was never ceasing, the demands they made upon the best of the Empire's manhood are now known. Yet throughout all those years and amid the hopes and disappointments they brought with them, the confidence of our troops in final victory never wavered. Their courage and resolution rose superior to every test, their cheerfulness never failing, however terrible the conditions in which they lived and fought. By the long road they took with so much faith and with such devoted and self-sacrificing bravery we have arrived at victory."

" See ye to it that their names be not forgotten."

---

[1] " Battalion by battalion was relieved by a Highland battalion, our battalion not going until the Highland battalion had arrived. There was a considerable overlap, and accommodation was difficult to arrange. The majority of our battalions were reduced to cadre, but one or two went to other Divisions; for instance, I think the 5th K.O.Y.L.I. went to the Midland Division."

THE UNVEILING OF THE WAR MEMORIAL TO THE 62nd (W.R.) DIVISION, AT HAVRINCOURT, IN JUNE, 1922.

I.

Folkestone, Tuesday, 5/6/22.

Victoria Station, London, this morning resembled something of its wartime appearance when representatives of the 62nd (West Riding) Division gathered on the platform preparatory to leaving for Havrincourt, where a memorial to their gallant dead is to be unveiled on Wednesday.

About 150 khaki-clad soldiers jostled in the crowd with as many naval men going off to join their ships. It was a picture which brought back vivid memories to all ex-Service men, and as one in " civies " remarked : " We only need to see the old coffee stalls and some red caps to make me feel my kit is on my back again."

CHANGE IN TRAVELLING.

Special train facilities had been arranged for the party by Messrs. Dean and Dawson, and travelling was, therefore, considerably more comfortable than in the bad old days. True, the soldiers were lined up in regulation style, but there was an absence of that rigid discipline which formerly existed.

The regiments represented were the R.A.M.C., West Yorks., Duke of Wellington's, King's Own Royal Engineers, York and Lancasters, and representatives of the Artillery. In addition, large numbers travelled in mufti.

Shortly before the train was timed to leave, the official party appointed by the Leeds City Council to attend the ceremony and proceed to Paris to confer the freedom of Leeds on Marshal Foch, walked on to the platform.

LEEDS REPRESENTATIVES.

The party consisted of the Lord Mayor, Councillor W. Hodgson, Aldermen C. H. Wilson, A. Braithwaite, G. Ratcliffe, H. Brown, and J. Eddison ; Councillors O. Connellan, L. Bathurst, T. Spencer and J. Thompson. The three last named are ex-Servicemen, having served with local units in the 49th and 62nd Divisions.

The party was accompanied by Mr. Graham, Director of Education, as interpreter, and Macebearer Jones.

The crossing was by way of Folkestone to Boulogne. The arrangements provide that we reach Arras at about seven o'clock to-night, and leave there in the morning to attend the ceremony at Havrincourt.

62ND (W.R.) DIVISION WAR MEMORIAL.
THE UNVEILING CEREMONY AT HAVRINCOURT.

After the ceremony, the Leeds civic party will travel from the scene of the memorial to Paris direct by motor, and will be accommodated at the Hotel Carlton in the Champs Elysée. The ceremony in which Marshal Foch will figure is fixed to take place at two o'clock on Thursday at the Boulevard des Invalides.

The civic party carries with it a wreath from the Lord Mayor and citizens of Leeds to the memory of the fallen.

ARRIVAL IN ARRAS.
Party impressed by the Ravages of War.

Arras, Tuesday Night.

The Yorkshire party arrived here this evening. They were joined on the boat by representatives of the Devons, who served with the Division.

There were affecting scenes when the party arrived at Arras Station, so well known to Yorkshire troops. The khaki-clad soldiers set the station ringing with army songs, but a pathetic note was struck by the presence of many wives and mothers of the fallen men, carrying boxes containing wreaths.

Captain Hirst, of Dewsbury, brought with him a number of wreaths which had been made from flowers grown in Crow Nest Park, Dewsbury, and sent by the citizens of that borough, which raised many men for the famous " Koylis."

French men and women fraternised with the visitors, in laboured conversation, and there were animated scenes at each stop *en route*. The guard of the train, who wore the Croix de Guerre on his blue coat and had been nine times wounded in the war, was a very popular figure with the party.

After leaving St. Pol behind, signs of the war began to appear, and those of the party who were visiting the war zone for the first time were deeply impressed by the partly filled-in shell holes which pock-marked the ground; the crumbling trenches which seared the countryside; and the gaping gunpits which no longer contained their deadly weapons.

Shell-torn and battered Arras, with the ruins of its noble cathedral still standing proudly in its midst, is now filled with hard-working inhabitants, who are putting in long hours of strenuous toil in an effort to repair the cruel ravages of the war. All the accommodation in the town has been taken up by the party, which includes the Mayor of Pontefract in his official capacity.

From " THE LEEDS MERCURY " 7/6/22.

II.
DESCRIPTIVE ACCOUNT OF THE HAVRINCOURT CEREMONY.
FROM THE " LEEDS MERCURY," 7/6/22.

Havrincourt, Wednesday Night, 6/6/22.

Whatever triumphal entry into Havrincourt the 62nd Division may have made during the war, they were never more warmly welcomed than they were to-day.

True it is they were welcomed in a hotter and livelier sense; but even the glory of that adventure was eclipsed by the glamour of to-day's visit.

After an interesting journey from Arras, during which they passed through Achicourt, Boisleux, Courcelles, Achiet-le-Grand, Bapaume, Velu, and Hermies, they reached shell-shocked, war-wounded Havrincourt, to be received by the village band, or " fanfare," as it is called, and Monsieur le Maire, Comte de Havrincourt, and the local councillors.

SIGNS OF HAVOC.

As the train entered the station, or the hutments which stood for the station, the musicians, all of whom were in uniform, struck up a stirring French tune, which was continued during the time the troops—khaki-clad—and civilians and the numerous visitors—about 350 in all—disembarked.

It was a changed Havrincourt which the excited soldiers found. Ruins, shattered trees, remnants of equipment, broken bricks, and undisguisable shell-holes were everywhere to be seen.

But amidst the foul signs of the tragic past there appeared wooden and brick buildings, " nissen " huts, and office of the " postes et telegraphes," the stationmaster's hutment, and numerous cafés, all of which were decorated with Union Jacks, tricolour flags, and any bunting which could be roused out from family possessions.

Charming mademoiselles, elegantly dressed madames, sunburnt youngsters, and " stiff and starchy " husbands and fathers lined the station rails—there were no platforms—in full strength.

A war-time scene followed: The band ceased its music, and the men in khaki and the soldiers in mufti were lined up alongside the rail track.

Having been put through the usual formalities of drill, preparatory to marching off, they were ready to fall into line behind the village band, which was headed by two banners, the one bearing the letters in gold " Les combatants de 1914-18," and the other inscription, " Fanfare de Havrincourt."

It was noticeable that the majority of the French bandsmen were ex-soldiers, each proudly carrying his medal, amongst which the " Croix de Guerre " was prominent.

EX-SOLDIERS THRILLED.

To quick-step, martial strains, and to sensations and feelings which none of the English ex-Service men could describe, but all could feel thrill them, the smart column swung down the " high street," flanked by shattered trees and bushes, to the " Grand Place," or village square, where the men were brought to a halt.

Short introductions concluded, warrant officers, N.C.O.'s, and men were asked to partake of refreshments, provided in a hut behind the wooden building dignified by the name of " Mairie."

Afterwards the visiting ex-fighters were dismissed for several hours, to wander at leisure amongst the scenes of their historic activities.

Havrincourt was reached about 10.30 in the morning ; and for an hour or more the sun had been making the railway carriages uncomfortably hot. The luckiest fellows were those who travelled in one of the open-sided trucks, labelled " 40 Hommes." They were able to sit on the step and enjoy the gentle breeze created by the movement of the train, which was not by any means an express. It was not so bad, however, as the " leave trains " of unforgetable memory.

The evacuation of the train brought but little relief. A strong sun burnt down with tropical ferocity, and several people began to be affected by the sun's rays. These visitors very wisely sought the frugal shade afforded by the war-scarred trees which remain standing in the grounds of the chateau.

The great majority, however, drawn by the magnetic attraction which old battlefields will always have for those who have fought over them, wandered over, searched, and viewed again fields of which they had a most intimate knowledge.

" Look ! There's Yorkshire Bank," was one cry from an old Yorkshire Light Infantry officer ; and on the instant a conversation arose concerning those days in November, 1917, when the " Duke's " and " Koylis " were engaged in hot conflict with the German horde in an endeavour to drive him from his hold in the vicinity of the Canal du Nord.

Really, the whole of the region, with the exception of the open country, which has been tilled and is now growing fine crops, was just like a battlefield which had been evacuated but a few months in the face of a victorious attacking army.

Amidst it all, however, loomed the rusted, broken equipment of the armies, which had fought their fights.

GRIM RELICS OF THE WAR.

Here and there, as one progressed down or alongside old trenches, were the broken shrapnel disfigured " tin hats " of both German and British, each telling its own sad story of the fate of the wearer.

" Dud " trench mortar bombs, hand grenades, eighteen-pounders and " Jerry " shells lurked everywhere in the luxuriant grass. Equipment, boots, and barbed wire were piled high in all directions.

" Pill boxes," some deserted and left as on the day they were evacuated; others converted into storage barns and fowl houses were also prominent in the landscape.

These were the scenes which greeted the eye from Havrincourt Wood as far as sight or legs could take one to the vicinity of the scarred and broken Bourlon Wood.

Nature, however, is making amends. Derelict trees are breaking out into fresh greenness from limbs that are black and dead. Another year or two and the whole of war's ravages in this hard-contested district will be camouflaged by the verdure and the out-growths.

It was amidst such scenes as this that the representatives of the 62nd Division marched to the commanding position overlooking the rolling countryside, which stretched as far as the eye could reach from the dense Havrincourt Wood to the gas-saturated Bourlon Wood, where the majestic monument to the Division has been erected.

At the monument the Divisional representatives formed three sides of a square, while the children, the relatives of the fallen, the French and English civilians, and the visiting English civil representatives were accorded a place of honour on the right of the monument.

"YORKSHIRE HERALD" 8/6/22.

THE MONUMENT.

The monument itself stands in the centre of the town in the open square on the road towards another war-famed village, Ribecourt. It is a pyramid 50 feet high, in granite, and bears the names of battles famous in history. It is simple throughout, and, therefore, all the more impressive. The pedestal and obelisk stand on a flight of steps raised above the ground on a low platform, which measures about 36 feet in length and breadth alike. On the four faces of the obelisk are panels on which various commemorative inscriptions are carved. The front bears simply the name of the Division and the period of its service, namely, 1916-1918. On the two adjoining faces are enumerated the chief battles in which the division was engaged, and on the remaining face is inscribed the following dedication :—

To the memory of all ranks of the LXII. West Riding Division who gave their lives for King and Country in the Great War.

The site of the monument, which was generously granted by the Marquis d'Havrincourt, covers the position of a German dug-out, which still exists at a depth of some 30 feet below the surface of the ground. This has been walled up, and the ascending gallery, which provided access from it to an adjoining sunken road, has been filled in solid to render the foundations of the monument secure. A wrought iron grille is to be provided to separate the monument from the park of the marquis, and the metal work will be strengthened and supported by granite pillars on which is carved the badge of the division—a Pelican.

YORKSHIRE REPRESENTATIVES.

The ceremony, which was performed by General Berthelot, who commanded the Fifth French Army, in which the Division served in July, 1918, was attended by two hundred members of all ranks of the Division.

The company at the ceremony included, in addition to Lieut.-General Sir Robert Whigham, K.C.B. (a former General Officer Commanding the 62nd Division), Lieutenant-Colonel H. F. Lea, General Mends, Colonel Viscount Hampden (late Commander 185th Infantry Brigade), and Lady Hampden, Lieutenant-Colonel J. C. Burnett (late Commander 186th Infantry Brigade), Lieutenant-Colonel A. P. Anderson (late C. R. A.) and Major C. J. Saunders, who was in charge of the arrangements, the Count of Havrincourt, the Mayor of the town and the Town Council, the sub-Prefects of Bapaume and Cambrai, representatives of ex-Service men's organisations, the Rev. Father C. M. Chevasse (a padre of great popularity among the men), and the Abbé Ducrocq, and the Dean of Havrincourt. The Lord Mayor of Leeds (Mr. W. Hodgson) attended, accompanied by Alderman C. H. Wilson, Alderman A. Braithwaite, Alderman G. Ratcliffe, Alderman H. Brown, Alderman J. Eddison, and Councillors O. Connellan, L. Bathurst, T. Spencer, and J. Thompson (the three last-named are ex-Service men of the 49th and 62nd Divisions), with Mr. James Graham (Director of Education) as interpreter, and Inspector Jones (macebearer). The representatives from Sheffield were associated with the 457th, 460th, and 461st Field Companies of the West Riding Royal Engineers, under Company Sergeant-Major Artindale; the 2nd-4th Hallamshires, under Regimental Sergeant-Major Webster; and the 2nd-5th Hallamshires, in charge of Regimental Sergeant-Major Edwards, from Rotherham.

The other representatives of the units in the Division were,
2-5th, 2-6th, 2-7th and 8th West Yorks. Regiment.
2-4th, 5th, 2-6th, and 2-7th Duke of Wellington's Regiment.
2-4th and 5th K.O.Y.L.I.
1-5th Devonshire Regiment.
9th Durham Light Infantry.
2-4th Hampshire Regiment.
2-20th London Regiment.
310th, 311th and 312th Artillery Brigades.
2-1st, 2-2nd, and 2-3rd Field Ambulance and 62nd Divisional Train, R.A.S.C.

KEYNOTE OF PROCEEDINGS.

Shortly before two o'clock the ex-soldiers, preceded by the band of the Division, walked over ground sacred to them to the square. The sight of 60 French ex-Service men marching with their comrades-in-arms was most impressive. As the scene was approached the monument was hidden with the colours of the two nations, the unity between whom was the keynote of the whole proceedings.

The first act was one of prayer.

The service was conducted by the late senior Chaplain to the Division, the Rev. Father C. M. Chevasse, who was assisted by the Curé of Havrincourt.

FORM OF SERVICE FOR THE UNVEILING AND DEDICATION OF THE MEMORIAL TO THE 62nd (WEST RIDING) DIVISION AT HAVRINCOURT, ON JUNE 7th, 1922.

" They served for Liberty, for Life they died."

ORDER OF SERVICE.

HYMN.

Let saints on earth in concert sing
    With those whose work is done ;
For all the servants of our King
    In Heav'n and earth are one.

One family, we dwell in Him,
    One Church, above, beneath ;
Though now divided by the stream,
    The narrow stream of death.

One army of the living God,
    To His command we bow ;
Part of the host have cross'd the flood,
    And part are crossing now.

E'en now to their eternal home
    There pass some spirits blest ;
While others to the margin come,
    Waiting their call to rest.

Jesu, be Thou our constant Guide ;
    Then, when the word is given,
Bid Jordan's narrow stream divide,
    And bring us safe to Heav'n.   AMEN.

SENTENCES.

I am the Resurrection and the Life saith the Lord; he that believeth in Me, though he were dead, yet shall he live : and whosoever liveth and believeth in Me shall never die.—St. John xi., 25-26.

Greater love hath no man that this, that a man lay down his life for his friends.—St. John xv., 13.

I heard a voice from heaven saying unto me, write, Blessed are the dead which die in the Lord from henceforth : yea, saith the Spirit, that they may rest from their labours ; for their works follow with them.—Rev. xiv., 13.

THE LESSON.

Wisdom III., 1-9.

THE UNVEILING.

By Général de Division H. M. BERTHELOT,
Membre du Conseil Supérieur de la Guerre.

THE DEDICATION.

" In the Faith of Jesus Christ, we dedicate this Memorial to the Glory of God, who has at all times raised up valiant hearts to accomplish His purposes, and in memory of these brave men who, fully convinced of the righteousness of their cause, laid down their lives for us—in the Name of the Father, and of the Son, and of the Holy Ghost. Amen."

" *See ye to it that these Men have not Died in Vain.*"

A WREATH WILL BE LAID UPON THE MEMORIAL.

THE LAST POST.

Let us Pray.

Lord have mercy upon us.
Christ have mercy upon us.
Lord have mercy upon us.

THE LORD'S PRAYER.

Let us remember the fallen.

Priest : The souls of the Righteous are in the hand of God.
Answer : Because God made trial of them and found them worthy of Himself.

O God of the spirits of all flesh, we praise and magnify Thy Holy Name for all Thy servants, who having fought a good fight, have finished their course in Thy faith and fear; and we beseech Thee that, encouraged by their examples and strengthened by their fellowship, we with them may be found meet to be partakers of the inheritance of the Saints in light; through the merits of Thy Son Jesus Christ our Lord. AMEN.

Let us pray for the bereaved.

Priest : In all their affliction He was afflicted.
Answer : And the Angel of His Presence served them.

Comfort, O Lord, we pray Thee, all those who mourn the loss of those who are dear to them. Support them in Thy Love, and teach them to lean on Thee. Give them faith to look beyond the troubles of this present time, and to know that neither life nor death can separate us from the love of God which is in Jesus Christ our Lord, to whom with Thee and the Holy Ghost be all honour and glory now and for ever. AMEN.

Let us consecrate ourselves afresh to the service of Christ.

Priest : O Saviour of the World, who by Thy Cross and Precious Blood hast redeemed us.
Answer : Save us O Lord and help us, we humbly beseech Thee, O Lord.

O Lord Christ, Thou Prince of Peace, the Faithful and True, who in righteousness dost judge and make war; grant to us all, we beseech Thee, that, putting on the whole armour of God, we may follow Thee as Thou goest forth conquering and to conquer; and, fighting manfully under Thy banner against sin, the world and the devil, we may be found more than conquerors, and at the last may be refreshed with the multitude of peace in the heavenly Jerusalem, the holy city of our God; whose is the greatness and the power, the victory and the majesty, for ever. AMEN.

THE BLESSING.

ADDRESSES.

By Général Berthelot and Lieutenant-General Sir Robert Whigham.

THE MARSEILLAISE.

GOD SAVE THE KING.

" Their Name liveth for Evermore."

Just before the " Last Post " was sounded, General Berthelot stepped forward in dead silence and placed a magnificent wreath at the foot of the monument as a token from the French Army. After the playing of " The Marseillaise," the Rev. Father Chevasse delivered a brief address. Then Abbé Ducrocq blessed the memorial in a few moving words. A pull of the tape by General Berthelot and the flags fell aside to reveal the simple beauty of the monument.

GENERAL BERTHELOT'S TRIBUTE.

General Berthelot's speech was remarkable.

SPEECH BY GÉNÉRAL BERTHELOT AT HAVRINCOURT ON 7TH JUNE, 1922.

En inaugurant ce monument à la mémoire des Héros de la 62nd Division, j'apporte au nom de l'Armée française, le tribut de la reconnaissance de leurs compagnons d'armes francais.

La 62nd Division s'est taillé une large part de gloire pendant les deux années de combats sur le sol de France qu'elle a arrosé du sang de tant de ses soldats.

Dès son arrivée sur le front le Commandement britannique savait qu'elle confiance il pouvait avoir dans ses bataillons de l'armée territoriale du West Yorkshire. N'avaient-ils point, en quittant l'angleterre, reçu un message spécial d'adieux de S.M. le Roi. A peine entrée en ligne, elle prenait part à la poursuite de l'ennemi en fèvrier 1917. C'est dans la bataille de Cambrai qu'elle répondit à ce que le Roi avait attendu d'elle. Par sa vaillance, elle merita dès son premier combat les éloges du Haut Commandement britannique.

Le 20 novembre 1917, chargée d'enlever Havrincourt, elle conquiert ce village par une très brillante et irrésistible attaque. Non contente de ce succès elle continue sa marche en avant, elle franchit d'un élan magnifique la ligne de réserve que l'ennemi avait creusée derrière Flesquières, enlève le village fortifié de Graincourt. La nuit seule arrêta sa marche dans le village d'Anneux dont elle acheva la conquête le lendemain matin.

Général Berthelot—Lieut.-General Sir R. D. Whigham.

Le Commmandant en Chef envoya à la Division un message plein d'honneur, " cette attaque de la 62 Division fut un tour de force éclatant par lequel les troupes avancèrent de quatre miles et demi, envahissant deux positions de la defénse allemande, et trois villages."

Les chances de la guerre voulurent que la 62nd Division eut à reprendre une 2nd fois le village d'Havrincourt pendant la grande et suprême offensive des Alliées. Mais auparavant, elle avait montré encore ses splendides qualités militaires.

A l'époque si sombre de la fin de mars 1918, elle resista vaillamment à la ruée allemande. Elles se battit avec un courage et une abnégation magnifique. Plus de deux mille de ses soldats se sacrifièrent pour prenettre aux Alliés d'arrêter l'ennemi. La 62nd Division montra encore de plus brillantes vertus militaire en juillet 1918, alors qu'elle appartenait à la Va. Armée ; que j'avais l'honneur de commander.

Du 20 au 28 juillet, la Division marcha de succès en succès attaquant l'ennemi avec un élan redoutable au Sud-Ouest de Reims. C'est un de ses bataillons du 8th West Yorkshire, qui enleva de haute lutte la Montagne de Bligny-Montagne, où quelques semaines auparavant un autre bataillon britannique le 4 du King's Shropshire Light Infantry avait pour sa résistance acharnée gagné la Croix de Guerre que j'ai eu le grand plaisir de remettre il y a quelque jours, à Shrewsbury aux survivants et aux jeunes soldats du Comté de Shropshire.

Là encore, le Commandant de la 62nd Division montra cette merveilleuse coquetterie de na jamais annoncer la perte d'une position, avant de pouvoir rendre compte de la reprise.

La vaillance du 8th West Yorkshire lui valut aussi la Croix de Guerre avec palme, et une magnifique citation du Commandant en Chef : " Malgré une résistance vigoureuse et décidée, un progrès régulier fut obtenu..... L'artillerie et les tanks francais avaient rendu des secours appréciables. Les 51st et 62nd Division ont fait 1,200 prisonniers appartenant à 7 divisions différentes et evancé de plus de 4 miles."

C'est ainsi qu'une fois de plus s'est marquée dans de glorieux combats l'etroite amitié des soldats de nos deux armées. Amitie precieuse qui doit durée indissolublement parce qu'elle est née de sacrifices communs pour un but unique, le Triomphe de la Justice et du Droit.

(General Berthelot's speech was translated into English by Colonel Langiois, and the British troops punctuated it with frequent cheers).

GEN. WHIGHAM'S REPLY.

General Whigham delivered a stirring reply.

SPEECH BY LIEUT.-GENERAL SIR ROBERT WHIGHAM, K.C.B., AT HAVRINCOURT, ON 7TH JUNE, 1922.

Mon Général,

In the name of all ranks of the 62nd Division and of the people of the West Riding of Yorkshire, I thank you for the honour you have done us in unveiling this memorial and for the moving words in which you have referred to the achievements of the Division.

It is in accordance with the unanimous desire of its survivors that this monument has been erected on the Hill of Havrincourt, one of the key positions of the famous Hindenburg Line, which was twice wrested from the enemy by the 62nd Division.

This site we owe, Monsieur le Comte, Maire d'Havrincourt, to the generosity of your illustrious family. Speaking for myself, standing here in the presence of so many of those whom I had the honour to command in the final and victorious allied offensive, it is with deep emotion that I read graven on these granite blocks the glorious record of the Division. Truly it was undefeated; but what a story of valour and endurance and self-sacrifice!

If I may venture to record an opinion as to the cause of its success, I would say that it was due to the spirit of loyalty and brotherhood between all arms and all ranks which permeated every unit in the Division.

And when I see assembled on this devastated ground this gathering of " Anciens Combattants " of the Great French Army, I am reminded of that same spirit of brotherhood between French and British troops which was born of the first clash of arms in 1914, and which continued firm through more than four long years, until by our common effort our enemies were finally overcome. In further proof of this spirit of true comradeship between the French and British Armies, I have to-day received from General Girard, who formerly commanded the 62nd French Division, a most touching letter of sympathy on this great occasion. In that letter he begs that he and the survivors of his Division may be associated with us in rendering homage to our brave comrades who made the great sacrifice for the freedom of the world.

May this monument, on this historic spot to-day, in the presence of so great a gathering of representatives of both nations, made sacred to the glorious memory of our brothers-in-arms, remain throughout the ages a symbol of the true and lasting friendship between the French and British peoples.

Le Général Girard,
Etat-Major Caserne de Reuilly,
Paris XII.

Mon Général,

La 62nd Division britannique inauguré demain 7th Juin le monument éléve par ses soins a Havrincourt a la memoire de ses soldats tombes au Champ d'Honneur.

Voulez vous permettre au Général Commandant la 62nd Division francaise, division aujourd'hui dissoute, de s'associer et d'associer les anciens combattants de cette division a l'hommage rendu par leur frères d'arme aux vaillants de l'armée britanniques morts pour la liberté du monde ?

Avec plus d'autorité que moi, le Général Berthelot glorifiera à juste titre la mémoire de vos braves, mais j'ai pensé cependant, mon Général qu'il etait nécessaire que ceux là qui ont combattu dans les rangs de la 62nd Division francaise viennent, aussie en ce jour solennel apporter leur tribut d'admiration et de respect, à leur camarades de la 62nd division britannique honorés à Havrincourt.

Que nos morts communs pieusement entourés de notre profond respect, reposent en paix : leur tâche est accomplie. Que nous, les vivants, liés dans la vie par leur grand souvenir, perseverions dans cette sainte et puissante union qui a gagne la guerre, qui doit nous assurer la paix bienfai-sante aujourd'hui, tels sont les vœux que je veux formuler ici et que je vous demande de transmettre de la part des anciens combattants de la 62nd Division francaise a nos camarades de la 62nd division francaise a nos camarades de la 62nd division britannique.

Quant à vous, mon Général, je vous prie de vouloir bien agréer l'expression de mes sentiments de haute consideration et de cordiale camaraderie.

G. GIRARD.

Appendix I.

ORDER OF BATTLE OF THE 62ND (W.R.) DIVISION ON 28TH AUGUST, 1918.

General Officer Commanding : Major-General Sir R. D. Whigham, K.C.B., D.S.O.
A.D.C. : Lieut. J. Bury, 17th Lancers.
„ Capt. F. M. Freake, R.F.A.
G.S.O. 1 Lieut.-Col. C. R. Newman, C.M.G., D.S.O., R.A.
„ 2 Bt. Major F. W. L. Bissett, M.C., D.C.L.I.
„ 3 Capt. C. C. Chandler, M.C., W. Yorks. R. (T.F.).
       Lieut. T. Robbins, Lancs. Fus. (T.F.) (Acting).
A.A. & Q.M.G. : Lieut.-Col. H. F. Lea, D.S.O., late Yorks. R., R. of O.
D.A.A.G. : Major C. J. Saunders, M.C., London R. (T.F.).
D.A.Q.M.G. : Major F. J. Langdon, D.S.O. (late The King's), R. of O.
C.R.A. : Brig.-Gen. A. T. Anderson, C.M.G., R.A.
C.R.E. : Lieut.-Col. L. Chenevix Trench, D.S.O., R.E.
A.D.M.S. : Colonel H. Collinson, C.M.G., D.S.O., R.A.M.C. (T.F.).
D.A.D.M.S. : Major S. M. Hattersley, M.C., R.A.M.C.
D.A.D.V.S. : Major C. F. Neill, A.V.C. (T.F.).
D.A.D.O.S. : Major R. M. Holland, A.O.D.
D.A.P.M. : Major G. D. U. Rodwell, General List.

185TH INFANTRY BRIGADE.

G.O.C. : Brig.-Gen. J. W. Viscount Hampden, C.B., C.M.G.
Bde.-Major : Capt. H. S. Kreyer, D.S.O., Yorks. Regt.
Staff Capt. : Capt. C. C. Harland, M.C., South Stafford Regt.
1/5th Bn. Devonshire Regt. : Lieut.-Col. H. Bastow, Yorkshire Regt.
8th Bn. West Yorkshire Regt. : Lieut.-Col. N. England.
2/20th Bn. London Regt. : Lieut.-Col. W. St. A. Warde-Aldam.

186TH INFANTRY BRIGADE.

G.O.C. : Brig.-Gen. J. L. G. Burnett, D.S.O., Gordon Highlanders.
Bde.-Major : Capt. G. E. Wingfield-Stratford, M.C., R.W. Kent Regt.
Staff-Capt. : Major W. O. Wright, D.S.O., R. Lancs. Regt. (T.F.).
2/4th Bn. Hampshire Regt. : Lieut.-Col. F. Brook.

Appendix 169

2/4th Bn. Duke of Wellington's Regt.: Lieut.-Col. P. P. Wilson, D.L.I.
5th Bn. Duke of Wellington's Regt.: Lieut.-Col. J. Walker, D. of W.'s Regt.

187TH INFANTRY BRIGADE.

G.O.C.: Brig.-Gen. A. J. Reddie, D.S.O., South Wales Borderers.
Bde.-Major: Capt. J. K. Newbigging, M.C., K.O.S.B.
Staff Capt.: Capt. H. J. Impson, M.C., Norfolk Regt.
2/4th Bn. York and Lancs. Regt.: Lieut.-Col. L. H. P. Hart.
2/4th Bn. King's Own Yorkshire L.I.: Lieut.-Col. C. A. Chaytor, K.O.Y.L.I.
5th Bn. King's Own Yorkshire L.I.: Lieut.-Col. F. H. Peter.

62ND DIVISIONAL ROYAL ARTILLERY.

C.R.A.: Brig.-Gen. A. T. Anderson, C.M.G., R.A.
Bde.-Major: Major F. FitzGibbon, D.S.O., R.F.A.
Staff Capt.: Major A. J. Elston, R.F.A., (T.F.).
Reconnaissance Officer: Lieut. R. A. T. Anderson, R.F.A. (S.R.).

310TH BRIGADE R.F.A.

O.C.: Lieut.-Col. D. J. C. Sherlock, D.S.O.
A/Battery B.C.: Major J. F. K. Lockhart, D.S.O.
B/ „ „ Major J. M. Currie.
C/ „ „ Major C. A. Eeles, D.S.O.
D/ „ „ Major R. C. Foot, M.C.

312TH BRIGADE, R.F.A.

O.C.: Lieut.-Col. A. G. Eden.
A/Battery B.C.: Major R. Nickols.
B/ „ „ Major F. A. Arnold-Forster, D.S.O.
C/ „ „ Major E. Rotheray.
D/ „ „ Major G. A. Swain, M.C.

62ND DIVISIONAL AMMUNITION COLUMN.

O.C.: Lieut.-Col. F. A. Woodcock, D.S.O.
No. 1 Section: Capt. J. Fraser.
No. 2 „ Capt. T. C. Kewley.
No. 3 „ Capt. J. E. Edmondson, T.D.

ROYAL ENGINEERS.

C.R.E. : Lieut.-Col. L. Chenevix-Trench, D.S.O., R.E.
Adjutant : Capt. E. B. Hammond, M.C., R.E. (T.F.).
457th Field Coy. R.E. : Major Paul, M.C.
460th ,,   ,,   ,,   Capt. Tyack
461st ,,   ,,   ,,   Major W. Froggatt, M.C.

SIGNAL SERVICE.

62nd Division Signal Coy. : Major R. V. Montgomery, Som. L.I.

62ND DIVISIONAL PIONEER BATTALION.

9th Bn. Durham Light Infantry (T.F.) : Lieut.-Col. E. Crouch.

62ND BATTALION MACHINE-GUN CORPS.

O.C. : Lieut.-Col. G. H. Harrison.

MEDICAL UNITS.

A.D.M.S. : Colonel H. Collinson, C.M.G., D.S.O., R.A.M.C. (T.F.).
D.A.D.M.S. : Major S. M. Hattersley, M.C., R.A.M.C.
2/1st West Riding Field Ambulance : Major H. B. Pope.
2/2nd ,,   ,,   ,,   ,,   Lieut.-Col. C. W. Eames.
2/3rd ,,   ,,   ,,   ,,   Lieut.-Col. P. G. Williamson.

62ND DIVISION SANITARY SECTION.

ARMY SERVICE CORPS.

62nd Divisional Train : Lieut.-Col. H. H. Wilberforce.
525th Coy. A.S.C. :
526th ,,   ,,
527th ,,   ,,
528th ,,   ,,

MOBILE VETERINARY SECTION.

2/1st (W.R.) Mobile Veterinary Section : Capt. D. R. Crabb (T.F.).

Appendix II.

EXTRACT FROM "LONDON GAZETTE," 15th November, 1918.

No. 240194 Sgt. Laurence CALVERT, M.M., 5th K.O.Y.L.I. (Conisbro').

For most conspicuous bravery and devotion to duty in attack when the success of the operation was rendered doubtful owing to severe enfilade machine-gun fire. Alone and single-handed Sgt. Calvert, rushing forward against the machine-gun team, bayoneted three and shot four.

His valour and determination in capturing single-handed two machine guns and killing the crews thereof enabled the ultimate objective to be won. His personal gallantry inspired all ranks.

Appendix III.

EXTRACT FROM "LONDON GAZETTE," 14th December, 1918.

No. 34506 Pte. Henry TANDEY, D.C.M., M.M., 5th Bn., W. Rid. R. (T.F.) (Leamington).

For most conspicuous bravery and initiative during the capture of the village and the crossings at Marcoing, and the subsequent counter-attack on September 28th, 1918.

When, during the advance on Marcoing, his platoon was held up by machine-gun fire, he at once crawled forward, located the machine gun, and, with a Lewis gun team, knocked it out.

On arrival at the crossings he restored the plank bridge under a hail of bullets, thus enabling the first crossing to be made at this vital spot.

Later in the evening, during an attack, he with eight comrades was surrounded by an overwhelming number of Germans, and though the position was apparently hopeless, he led a bayonet charge through them, fighting so fiercely that 37 of the enemy were driven into the hands of the remainder of his company.

Although twice wounded, he refused to leave till the fight was won.

Appendix IV.

EXTRACT FROM "LONDON GAZETTE," 6th January, 1919.

No. 205353 Cpl. (A/Sjt.) John Brunton DAYKINS, 2/4th Bn. York & Lanc. R. (T.F.) (Jedburgh, Scotland).

For most conspicuous bravery and initiative at Solesmes on 20th October, 1918, when, with twelve remaining men of his platoon, he worked his way most skilfully, in face of heavy opposition, towards the church. By prompt action he enabled his party to rush a machine gun, and during subsequent severe hand-to-hand fighting he himself disposed of many of the enemy and secured his objective, his party in addition to heavy casualties inflicted, taking thirty prisoners.

He then located another machine gun which was holding up a portion of his company. Under heavy fire he worked his way alone to the post, and shortly afterwards returned with twenty-five prisoners and an enemy machine gun, which he mounted at his post.

His magnificent fighting spirit and example inspired his men, saved many casualties, and contributed very largely to the success of the attack.

Appendix V.
CASUALTIES AND CAPTURES OF THE 62ND DIVISION DURING THE OPERATIONS FROM 24TH AUGUST—11TH NOVEMBER, 1918:

From 24th August—3rd September.

Casualties: Officers, killed 19, wounded 74, missing 1; other ranks, killed 302, wounded 1,702, missing 325.

Captures: Officers 39, other ranks, 1,418. Field guns 3, machine guns 277, trench mortars 35, anti-tank rifles 35.

From 12th—15th September.

Casualties: Officers, killed 8, wounded 34, missing nil; other ranks, killed 194, wounded 1,058, missing 228.

Captures: Officers 18, other ranks, 866. Field guns 4, trench mortars 12, machine guns 46.

From 25th September—1st October.

Casualties: Officers, killed 20, wounded 42, missing 3; other ranks, killed 243, wounded 1,135, missing 262.

Captures: Officers, 24; other ranks, 1,495. Guns 65, including four 5·9-in. Howitzers, one Naval gun and one H.V. gun. Machine guns 358, trench mortars 25, anti-tank rifles 2, automatic rifles 2.

From 19th—20th October.

Casualties: Officers, killed nil, wounded 10, missing nil; other ranks, killed 57, wounded 370, missing 15.

Captures: Officers, 12; other ranks, 687. machine guns 71, trench mortars 13, guns 3.

From 4th—11th November.

Casualties: Officers, killed 2, wounded 26, missing nil; other ranks, killed 117, wounded 693, missing 61.

Captures: Officers, 13; other ranks, 900. Guns 24, machine guns 115, trench mortars 11.

Total Casualties.

Officers: Killed 49, wounded 186, missing 4 = 239.
Other ranks, Killed 918, wounded 3,976, missing 891 = 5,785.

Total Captures.

Officers, 106. Other ranks, 5,366.

Appendix VI.

REPORT ON BRIDGING OPERATIONS CARRIED OUT BY 62nd (WEST RIDING) DIVISIONAL R.E. ON THE NIGHT OF 19th/20th OCTOBER, 1918

1.—It was decided to make a minimum of eight foot bridges to the north of the town of Solesmes and four to the south. Later on, as soon as daylight allowed a correct reconnaissance to be made, two pontoon bridges to carry field guns were to be made.

2.—The northern set of bridges were to be made between V.30.c.o.1. and V.30. c. 1.7. Reconnaissances were carried out on the night of the 17th, and the width of the river at water level estimated to be about 25 feet, depth 3 to 4 feet, banks very steep and 6 to 10 feet high, and quite unclimbable by Infantry in fighting order.

The bed of the river had 1 to 2 feet of mud.

It was decided to use six light trestle bridges and two cork bridges carrying infantry in single file.

In addition, in case the bridges should fail for any reason, four wire netting mats were to be laid across the river to allow men to walk through the water over the mud.

Ropes were to be laid across the river at these crossing places from top to top of bank, to enable men to pull themselves up the steep banks.

Scaling ladders 10 feet high were also given to the Infantry for the same purpose.

Owing to the necessity for absolute silence throughout the operations and the steepness and height of the banks, petrol tin bridges, light pontoon bridges and barrels were ruled out.

The night of the 18th/19th was used for carrying up material and setting it out into bridges.

A carrying party of the 9th Battalion Durham Light Infantry (Pioneers) was organized in such a way that each party knew exactly what it had to do. The party was attached to a Field Company for two days before the operation and was given all possible instruction in handling the material, which had to be carried about 700 yards from the wagons.

On the night of the 19th/20th, Zero hour having been fixed for 0.200 hours on the 20th, the erection of the bridges was started at 0.130 hours and completed at or before Zero in every case.

A single cork float bridge was completed half an hour before Zero to enable a Company of Infantry to pass over as covering party. The Company lay under the far bank of the river.

The Infantry passed over the bridges without a check of any kind and the operation was completely successful.

3.—The southern set of bridges were to be made between D.18. b. 4.1. and D.18. b. 6.5. A reconnaissance on the night of the 17th having fixed these as the most suitable limits.

A second reconnaissance on the night of the 18th showed that the river had risen several feet owing to the enemy having dammed it between the northern and southern bridging places.

The site for the bridges was accordingly moved up D.18. d. 2.3.

It was decided to make two petrol tin and two cork float bridges on the night of the 19th, all material having been carried up in the same way as for the northern bridges, to the site of the work. Bridging was started at 23.00 hours on the 19th.

It was found that the river had risen still further and the bridges were not long enough to span it. Their number was accordingly reduced to three, and an existing foot bridge patched up to serve as a fourth.

The operation was quite successful, and the Infantry passed over without a check in due time.

4.—The light trestles which were used were made out of hexagonal 16 foot Signal Service telegraph poles.

They were four-legged, transoms 7 ft. 6 in. above foot of legs, the legs were splayed out 2 ft. 6 in. each pair of legs 4 ft 6 in. apart. Angle iron pickets were used as ledgers in order to sink the trestles. All lashings were of wire. Trestles were stiffly cross-braced and made up complete with the lashing fixed to the transom before leaving Camp.

The footways for the trestle bridges consisted of two 15 ft. duckboards, 2 ft. wide, runners were 3 in. by 3 in., slats, 3 in. by 1 in. placed 1½ in. apart. The duckboards thus formed were stiffly trussed underneath with heavy telegraph wire windlassed tight.

Three slats were left out of the trestle end of each duckboard, to allow for overlapping and difference in level, and the lashing, ready fixed to the transom, was used to lash them down.

Each trestle was carried out into mid-stream by two men wading, and stuck into the mud without difficulty.

5.—The cork bridges were formed of three pairs of cork piers at 7 ft. centres, the centre pier was anchored back to each bank.

6.—The wire netting mats were made of German wire netting, one metre wide, with slats 1½ in. by 1 in. fastened on the top side of the wire 18 in. apart. These were fixed down with screw pickets at the shore end, and rolled across the bed of the river by a man wading along and shoving the roll in front of him with his foot, and picketted down on the far bank.

Slung ropes were placed alongside each mat to guide men over and help them down and up the banks.

The mats were not used owing to the success of the bridges.

Petrol tin float in pairs were made with two frames, each holding twenty-four tins, spaced at 9 in. centres, tins being encased in a crate of rabbit wire and wedged tightly in a 3 in. by 3 in. timber framing.

On the southern site, mauls, muffled with sandbags, could be used to drive pickets but at the northern site screw pickets had to be used. Some specially strong kite balloon crew anchorage pickets were obtained, and found very successful on the northern site.

Absolute silence was necessary, as the nearest enemy post was found to be only fifty yards off.

7.—The approaches to the bridges were marked with tapes. The river ends of the approaches were marked with number boards painted white on black, one foot square. The other ends were marked with petrol tins punched with corresponding numbers, with candles in them.

These candles were quickly put out by shelling, but the moon gave sufficient light for the tapes to be found. Electric torches might be useful on a similar occasion instead of candles.

The duckboards should have been covered with wire netting to prevent men slipping on them, but in this case, they worked successfully without wire netting.

8.—Organization was based on each party of R.E. having its own carrying party of requisite strength and having one job only to do.

Thus each trestle bridge had five Sappers and ten carriers. Each cork float bridge six Sappers and twelve carriers. Each wire netting mat three Sappers and so on.

9.—It rained steadily throughout the night of 19th/20th, and this possibly accounted for the operations being unheard. They were only harassed by ordinary machine-gun fire, but when the hostile barrage came down after completion of work, working parties had to take to the cellars for some time before they could get back.

10.—The pontoon bridges, of which two were made, were successfully completed in time for the artillery to use them. Their construction was only difficult on account of hostile shell fire.

The 457th Field Company, R.E., made the pontoon bridges.

Half 460th Field Company, R.E., made the southern foot bridges.

461st Field Company, R.E., and half 460th Field Company, R.E., made the northern ones.

Total casualties among the R.E. and Pioneers were one officer killed, seven other ranks wounded.

Appendix VII.
V. Armêe Etat-Major.
Q.C. le 10 Decembre, 1918.

No. 5575/P.
Bureau du Personnel.

EXTRAIT DE L'ORDRE GENERAL NO. 430.

Le Général Commandant la V. Armée cite à l'ordre de l'Armée.

Le 8 Bataillon du West Yorkshire Rgt.

" Bataillon d'élite ; sous le commandement énergique du Lieutenant-Colonel Norman Ayrton England, a participé brilliament aux durs combats du 20 au 30 Juillet qui ont valu la conquête de la vallée de l'Ardre. Le 23 Juillet 1918 après s'être frayé un chemin dans les fourrés épais du Bois du Petit Champs, s'est emparé d'une position importante malgré un feu nourri des mitrailleuses ennemies. Le 28 Juillet 1918 dans un brio magnifique, a enlevé la Montagne de Bligny, fortement défendue par des forces ennemies supérieures en nombre, s'y est maintenu malgré les pertes subies, et les efforts désespérés de l'adversaire pour la position." (Décision G.Q.G. No. 22389 en date du 16 Octobre 1918).

Le General Commandant La V. Armée,
GUILLAUMAT.

Pour extrait certifié conforme
Q.G. le 3 Decembre 1918.
Le Général Commandant la V. Armée
C.O. Le Chef du Bureau du Personnel
CHAMOUZ.

True copy of an official copy.
Horatio Mends,
B.G.

10.1.25.

Appendix VII.
TRANSLATION.
Vth Army Staff.
H.Q., 10th December, 1918.

Personal Services Department.
No. 5575/P.

EXTRACT FROM GENERAL ORDER NO. 430.

The General Officer Commanding the Vth Army mentions in his Army Orders:—

The 8th Battalion the West Yorkshire Regiment.

" A most distinguished battalion. Under the energetic command of Lieutenant-Colonel Norman Ayrton England it took a brilliant part in the hard fighting between the 20th and the 30th July which resulted in the capture of the valley of the Ardre. On the 23rd July, 1918, after forcing a way through the thick undergrowth of the Bois du Petit Champs, it carried an important position in the face of sustained fire of enemy machine guns. On the 28th July, 1918, it captured the Montagne de Bligny with magnificent dash though this hill was strongly defended by superior enemy forces, and held it in spite of heavy losses and the determined efforts of the enemy to recapture it."

(G.H.Q. Decision No. 22389 dated 16th October, 1918).

GUILLAUMAT,
General Officer Comanding the Vth Army.

Certified true copy.
H.Q. 3rd Dec., 1918.
By order of the General Officer Commanding the Vth Army.

CHAMOUZ,
Chief of the Personal Services Department.

Appendix VIII.
OFFICER CASUALTIES, 62ND (W.R.) DIVISION, 1917-1918.

1917.
DURING THE ADVANCE TO THE HINDENBURG LINE, 11TH JANUARY-13TH MARCH.

2/2/17	2/Lieut. E. J. Trubshawe, 460th Field Coy. R.E.—Killed.
6/2/17	2/Lieut. N. E. Bentley, 2/5th W. Riding Regt.—Missing.
11/2/17	Capt. H. C. Lasbrey, 310th Bde. R.F.A.—Wounded.
15/2/17	Capt. G. R. Nevitt, 2/8th W. Yorks. Regt.—Wounded.
16/2/17	Lieut. H. Sinclair, 2/4th W. Riding Regt.—Killed.
17/2/17	2/Lieut. H. A. Girling, 2/5th W. Yorks. Regt.—Wounded.
18/2/17	Lieut. D. L. E. Davies, 2/6th W. Yorks. Regt.—Wounded.
19/2/17	Major F. A. Lupton, 2/8th W. Yorks. Regt.—Missing (later found dead).
19/2/17	2/Lieut. S. A. Smith, 457th Field Coy. R.E.—Wounded.
20/2/17	Capt. C. R. Bramley, 2/5th K.O.Y.L.I.—Killed.
,,	2/Lieut. S. D. Lang, 2/5th K.O.Y.L.I.—Wounded, died of wounds 24/2/17.
,,	Rev. F. L. Suggett, C.F., attd. 2/6th W. Riding Regt.—Wounded.
,,	Lieut. G. K. Brown, 2/6th W. Yorks. Regt.—Wounded.
21/2/17	Lieut. H. G. Hodgkinson, 2/5th W. Riding Regt.—Wounded.
,,	Capt. R. J. Preston, 2/5th K.O.Y.L.I.—Wounded.
22/2/17	Capt. A. S. Furniss, 2/5th Y. and L. Regt.—Missing.
,,	Lieut. A. H. Hicks, 2/5th Y. and L. Regt.—Missing.
,,	Capt. W. N. Gale, 2/4th Y. and L. Regt.—Wounded.
23/2/17	Lieut. A. E. Furniss, 2/5th Y. and L. Regt. Wounded.
25/2/17	2/Lieut. T. B. Lyth, 2/5th Y. and L. Regt.—Wounded.
26/2/17	Major R. E. Negus, 2/8th W. Yorks. Regt.—Wounded.
,,	2/Lieut. J. S. McEwen, 461st Field Coy. R.E.—Wounded.
1/3/17	Major A. P. Dale, 2/5th W. Yorks. Regt.—Killed.
,,	Major R. C. Williams, 310th Bde. R.F.A.—Wounded.
,,	2/Lieut. W. O. de W. Silmon, 2/8th W. Yorks. Regt.—Killed.

1/3/17	Lieut. K. S. Sexton, 2/6th W. Riding Regt.—Wounded.
2/3/17	2/Lieut. R. G. Pickard, 2/4th K.O.Y.L.I.—Died of Wounds.
3/3/17	2/Lieut. G. Ambler, 2/6th W. Yorks. Regt.—Wounded.
,,	2/Lieut. E. S. Smith, 2/6th W. Yorks. Regt.—Missing.
,,	Lieut. C. G. Fowler, 2/8th W. Yorks. Regt.—Wounded Accidentally.
,,	2/Lieut. H. A. Sabelli, 310th Bde. R.F.A.—Wounded.
5/3/17	Lieut. E. N. J. Wethey, 2/6th W. Yorks. Regt.—Wounded.
,,	Lieut. E. W. F. Jephson, 310th Bde. R.F.A.—Wounded.
6/3/17	2/Lieut. R. Holburn, 310th Bde. R.F.A.—Wounded.
,,	2/Lieut. J. C. McIlroy, 310th Bde. R.F.A.—Wounded.
7/3/17	Lieut. J. D. Conyers, 2/8th W. Yorks. Regt.—Wounded.
,,	2/Lieut. F. Warner, 2/5th Y. and L. Regt.—Killed.
,,	2/Lieut. J. W. McHattie, 2/5th Y. and L. Regt.—Wounded.
,,	Capt. F. Wilson, R.A.M.C., att. 2/5th Y. and L. Regt.—Wounded.
9/3/17	Capt. W. H. Smith, 2/4th K.O.Y.L.I.—Wounded.
,,	2/Lieut. A. Morris, 2/4th K.O.Y.L.I.—Wounded.
11/3/17	Lieut. R. E. Mainprice, 2/4th Y. and L. Regt.—Wounded.
,,	Lieut.-Col. P. Prince, Cmdg. 2/5th Y. and L. Regt.—Wounded.
,,	Lieut. S. S. Mainwright, 2/4th K.O.Y.L.I.—Killed.
12/3/17	Capt. C. E. Stuart, 2/4th Y. and L. Regt.—Died of Wounds, 15/3/17.
13/3/17	Capt. F. H. Seaman, 310th Bde. R.F.A.—Wounded (gas).
,,	2/Lieut. R. E. F. Russell, 2/5th Y. and L. Regt.—Wounded.

DURING THE GERMAN RETREAT TO THE HINDENBURG LINE, 14TH MARCH—5TH APRIL, 1917.

14/3/17	Capt. H. E. Jenkinson, 2/4th Y. and L. Regt.—Wounded.
,,	Lieut. E. B. Bilton, 2/5th K.O.Y.L.I.—Killed.
,,	2/Lieut. G. S. High, 2/5th K.O.Y.L.I.—Killed.
,,	Lieut. J. Mailer, 2/5th K.O.Y.L.I.—Wounded.
,,	Lieut. C. Boden, 2/5th K.O.Y.L.I.—Wounded.
,,	2/Lieut. J. H. Lister, 2/4th W. Riding Regt.—Wounded.
15/3/17	Capt. W. Bell, 2/4th K.O.Y.L.I.—Killed.
20/3/17	Capt. W. Graham, 2/4th W. Riding Regt.—Wounded.

Appendix

21/3/17	Major F. A. Lupton, 2/8th W. Yorks. Regt.—Found dead, missing since 21/2/17.
22/3/17	2/Lieut. C. M. Pullan, 312th Bde. R.F.A.—Killed.
5/4/17	2/Lieut. J. M. Rivington, 2/7th W. Yorks. Regt.—Wounded.

IN TRENCH WARFARE.

6/4/17	Lieut. R. S. Greenwood, 186th Bde. Hqs.—Wounded.
7/4/17	Capt. J. Willey, 310th Bde. R.F.A.—Wounded.
,,	Capt. C. Dyson, 2/8th W. Yorks. Regt.—Killed.
,,	Lieut. C. G. Fowler, 2/8th W. Yorks. Regt.—Killed.
,,	2/Lieut. H. C. Waite, 2/8th W. Yorks. Regt.—Killed.
,,	Major F. A. Arnold Forster, 310th Bde. R.F.A.—Wounded.
,,	Lieut. P. K. B. Reynolds, 310th Bde. R.F.A.—Wounded.
,,	Lieut. H. C. Ashby, 310th Bde. R.F.A.—Wounded.
,,	2/Lieut. A. R. Moore, 2/8th W. Yorks. Regt.—Wounded.
10/4/17	Capt. R. M. Waddington, 2/8th W. Yorks. Regt.—Wounded.

IN THE FIRST ATTACK ON BULLECOURT, 11TH APRIL, 1917.

11/4/17	Lieut. C. F. R. Pells, 2/6th W. Yorks. Regt.—Killed.
,,	2/Lieut. A. G. Harris, 2/6th W. Yorks. Regt.—Killed.
,,	Capt. R. B. Armistead, 2/6th W. Yorks. Regt.—Wounded.
,,	Capt. R. M. Waddington, 2/8th W. Yorks. Regt.—Wounded.

IN TRENCH WARFARE.

12/4/17	2/Lieut. A. R. Moore, 2/8th W. Yorks. Regt.—Killed.
13/4/17	Capt. G. L. C. Hudson, 312th Bde. R.F.A.—Wounded.
14/4/17	Lieut. K. B. Nicholson, 312th Bde. R.F.A.—Wounded.
15/4/17	Lieut. L. D. Goldseller, 2/5th W. Riding Regt.—Killed.
17/4/17	Lieut. J. S. Shackleton, 2/4th W. Riding Regt.—Killed.
,,	2/Lieut. W. S. Masse, 2/4th W. Riding Regt.—Wounded.
18/4/17	Capt. N. C. Prince, 2/6th W. Riding Regt.—Killed.
,,	Capt. S. J. Rhodes, 2/6th W. Riding Regt.—Wounded.
,,	Lieut. D. D. F. Hazel, 2/6th W. Riding Regt.—Wounded.
,,	2/Lieut. E. W. D. Walker, 2/7th W. Riding Regt.—Wounded.
20/4/17	2/Lieut. F. V. Sykes, 2/5th W. Riding Regt.—Wounded.
24/4/17	Lieut. C. P. Senior, 310th Bde. R.F.A.—Wounded.
28/4/17	2/Lieut. A. Haythorne, 2/7th W. Riding Regt.—Wounded.

184 Appendix

28/4/17 Lieut. C. T. Luytens, 310th Bde. R.F.A.—Wounded.
„ Lieut. S. C. Ball, 310th Bde. R.F.A.—Wounded.
„ Lieut. R. Forrest, 310th Bde. R.F.A.—Wounded.
„ Lieut. J. W. Proctor, 310th Bde. R.F.A.—Wounded.
30/4/17 2/Lieut. Petrie, 2/6th W. Riding Regt.—Wounded (Acc.).

IN THE BATTLE OF BULLECOURT, 3RD MAY, 1917.

3/5/17 Capt. F. H. Knowles, 2/5th W. Yorks. Regt.—Missing, believed killed.
„ Lieut. C. H. Churchman, 2/5th W. Yorks. Regt.—Missing.
„ 2/Lieut. E. S. Annely, 2/5th W. Yorks. Regt.—Missing.
„ 2/Lieut. A. Wilson, 2/5th W. Yorks. Regt.—Missing.
„ Capt. C. Bulmer, 2/5th W. Yorks. Regt.—Wounded.
„ Capt. A. E. Green, 2/5th W. Yorks. Regt.—Wounded.
„ Lieut. A. W. L. Smith, 2/5th W. Yorks. Regt.—Wounded.
„ Lieut. J. L. Wesley Smith, 2/5th W. Yorks. Regt.—Wounded.
„ 2/Lieut. G. B. Foster, 2/5th W. Yorks. Regt.—Wounded.
„ 2/Lieut. C. S. Almond, 2/5th W. Yorks. Regt.—Wounded.
„ Capt. G. S. Gordon, 2/6th W. Yorks. Regt.—Wounded.
„ Capt. E. C. Gregory, 2/6th W. Yorks. Regt.—Wounded.
„ Lieut. T. Armistead, 2/6th W. Yorks. Regt.—Killed.
„ Lieut. V. B. Dowling, 2/6th W. Yorks. Regt.—Wounded.
„ 2/Lieut. R. Frost, 2/6th W. Yorks. Regt.—Wounded.
„ 2/Lieut. H. Rhodes, 2/6th W. Yorks. Regt.—Wounded.
„ 2/Lieut. V. Wilson, 2/6th W. Yorks. Regt.—Wounded.
„ 2/Lieut. B. Bickerdike, 2/6th W. Yorks. Regt.—Wounded.
„ 2/Lieut. J. G. Hall, 2/6th W. Yorks. Regt.—Missing.
„ 2/Lieut. E. S. Fletcher, 2/6th W. Yorks. Regt.—Missing.
„ 2/Lieut. G. Charlesworth, 2/6th W. Yorks. Regt.—Missing.
„ Major G. W. Lawson, S.L.I., 2/7th W. Yorks. Regt.—Wounded.
„ Capt. G. L. Clark, 2/7th W. Yorks. Regt.—Wounded.
„ Lieut. J. Bazley-White, 2/7th W. Yorks. Regt.—Wounded.
„ Lieut. E. S. Moeran, 2/8th W. Yorks. Regt.—Wounded.
„ 2/Lieut. R. P. Nethercott, 2/8th W. Yorks. Regt.—Wounded.
„ 2/Lieut. B. W. Thornhill, 2/8th W. Yorks. Regt.—Wounded.
„ Lieut. V. Tansley, 2/8th W. Yorks. Regt.—Missing.

Appendix

3/5/17	2/Lieut. W. D. Muirhead, 2/8th W. Yorks. Regt.—Missing.
,,	2/Lieut. W. A. Newman, M.G. Corps.—Wounded.
,,	Capt. W. Graham, 2/4th W. Riding Regt.—Killed.
,,	2/Lieut. A. G. Priestley, 2/4th W. Riding Regt.—Killed.
,,	2/Lieut. H. L. Arnott, 2/4th W. Riding Regt.—Wounded.
,,	2/Lieut. T. G. Roberts, 2/4th W. Riding Regt.—Wounded.
,,	2/Lieut. J. L. Lister, 2/4th W. Riding Regt.—Wounded.
,,	2/Lieut. F. E. Meadows, 2/4th W. Riding Regt.—Wounded.
,,	2/Lieut. G. E. H. Peskett, 2/4th W. Riding Regt.—Missing.
,,	2/Lieut. P. R. A. Appleton, 2/4th W. Riding Regt.—Missing, believed killed.
,,	Capt. and Adjt. T. Bentley, 2/5th W. Riding Regt.—Died of Wounds, 4/5/17.
,,	Lieut. O. Walker, 2/5th W. Riding Regt.—Killed.
,,	Capt. W. Shaw, 2/5th W. Riding Regt.—Wounded.
,,	Capt. J. Walker, 2/5th W. Riding Regt.—Wounded.
,,	2/Lieut. A. M. Fisher, 2/5th W. Riding Regt.—Wounded.
,,	Lieut. P. R. Ridley, 2/5th W. Riding Regt.—Wounded and Missing.
,,	2/Lieut. H. A. Simmonds, 2/5th W. Riding Regt.—Wounded.
,,	2/Lieut. E. T. Sykes, 2/5th W. Riding Regt.—Wounded and Missing.
,,	Capt. G. Glover, 2/5th W. Riding Regt.—Missing.
,,	2/Lieut. T. C. Jacobs, 2/5th W. Riding Regt.—Missing.
,,	2/Lieut. W. Heaton, 2/5th W. Riding Regt.—Missing.
,,	2/Lieut. W. M. Hutton, 2/5th W. Riding Regt.—Missing.
,,	2/Lieut. C. T. Darwent, 2/5th W. Riding Regt.—Missing.
,,	Lieut. R. O. Niel, 2/6th W. Riding Regt.—Killed.
,,	Capt. S. J. Rhodes, 2/6th W. Riding Regt.—Wounded.
,,	Capt. C. D. Bennett, 2/6th W. Riding Regt.—Wounded.
,,	Capt. J. M. Somervell, 2/6th W. Riding Regt.—Wounded.
,,	2/Lieut. R. M. Wimbush, 2/6th W. Riding Regt.—Wounded.
,,	2/Lieut. W. G. Kinghorn, 2/6th W. Riding Regt. Wounded and Missing.
,,	Capt. W. K. Law, 2/6th W. Riding Regt.—Missing.

Appendix

3/5/17	2/Lieut. C. Holroyd, 2/6th W. Riding Regt.—Missing, believed killed.
,,	2/Lieut. W. Stockdale, 2/6th W. Riding Regt.—Missing, believed killed.
,,	2/Lieut. J. J. Shackleton, 2/6th W. Riding Regt.—Killed.
,,	2/Lieut. E. P. Kaye, 2/7th W. Riding Regt.—Killed.
,,	Major G. E. C. Cockburn, 2/6th W. Riding Regt.—Wounded.
,,	Capt. W. V. Haigh, 2/7th W. Riding Regt.—Wounded.
,,	Lieut. A. F. Gloag, 2/7th W. Riding Regt.—Wounded.
,,	2/Lieut. T. Hawkesfield, 2/7th W. Riding Regt.—Wounded.
,,	2/Lieut. E. Tanner, 2/7th W. Riding Regt.—Wounded.
,,	2/Lieut. S. Rhodes, 2/7th W. Riding Regt.—Wounded.
,,	2/Lieut. J. I. Brierley, 2/7th W. Riding Regt.—Wounded.
,,	2/Lieut. I. V. Haughton, 2/7th W. Riding Regt.—Wounded.
,,	2/Lieut. H. Furness, 2/7th W. Riding Regt.—Wounded.
,,	2/Lieut. E. Marlow, 2/7th W. Riding Regt.—Wounded.
,,	2/Lieut. H. E. Street, 2/7th W. Riding Regt.—Wounded.
,,	2/Lieut. M. O. Walsh, 2/4th K.O.Y.L.I.—Killed.
,,	Capt. A. L. Pyrah, 2/4th K.O.Y.L.I.—Wounded.
,,	Lieut. A. R. Mosley, 2/4th K.O.Y.L.I.—Wounded.
,,	2/Lieut. A. Ireland, 2/4th K.O.Y.L.I.—Wounded.
,,	2/Lieut. W. B. Driver, 2/4th K.O.Y.L.I.—Wounded.
,,	2/Lieut. J. E. V. Hill, 2/4th K.O.Y.L.I.—Wounded.
,,	2/Lieut. T. R. P. Butcher, 2/4th K.O.Y.L.I.—Wounded.
,,	2/Lieut. B. N. Smith, 2/4th K.O.Y.L.I.—Wounded.
,,	2/Lieut. C. H. Johnson, 2/4th K.O.Y.L.I.—Wounded.
,,	Lieut. Col. W. Watson, Cmdg. 2/5th K.O.Y.L.I.—Killed.
,,	Lieut. F. P. Pattinson, 2/5th K.O.Y.L.I.—Killed.
,,	2/Lieut. B. S. Brewster, 2/5th K.O.Y.L.I.—Killed.
,,	2/Lieut. F. A. Moorcock, 2/5th K.O.Y.L.I.—Missing.
,,	Major O. C. S. Watson, 2/5th K.O.Y.L.I.—Wounded.
,,	Capt. S. S. Chappell, 2/5th K.O.Y.L.I.—Wounded.
,,	Capt. T. W. Mottram, 2/5th K.O.Y.L.I.—Wounded.
,,	Capt. W. J. Oswald, 2/5th K.O.Y.L.I.—Wounded.
,,	Lieut. and Adjt. A. Robinson, 2/5th K.O.Y.L.I.—Wounded.
,,	Lieut. C. C. Snow, 2/5th K.O.Y.L.I.—Wounded.

Appendix

3/5/17 Lieut. E. R. Woodhouse, 2/5th K.O.Y.L.I.—Wounded.
,, Lieut. J. L. Somers, 2/5th K.O.Y.L.I.—Wounded.
,, Lieut.-Col. F. St. J. Blacker, Cmdg. 2/4th Y. and L. Regt.—Wounded.
,, Major J. W. Richardson, 2/4th Y. and L. Regt.—Killed.
,, Capt. H. E. Jenkinson, 2/4th Y. and L. Regt.—Wounded.
,, Lieut. J. Rodgers, 2/4th Y. and L. Regt.—Wounded.
,, Lieut. P. H. Lonsdale, 2/4th Y. and L. Regt.—Wounded.
,, 2/Lieut. Seagrave, 2/4th Y. and L. Regt.—Wounded.
,, Capt. W. S. M. Beeby, 2/4th Y. and L. Regt.—Killed.
,, 2/Lieut. J. H. Clively, 2/4th Y. and L. Regt.—Killed.
,, Lieut. J. A. Conmee, 2/4th Y. and L. Regt.—Killed.
,, Capt. W. N. Gale, 2/4th Y. and L. Regt.—Missing.
,, Lieut. G. D. Gray, 2/4th Y. and L. Regt.—Died of Wounds, 5/5/17.
,, 2/Lieut. D. H. Wells, 2/5th Y. and L. Regt.—Killed.
,, 2/Lieut. W. P. Taylor, 2/5th Y. and L. Regt.—Killed.
,, 2/Lieut. T. E. F. Russell, 2/5th Y. and L. Regt.—Killed.
,, 2/Lieut. S. Spencer, 2/5th Y. and L. Regt. Killed.
,, Capt. J. B. Phillips, 2/5th Y. and L. Regt.—Wounded.
,, Capt. A. C. Lancaster, 2/5th Y. and L. Regt.—Wounded.
,, Lieut. J. Ellse, 2/5th Y. and L. Regt.—Wounded.
,, 2/Lieut. G. C. Jenkins, 2/5th Y. and L. Regt.—Missing.
4/5/17 Lieut. G. K. Brown, 2/6th W. Yorks. Regt.—Killed.
,, Lieut. J. G. Anderson, M.G. Corps.—Wounded.
5/5/17 2/Lieut. P. Holroyd, 2/5th K.O.Y.L.I.—Killed.
7/5/17 Lieut. C. Punchard, R.F.A.—Wounded.
8/5/17 Lieut.-Col. C. K. James, 2/7th W. Yorks. Regt.—Wounded.
9/5/17 2/Lieut. H. Lupton, 2/5th W. Yorks. Regt.—Wounded.
12/5/17 Lieut. G. H. Kitson, R.F.A.—Wounded.
,, Capt. J. Moffatt, 185th T.M.B.—Wounded.
13/5/17 2/Lieut. G. L. Jefferson, 2/4th Y. and L. Regt.—Wounded.
,, Lieut. C. V. Montgomery, R.F.A.—Wounded.
14/5/17 2/Lieut. B. C. Johnson, 2/7th W. Riding. Regt.—Killed.
,, 2/Lieut. Haythorne, 2/7th W. Riding Regt.—Wounded.
15/5/17 Lieut. A. J. Edwards, R.F.A.—Wounded.
,, Lieut. E. W. Jephson, R.F.A.—Wounded.

IN TRENCH WARFARE.

19/5/17	Capt. E. H. Watson, 2/7th W. Riding Regt.—Wounded.
,,	Lieut. C. H. Lockwood, 2/7th W. Riding Regt.—Wounded.
,,	2/Lieut. J. Maden, 2/7th W. Riding Regt.—Wounded.
,,	2/Lieut. T. P. Crosland, 2/7th W. Riding Regt.—Wounded (Acc.).
23/5/17	2/Lieut. F. C. Lambert, 2/5th K.O.Y.L.I.—Wounded.
,,	Lieut. A. C. Lynn, 2/5th K.O.Y.L.I.—Wounded.
24/5/17	Lieut. H. O. Brown, 2/5th K.O.Y.L.I.—Wounded.
26/5/17	Capt. H. B. Gillmore, 312th Bde. R.F.A.—Killed.
,,	Lieut. G. Hardy, 312th Bde. R.F.A.—Wounded.
27/5/17	2/Lieut. J. Maud, 2/7th W. Riding Regt.—Wounded.
12/6/17	2/Lieut. F. Akroyd, 2/4th W. Riding Regt.—Wounded (Accidentally).
17/6/17	2/Lieut. J. Broughton, 2/6th W. Riding Regt.—Injured.
18/6/17	2/Lieut. G. E. Gee, 2/4th Y. and L. Regt.—Wounded (Accidentally).
19/6/17	2/Lieut. F. G. Hay, 312th Bde. R.F.A.—Wounded (Acc.).
25/6/17	2/Lieut. J. H. Irons, 2/4th W. Riding Regt.—Wounded (Accidentally).
,,	2/Lieut. E. G. Harris, 2/7th W. Riding Regt.—Wounded (Accidentally) (Died of Wounds, 26/6).
2/7/17	Capt. C. S. Wilson, 2/7th W. Riding Regt.—Wounded.
4/7/17	Capt. H. N. Waller, 2/4th W. Riding Regt.—Died of Wounds, 4/7/17.
,,	2/Lieut. T. F. Galpine, 2/7th W. Yorks. Regt.—Wounded.
7/7/17	Lieut. J. A. Brown, 312th Bde. R.F.A.—Wounded.
8/7/17	Lieut. F. L. Davies, 2/8th W. Yorks. Regt.—Killed.
9/7/17	2/Lieut. J. L. Rodger, 2/4th K.O.Y.L.I.—Wounded.
11/7/17	2/Lieut. R. L. Pickard, 310th Bde. R.F.A.—Wounded.
13/7/17	Capt. H. J. Behrens, 2/6th W. Yorks. Regt.—Wounded.
,,	2/Lieut. G. Ambler, 2/6th W. Yorks. Regt.—Wounded.
,,	2/Lieut. A. H. Metcalfe, 2/4th K.O.Y.L.I.—Wounded.
,,	2/Lieut. A. Butler, 2/5th K.O.Y.L.I.—Wounded.
14/7/17	2/Lieut. T. B. Wills, 310th Bde. R.F.A.—Wounded.
17/7/17	2/Lieut. W. H. Dawson, 2/7th W. Yorks. Regt.—Wounded.
,,	Lieut.-Col. P. Prince, Cmdg. 2/5th Y. and L. Regt.—Wounded.

Appendix

17/7/17	2/Lieut. E. H. Vanderpump, 310th Bde. R.F.A.—Wounded.
,,	2/Lieut. H. C. O. Lawrie, 310th Bde. R.F.A.—Wounded.
,,	2/Lieut. T. B. Wills, 310th Bde. R.F.A.—Wounded.
18/7/17	Capt. C. D. Bennett, 2/6th W. Riding Regt.—Died of Wounds.
27/7/17	Lieut. C. G. Edwards, 2/7th W. Riding Regt.—Wounded.
28/7/17	2/Lieut. F. Muff, 2/7th W. Riding Regt.—Wounded.
30/7/17	2/Lieut. F. Abrahams, 310th Bde. R.F.A.—Wounded.
7/8/17	2/Lieut. A. Q. Bennett, V/62 T.M.B.—Wounded.
10/8/17	Lieut.-Col. F. G. Chamberlin, Cmdg. 2/7th W. Riding Regt.—Wounded.
11/8/17	2/Lieut. G. H. Haigh, 2/6th W. Yorks. Regt.—Wounded.
13/8/17	2/Lieut. H. Broomfield, 2/6th W. Yorks. Regt.—Wounded.
20/8/17	2/Lieut. G. Spedding, 2/4th K.O.Y.L.I.—Killed.
26/8/17	2/Lieut. A. A. Gould, 2/7th W. Riding Regt.—Wounded.
,,	Lieut. J. E. David, 2/4th K.O.Y.L.I.—Wounded.
27/8/17	Lieut.-Col. J. J. Josselyn, Cmdg. 2/5th W. Yorks. Regt.—Wounded, shell shock.
1/9/17	Lieut. H. Hutchinson, 2/5th W. Yorks. Regt.—Died of Wounds.
7/9/17	Capt. A. H. Willatts, 2/5th Y. and L. Regt.—Killed.
8/9/17	2/Lieut. T. B. Wakefield, 2/6th W. Yorks. Regt.—Killed.
,,	2/Lieut. J. N. Parker, 2/6th W. Yorks. Regt.—Killed.
9/9/17	Capt. C. F. C. Taylor, 2/5th Y. and L. Regt.—Wounded.
10/9/17	Capt. J. Ellse, 2/5th Y. and L. Regt.—Wounded.
11/9/17	2/Lieut. B. Bentley, 2/5th Y. and L. Regt.—Killed.
13/9/17	Capt. G. C. Turner, 2/6th W. Yorks. Regt.—Killed.
14/9/17	2/Lieut. J. Buckley, 2/7th W. Riding Regt.—Wounded.
,,	2/Lieut. J. H. Grisdale, 213th M.G. Coy.—Wounded.
15/9/17	Lieut. W. E. Harris, Y/62 T.M.B.—Killed.
,,	Lieut. G. A. Craven, Z/62 T.M.B.—Died of Wounds.
,,	Capt. G. F. Fitzgerald, 2/4th Y. and L. Regt.—Wounded (Accidentally).
17/9/17	2/Lieut. A. Bray, 2/6th W. Riding Regt.—Wounded.
19/9/17	2/Lieut. F. Calvert, 2/4th K.O.Y.L.I.—Wounded.
20/9/17	Capt. G. B. Faulder, 2/4th K.O.Y.L.I.—Wounded.
21/9/17	2/Lieut. E. N. Kitcat, 2/7th W. Yorks. Regt. Wounded.
26/9/17	2/Lieut. G. C. Beetham, 2/5th Y. and L. Regt.—Wounded
3/10/17	2/Lieut. T. B. Lyth, 2/5th Y. and L. Regt.—Wounded.

4/10/17 Capt. S. Coates, 2/8th W. Yorks. Regt.—Wounded.
„ Lieut. G. Bevington, 2/5th W. Riding Regt.—Wounded (Accidentally).
29/10/17 Lieut. H. Sutherland, 312th Bde. R.F.A.—Killed.

IN THE CAMBRAI OPERATIONS, 1917.*

2/Lieut. W. B. Diver, 2/4th K.O.Y.L.I.—Wounded.
Lieut. J. E. David, 2/4th K.O.Y.L.I.—Wounded.
2/Lieut. E. W. Davis, 310th Bde. R.F.A.—Wounded.
2/Lieut. N. H. Smith, 2/5th W. Yorks. Regt.—Killed.
2/Lieut. N. G. Airey, 2/5th W. Yorks. Regt.—Killed.
2/Lieut. A. J. Watson, 2/5th W. Yorks. Regt.—Wounded.
2/Lieut. L. F. Walker, 2/5th W. Yorks. Regt.—Wounded.
2/Lieut. R. M. Davidson, 2/5th W. Yorks. Regt.—Wounded.
Capt. R. Bickerdike, 2/6th W. Yorks. Regt.—Killed.
Capt. G. Barker, 2/6th W. Yorks. Regt. Killed.
2/Lieut. A. W. Bedford, 2/6th W. Yorks. Regt.—Killed.
2/Lieut. J. G. Booth, 2/6th W. Yorks. Regt.—Killed.
2/Lieut. P. Haywood, 2/6th W. Yorks. Regt.—Killed.
2/Lieut. W. Moorhouse, 2/6th W. Yorks. Regt.—Killed.
Capt. C. E. J. Brooksbank, 2/6th W. Yorks. Regt.—Wounded.
Capt. G. R. S. Walker, 2/6th W. Yorks. Regt.—Wounded.
2/Lieut. J. W. Worth, 2/6th W. Yorks. Regt.—Wounded.
2/Lieut. J. R. Allett, 2/6th W. Yorks. Regt.—Wounded.
Lieut. E. C. Lawrence, 2/6th W. Yorks. Regt.—Wounded.
2/Lieut. J. Moor, 2/6th W. Yorks. Regt.—Wounded.
2/Lieut. H. Potterton, 2/6th W. Yorks. Regt.—Wounded.
2/Lieut. G. L. Bonsor, 2/6th W. Yorks. Regt.—Wounded.
2/Lieut. D. N. Vize, 2/6th W. Yorks. Regt.—Wounded.
Lieut.-Col. C. H. Hoare, Cmdg. 2/6th W. Yorks. Regt.—Wounded.
2/Lieut. W. Mellor, 2/6th W. Yorks. Regt.—Wounded.
2/Lieut. B. J. A. Pratt, 2/6th W. Yorks. Regt.—Missing.
Capt. H. Smith, 2/6th W. Yorks. Regt.—Missing.
2/Lieut. W. R. Brown, 2/7th W. Yorks. Regt.—Killed.
2/Lieut. J. Swift, 2/7th W. Yorks. Regt.—Killed.
2/Lieut. W. R. Hutchinson, 2/8th W. Yorks. Regt.—Killed.
Capt. H. R. Burrows, 2/8th W. Yorks. Regt.—Wounded.
Lieut. T. A. H. Orr, 2/8th W. Yorks. Regt.—Wounded.
Lieut. P. Jowett, 2/8th W. Yorks. Regt.—Wounded.

* No dates are given in the "A" and "Q" Diary.

Appendix 191

Lieut. G. M. Hirst, 2/8th W. Yorks. Regt.—Wounded.
2/Lieut. O. R. Pogson, 2/8th W. Yorks. Regt.—Wounded.
2/Lieut. V. L. Patch, 2/4th W. Riding Regt.—Killed.
Lieut. L. Cordingley, 2/4th W. Riding Regt.—Wounded.
Lieut. W. L. Oldroyd, 2/4th W. Riding Regt.—Wounded.
2/Lieut. H. E. Hoyle, 2/4th W. Riding Regt.—Wounded.
2/Lieut. G. R. U. Peel, 2/4th W. Riding Regt.—Wounded.
2/Lieut. G. F. Hotson, 2/4th W. Riding Regt.—Wounded.
2/Lieut. H. A. Esden, 2/4th W. Riding Regt.—Wounded.
2/Lieut. W. Kennett, 2/4th W. Riding Regt.—Wounded.
2/Lieut. J. P. Castle, 2/4th W. Riding Regt.—Wounded.
Lieut.-Col. T. A. D. Best, Cmdg. 2/5th W. Riding Regt.—Killed.
Lieut. J. E. Ridgway, 2/5th W. Riding Regt.—Killed.
Lieut. J. G. Bodker, 2/5th W. Riding Regt.—Killed.
Capt. G. S. Moxon, 2/5th W. Riding Regt.—Wounded.
Lieut. J. A. Haigh, 2/5th W. Riding Regt.—Wounded.
Lieut. W. L. Thomas, 2/5th W. Riding Regt.—Wounded.
2/Lieut. C. Wright, 2/6th W. Riding Regt.—Killed.
Lieut. J. Stocks, 2/6th W. Riding Regt.—Wounded.
Lieut. H. H. Peet, 2/6th W. Riding Regt.—Wounded.
Capt. J. C. K. Alexander, 2/7th W. Riding Regt.—Wounded.
Capt. A. F. Gloag, 2/7th W. Riding Regt.—Wounded.
Lieut. C. G. Stott, 2/7th W. Riding Regt.—Wounded.
Lieut. J. Maden, 2/7th W. Riding Regt.—Wounded.
2/Lieut. A. E. Crookson, 2/7th W. Riding Regt.—Wounded.
2/Lieut. C. Hirst, 2/4th K.O.Y.L.I.—Wounded.
2/Lieut. H. A. E. Barker, 2/4th K.O.Y.L.I.—Killed.
2/Lieut. C. P. Maddox, 2/4th K.O.Y.L.I.—Killed.
2/Lieut. A. G. Hill, 2/4th K.O.Y.L.I.—Wounded.
Capt. G. H. Roberts, 2/4 K.O.Y.L.I.—Wounded.
Capt. M. McNicoll, 2/4th K.O.Y.L.I.—Wounded.
Lieut. A. R. Mosley, 2/4th K.O.Y.L.I.—Wounded.
Lieut. R. Hale-White, 2/4th K.O.Y.L.I.—Wounded.
2/Lieut. H. Anderson, 2/4th K.O.Y.L.I.—Wounded.
2/Lieut. S. A. V. Butler, 2/4th K.O.Y.L.I.—Wounded.
2/Lieut. A. Kilner, 2/4th K.O.Y.L.I.—Wounded.
2/Lieut. E. Morris, 2/5th K.O.Y.L.I.—Wounded.
2/Lieut. J. A. V. Jago, 2/5th K.O.Y.L.I.—Wounded.
Capt. A. Robinson, 2/5th K.O.Y.L.I.—Wounded.
2/Lieut. E. McLaren, 2/4th Y. and L. Regt.—Killed.

Appendix

Capt. C. G. Vickers, 2/4th Y. and L. Regt.—Killed.
2/Lieut. W. E. Laidlaw, 2/4th Y. and L. Regt.—Wounded.
Capt. R. C. Hall, 2/5th Y. and L. Regt.—Killed.
2/Lieut. C. A. G. Bertram, 2/5th Y. and L. Regt.—Wounded.
Capt. S. O. R. Surridge, 2/5th Y. and L. Regt.—Wounded.
Rev. C. M. Chevasse, 62nd Divisional Hqs.—Wounded.
Rev. A. B. Wright, 62nd Divisional Hqs.—Wounded.
Brig.-Genl. R. B. Bradford, V.C., Hqs. 186th Bde.—Killed.
Lieut. G. B. Foster, 2/5th W. Yorks. Regt.—Wounded.
2/Lieut. G. R. Hutchinson, 2/5th W. Yorks. Regt.—Killed.
2/Lieut. T. E. Gibson, 2/5th W. Yorks. Regt.—Killed.
2/Lieut. B. Hick, 2/6th W. Yorks. Regt.—Wounded.
Capt. C. L. Sagar-Musgrave, 2/7th W. Yorks. Regt.—Wounded.
Lieut. A. E. Leeson, 2/7th W. Yorks. Regt.—Wounded.
2/Lieut. G. W. Curry, 2/7th W. Yorks. Regt.—Wounded.
2/Lieut. J. W. Pugh, 2/7th W. Yorks. Regt.—Wounded.
Lieut. G. E. Raven, 2/7th W. Yorks. Regt.—Wounded.
Capt. G. R. Nevitt, 2/8th W. Yorks. Regt.—Killed.
Lieut. E. M. Boxall, 2/8th W. Yorks. Regt.—Wounded.
Lieut. H. Coles, 2/8th W. Yorks. Regt.—Wounded.
2/Lieut. A. W. Shann, 2/8th W. Yorks. Regt.—Killed.
Lieut. A. T. Hodgson, 2/8th W. Yorks. Regt.—Wounded.
Capt. G. M. Fletcher, 2/4th W. Riding Regt.—Wounded.
Lieut. G. F. Robertshaw, 2/4th W. Riding Regt.—Wounded.
2/Lieut. B. Stott, 2/4th W. Riding Regt.—Wounded.
2/Lieut. A. Shaw, 2/4th W. Riding Regt.—Wounded.
2/Lieut. W. Saunders, 2/4th W. Riding Regt.—Wounded.
2/Lieut. H. Metcalfe, 2/4th W. Riding Regt.—Wounded.
2/Lieut. G. Liddle, 2/5th W. Riding Regt.—Wounded.
Capt. F. A. Sykes, 2/5th W. Riding Regt.—Wounded.
Lieut. E. W. Harris, 2/5th W. Riding Regt.—Wounded.
Lieut. D. Black, 2/5th W. Riding Regt.—Wounded.
2/Lieut. A. S. Jack, 2/5th W. Riding Regt.—Wounded.
2/Lieut. J. Bower, 2/5th W. Riding Regt.—Wounded.
2/Lieut. V. Greaves, 2/5th W. Riding Regt.—Wounded.
2/Lieut. W. O. Davies, 2/5th W. Riding Regt.—Killed.
2/Lieut. J. Melville, 2/5th W. Riding Regt.—Missing.
Capt. W. Robertson, R.A.M.C., att. 2/5th W. Riding Regt.—Wounded.
Capt. W. F. Luckman, 2/6th W. Riding Regt.—Wounded.

Appendix 193

Capt. B. S. Mann, 2/6th W. Riding Regt.—Killed.
2/Lieut. A. F. Melton, 2/6th W. Riding Regt.—Killed.
2/Lieut. A. J. Alexander, 2/6th W. Riding Regt.—Killed.
Capt. A. Somervell, 2/6th W. Riding Regt.—Wounded.
Capt. T. J. Howell, 2/6th W. Riding Regt.—Wounded.
2/Lieut. M. Elwin, 2/6th W. Riding Regt.—Wounded.
2/Lieut. T. C. Sharples, 2/6th W. Riding Regt.—Wounded.
2/Lieut. G. A. Cartwright, 2/7th W. Riding Regt.—Wounded.
2/Lieut. H. Hartley, 2/7th W. Riding Regt.—Wounded.
2/Lieut. C. Sexton, 2/7th W. Riding Regt.—Wounded.
2/Lieut. A. V. Spafford, 2/7th W. Riding Regt.—Wounded.
Lieut. N. T. Lawton, 2/7th W. Riding Regt.—Wounded.
2/Lieut. J. W. Berryman, 2/4th K.O.Y.L.I.—Died of Wounds.
2/Lieut. F. MacCunn, 2/4th K.O.Y.L.I.—Wounded.
Lieut. H. L. Hollard, 2/4th K.O.Y.L.I.—Wounded.
Lieut. A. E. Earle, 2/4th K.O.Y.L.I.—Wounded.
2/Lieut. F. Cocker, 2/4th K.O.Y.L.I.—Wounded.
2/Lieut. A. Brealey, 2/4th K.O.Y.L.I.—Wounded.
Capt. O. S. Roper, 2/5th K.O.Y.L.I.—Killed.
2/Lieut. G. A. Eardley, 2/5th K.O.Y.L.I.—Killed.
2/Lieut. L. Melhuish, 2/5th K.O.Y.L.I.—Killed.
Capt. H. O. Brown, 2/5th K.O.Y.L.I.—Wounded.
2/Lieut. R. A. Waters, 2/5th K.O.Y.L.I.—Wounded.
2/Lieut. P. Cartwright, 2/5th K.O.Y.L.I.—Wounded.
2/Lieut. C. E. Townend, 2/5th K.O.Y.L.I.—Wounded.
2/Lieut. W. McArthur, 2/5th K.O.Y.L.I.—Wounded.
2/Lieut. C. W. V. Hughes, 2/5th K.O.Y.L.I.—Wounded.
Lieut. C. H. Wilson, 2/5th K.O.Y.L.I.—Wounded.
Lieut. H. L. Field, 2/5th K.O.Y.L.I.—Wounded.
Capt. M. Barber, 2/4th Y. and L. Regt.—Killed.
Capt. C. Walker, 2/4th Y. and L. Regt.—Wounded.
2/Lieut. P. Wortley, 2/4th Y. and L. Regt.—Wounded.
2/Lieut. A. H. Halliday, 2/4th Y. and L. Regt.—Wounded.
Capt. G. A. G. Hewitt, 2/5th Y. and L. Regt.—Killed.
Capt. J. Ellse, 2/5th Y. and L. Regt.—Wounded.
Capt. S. O. R. Surridge, 2/5th Y. and L. Regt.—Wounded.
2/Lieut. H. E. Newton, 2/5th Y. and L. Regt.—Wounded.
Lieut. E. L. H. Dunkerton, 2/5th Y. and L. Regt.—Wounded.
Lieut. G. Thompson, 2/5th Y. and L. Regt.—Wounded.
2/Lieut. H. Ashton, 2/5th Y. and L. Regt.—Wounded and Missing.

194 Appendix

2/Lieut. W. Barber, 2/5th Y. and L. Regt.—Wounded and Missing.
Lieut. C. G. Harrison, 2/5th Y. and L. Regt.—Missing.
Capt. C. B. R. King, 208th M.G. Coy.—Wounded.
2/Lieut. A. P. McClare, 208th M.G. Coy. —Wounded.
2/Lieut. J. S. Quarmby, 2/7th W. Riding Regt.—Killed.
2/Lieut. H. Hinchliffe, 2/7th W. Riding Regt.—Wounded.
2/Lieut. G. Binns, 2/7th W. Yorks. Regt.—Wounded.
2/Lieut. L. Clack, 2/5th K.O.Y.L.I.—Wounded.

IN TRENCH WARFARE.

26/11/17 2/Lieut. G. R. Maskell, 2/4th W. Riding Regt.—Wounded, Shell Shock.
27/11/17 2/Lieut. L. Keen, 2/5th K.O.Y.L.I.—Wounded, Shell Shock.
27/11/17 2/Lieut. L. B. Clack, 2/5th K.O.Y.L.I.—Wounded, Shell Shock.

1918.

IN TRENCH WARFARE.

9/1/18 2/Lieut. L. M. C. Collins, att. 2/5th Y. and L. Regt.—Missing.
20/1/18 2/Lieut. E. G. Mackenzie, 2/5th W. Riding Regt.—Missing, believed killed.
„ 2/Lieut. T. R. Sykes, 2/5th W. Riding Regt.—Wounded.
25/1/18 2/Lieut. F. Williams, 2/5th Y. and L. Regt.—Killed (Acc.)
28/1/18 Capt. J. L. Thompson, 2/5th W. Yorks. Regt.—Wounded.
29/1/18 2/Lieut. E. Morton, 2/5th K.O.Y.L.I.—Wounded.
31/1/18 Lieut. S. A. Thorn, 2/7th W. Yorks.—Wounded.
2/2/18 Capt. C. S. Wilson, 2/7th W. Yorks.—Wounded.
6/2/18 2/Lieut. C. R. Witcher, 310th Bde. R.F.A.—Wounded.
7/2/18 2/Lieut. J. A. Hawkins, 8th W. Yorks. Regt.—Wounded. Died of Wounds, 8/2/18.
7/3/18 2/Lieut. C. H. Croft, 5th K.O.Y.L.I.—Wounded.
9/3/18 2/Lieut. P. Kirk, 2/4th W. Riding Regt.—Wounded.
11/3/18 Capt. J. H. Irons, 2/4th W. Riding Regt.—Wounded.
„ 2/Lieut. B. Sheldon, 2/4th W. Riding Regt.—Wounded.
16/3/18 Lieut. J. R. Symons, 8th W. Yorks. Regt.—Wounded.
17/3/18 Capt. C. B. Stead, 8th W. Yorks. Regt.—Wounded.
„ 2/Lieut. J. F. Blakey, 9th Durham L.I.—Wounded.
„ 2/Lieut. C. J. Easton, 62nd Bn. M.G.C.—Wounded.

Appendix 195

18/3/18 2/Lieut. A. Naylor, 8th W. Yorks. Regt.—Wounded.
„ 2/Lieut. S. W. Allen, 8th W. Yorks. Regt.—Wounded.
„ 2/Lieut. R. G. Wright, 8th W. Yorks. Regt.—Wounded.
20/3/18 2/Lieut. S. E. Perry, 8th W. Yorks. Regt.—Wounded.
21/3/18 2/Lieut. H. G. Goldsmith, 310th Bde. R.F.A.—Wounded.
„ 2/Lieut. L. W. Nott, 461st Field Coy. R.E.—Wounded.

DURING THE GERMAN OFFENSIVES, 1918.

26/3/18 Lieut.-Col. A. H. James, Cmdg. 8th W. Yorks. Regt.—Killed.
„ Capt. E. Murgatroyd, 8th W. Yorks. Regt.—Killed.
„ Lieut. H. Evans, 8th W. Yorks. Regt.—Killed.
„ Lieut. J. H. Hussey, 8th W. Yorks. Regt.—Wounded.
„ 2/Lieut. W. H. Hartley, 8th W. Yorks. Regt.—Wounded.
„ 2/Lieut. C. J. Priestley, 8th W. Yorks. Regt.—Wounded.
„ 2/Lieut. C. Waite, 8th W. Yorks. Regt.—Wounded.
„ 2/Lieut. W. D. Cattermole, 8th W. Yorks. Regt.—Wounded.
„ 2/Lieut. J. L. Percival, 8th W. Yorks. Regt.—Wounded.
„ Lieut.-Col. J. Walker, Cmdg. 5th W. Riding Regt.—Wounded.
„ 2/Lieut. F. J. B. Dixon, 62nd Bn. M.G.C.—Wounded.
„ Capt. H. K. Wilson, 2/4th Y. and L. Regt.—Wounded.
„ Capt. R. C. Barnes, 2/4th Y. and L. Regt.—Wounded.
„ Lieut. G. F. Bolam, 9th Durham L.I.—Wounded.
„ Major P. P. Wilson, 9th Durham L.I.—Wounded.
27/3/18 2/Lieut. F. W. Potter, 2/7th W. Yorks. Regt.—Wounded.
„ 2/Lieut. J. A. Webdale, 8th W. Yorks. Regt. and 185th T.M.B.—Wounded.
„ Capt. H. O. Browning, 5th W. Riding Regt.—Wounded.
„ 2/Lieut. T. Lawson, 2/7th W. Riding Regt.—Wounded.
„ Capt. F. H. Threappleton, 2/4th W. Riding Regt.—Wounded.
„ 2/Lieut. J. McFarlane, 62nd Bn. M.G.C.—Wounded.
„ 2/Lieut. F. Drake, 2/4th K.O.Y.L.I.—Killed.
„ J. Rainford, 2/4th K.O.Y.L.I.—Wounded.
„ 2/Lieut. J. W. Parr, 2/4th K.O.Y.L.I.—Wounded, Died of Wounds, 29/3/18.
„ Capt. A. E. Pilley, 2/4th K.O.Y.L.I.—Missing.
„ Capt. G. L. Hudson, 2/4th K.O.Y.L.I.—Missing.

27/3/18	2/Lieut. D. O. C. Maggs, 2/4th K.O.Y.L.I.—Missing.
,,	2/Lieut. H. W. Spink, 2/4th K.O.Y.L.I.—Missing.
,,	Lieut.-Col. F. St. J. Blacker, Cmdg. 2/4th Y. and L. Regt.—Missing.
,,	2/Lieut. J. C. Fernley, 2/4th Y. and L. Regt.—Missing.
,,	Lieut. J. Fisher, 9th Durham L.I.—Missing.
28/3/18	Capt. J. D. Ballantyne, 8th W. Yorks. Regt.—Missing.
,,	Lieut. W. H. C. Jeffcock, 2/7th W. Yorks. Regt.—Missing.
,,	2/Lieut. J. G. Hewitt, 2/7th W. Yorks. Regt.—Missing.
,,	2/Lieut. T. F. Galpine, 2/7th W. Yorks. Regt.—Missing.
,,	2/Lieut. A. E. Targett, 2/7th W. Yorks. Regt.—Missing.
,,	Capt. B. H. Pickering, 2/7th W. Yorks. Regt.—Missing.
,,	2/Lieut. P. Mosley, 5th W. Riding Regt.—Killed.
,,	2/Lieut N. H. Weighill, 1st W. Yorks. att. 5th W. Riding Regt.—Wounded.
,,	Lieut. B. Mollett, 5th W. Riding Regt.—Wounded.
,,	Major F. Brook, K.O.Y.L.I. att. 5th W. Riding Regt.—Wounded.
,,	Lieut. J. W. Sherrick, U.S.M.C. att. 5th W. Riding Regt.—Wounded.
,,	Capt. J. Groves, 2/4th W. Riding Regt.—Wounded.
,,	Lieut. R. M. Skelsey, 2/4th W. Riding Regt., 186th T.M.B.—Missing.
,,	2/Lieut. W. H. Baillie, 62nd Bn. M.G.C.—Wounded.
,,	2/Lieut. H. A. Waterhouse, 62nd Bn. M.G.C.—Wounded.
,,	2/Lieut. L. C. Gane, 310th Bde. R.F.A.—Wounded.
,,	Lieut. C. V. Montgomery, 312th Bde. R.F.A.—Wounded.
,,	Lieut.-Col. O. C. S. Watson, Cmdg. 5th K.O.Y.L.I.—Killed.
,,	2/Lieut. G. C. M. Green, 5th K.O.Y.L.I.—Killed.
,,	2/Lieut. F. C. Lambert, 5th K.O.Y.L.I.—Killed.
,,	Lieut. E. H. Shank, 5th K.O.Y.L.I.—Wounded.
,,	Capt. B. A. Beack, 5th K.O.Y.L.I.—Missing.
,,	Capt. A. D. Thomson, 5th K.O.Y.L.I.—Missing.
,,	Capt. E. Roberts, 5th K.O.Y.L.I.—Missing.
,,	Lieut. R. Crigg, 5th K.O.Y.L.I.—Missing.
,,	2/Lieut. R. Appleton, 5th K.O.Y.L.I.—Missing.
,,	2/Lieut. T. Weldon, 5th K.O.Y.L.I.—Missing.
,,	2/Lieut. W. C. Ibbott, 5th K.O.Y.L.I.—Missing.
,,	2/Lieut. B. P. Jenkinson, 5th K.O.Y.L.I.—Missing.

Appendix 197

28/3/18	2/Lieut. M. Hamer, 5th K.O.Y.L.I.—Missing.
,,	2/Lieut. H. G. Northey, 5th K.O.Y.L.I.—Missing.
,,	Lieut. R. A. Hamilton, 5th K.O.Y.L.I.—Killed.
,,	2/Lieut. J. W. Pownall, 2/4th K.O.Y.L.I.—Missing.
,,	2/Lieut. H. Rogerson, 2/4th K.O.Y.L.I.—Missing.
,,	2/Lieut. J. R. Draper, 2/4th Y. and L. Regt.—Wounded.
,,	2/Lieut. H. Mitchell, 2/4th Y. and L. Regt.—Wounded.
,,	2/Lieut. E. Butterfield, 2/4th Y. and L. Regt.—Wounded.
,,	Lieut. P. Reid, 2/4th Y. and L. Regt.—Wounded.
,,	2/Lieut. J. W. Thornton, 2/4th Y. and L. Regt.—Wounded.
,,	Lieut. W. G. Wylie, 9th Durham L.I.—Killed.
,,	2/Lieut. A. W. Bell, 9th Durham L.I.—Killed.
29/3/18	Bt.-Major F. W. L. Bissett, G.S.O. II., 62nd Division—Wounded.
,,	Capt. B. Hutchinson, 8th W. Yorks. Regt.—Wounded.
,,	2/Lieut. H. Sowden, 8th W. Yorks. Regt.—Wounded.
,,	2/Lieut. J. Sugden, 5th W. Riding Regt.—Killed.
,,	Capt. G. L. Tinker, 5th W. Riding Regt.—Wounded.
,,	Capt. T. Goodall, 5th W. Riding Regt.—Wounded.
,,	2/Lieut. A. Cawthra, 5th W. Riding Regt.—Missing.
,,	2/Lieut. F. Chapman, 5th W. Riding Regt.—Wounded.
30/3/18	2/Lieut. J. Martindale, 2/4th W. Riding Regt.—Killed.
,,	Capt. R. E. B. Lisle, 9th Durham L.I.—Killed.
,,	Major, P. P. Wilson, 9th Durham L.I.—Wounded.
,,	Lieut. J. G. Weightman, 9th Durham L.I.—Wounded.
31/3/18	Capt. W. G. Kemp, 8th W. Yorks. Regt.—Wounded.
3/4/18	Major J. Willey, 312th Bde. R.F.A.—Killed.

IN TRENCH WARFARE.

5/4/18	Lieut. J. C. F. Nowill, 310th Bde. R.F.A.—Wounded.
,,	2/Lieut. F. W. G. Sharpling, 310th Bde. R.F.A.—Wounded.
6/4/18	Major M. R. H. Crofton, 312th Bde. R.F.A.—Wounded (gas).
,,	Capt. A. Senior, 312th Bde. R.F.A.—Wounded (gas).
,,	Lieut. J. B. Boden, 312th Bde. R.F.A.—Wounded (gas).
,,	Lieut. S. A. Rissik, 312th Bde. R.F.A.—Wounded (gas).
,,	2/Lieut. E. J. W. Puttock, 312th Bde. R.F.A.—Wounded (gas).
,,	2/Lieut. A. E. Stuttle, 312th Bde. R.F.A.—Wounded (gas).

7/4/18	Lieut. E. H. Vanderpump, 310th Bde. R.F.A.—Wounded (gas).
,,	Capt. T. Whitelaw, R.A.M.C. att. 2/7th W. Yorks. Regt.—Killed.
,,	2/Lieut. E. N. Temple, 2/7th W. Yorks. Regt.—Wounded.
,,	2/Lieut. H. D. Forrest, 5th W. Riding Regt.—Killed.
8/4/18	Lieut. A. A. Campbell, 9th Durham L.I.—Wounded.
9/4/18	2/Lieut. A. Walker, 5th W. Riding Regt.—Wounded.
10/4/18	Lieut. W. O. P. Gibb, 2/4th K.O.Y.L.I..—Wounded.
11/4/18	2/Lieut. E. C. J. Sheppard, 310th Bde. R.F.A.—Wounded.
12/4/18	Lieut. Sir R. C. Muir-Mackenzie, 9th Durham L.I.—Killed.
,,	2/Lieut. R. J. Dangerfield, 62nd Bn. M.G.C.—Wounded.
,,	Capt. A. J. Neilan, 312th Bde. R.F.A.—Wounded.
13/4/18	Lieut. W. Douglas, 9th Durham L.I.—Wounded.
,,	2/Lieut. F. J. Doherty, 5th K.O.Y.L.I.—Wounded.
14/4/18	2/Lieut. A. H. Fehr, 5th K.O.Y.L.I.—Missing.
,,	Lieut. T. F. B. Hall, 5th K.O.Y.L.I., 187th T.M.B.—Wounded (gas).
15/4/18	Capt. C. A. McK. Morant, 2/5th W. Yorks. Regt.—Killed.
,,	2/Lieut. O. C. Gardiner, 461st Field Coy. R.E.—Wounded.
16/4/18	2/Lieut. J. M. Wilson, 2/4th K.O.Y.L.I.—Wounded.
17/4/18	2/Lieut. A. Hall, 2/7th W. Yorks. Regt.—Wounded.
,,	Lieut. J. P. McIlroy, 310th Bde. R.F.A.—Wounded.
18/4/18	2/Lieut. A. Marshall, 2/7th W. Yorks. Regt.—Wounded.
19/4/18	2/Lieut. J. S. Green, 310th Bde. R.F.A.—Wounded (gas).
22/4/18	Major W. F. Tuthill, 312th Bde. R.F.A.—Wounded (gas).
,,	2/Lieut. A. E. Cockerell, 312th Bde. R.F.A.—Wounded (gas).
,,	Capt. W. Vero, 2/5th W. Yorks. Regt.—Wounded.
,,	Lieut.-Col. N. A. England, Cmdg. 8th W. Yorks. Regt.—Wounded.
23/4/18	2/Lieut. R. J. Machin, 5th W. Riding Regt.—Wounded.
30/4/18	2/Lieut. S. H. Bell, 2/4th W. Riding Regt.—Wounded.
10/5/18	Lieut. J. Owen, 310th Bde. R.F.A.—Wounded.
16/5/18	Lieut. C. E. Morier, 5th W. Riding Regt.—Wounded.
,,	2/Lieut. R. B. Hill, 5th W. Riding Regt.—Wounded.
,,	2/Lieut. C. Scott, 2/7th W. Riding Regt.—Wounded.
18/5/18	Capt. W. G. James, 5th K.O.Y.L.I.—Wounded.
19/5/18	Lieut.-Col. C. K. James, Cmdg. 2/7th W. Yorks. Regt.—Killed.

Appendix

19/5/18	2/Lieut. S. Powell, 2/7th W. Yorks. Regt.—Wounded.
21/5/18	2/Lieut. R. Donkersley, 2/5th W. Yorks. Regt.—Wounded.
22/5/18	2/Lieut. C. H. Crofts, 5th K.O.Y.L.I.—Wounded.
24/5/18	2/Lieut. K. Lance, 8th W. Yorks. Regt.—Wounded.
,,	2/Lieut. R. J. Ingleby, 8th W. Yorks. Regt.—Wounded.
,,	Lieut. E. Pepper, 8th W. Yorks. Regt.—Missing.
,,	Capt. G. F. M. Ling, 2/7th W. Yorks. 185th T.M.B.—Killed.
,,	2/Lieut. A. C. Potter, 2/4th W. Riding Regt.—Wounded.
26/5/18	2/Lieut. A. McKinnon, 67th Bn. M.G.C.—Wounded.
29/5/18	2/Lieut. P. de Lacy, 2/5th W. Yorks. Regt.—Wounded.
,,	2/Lieut. H. Newton, 2/4th Y. and L. Regt.—Wounded.
,,	Lieut. A. P. H. Sage, M.O.R.C., U.S.A., att. 2/1st W.R.F.A.—Killed.
30/5/18	Capt. J. J. G. Greenwood, 2/5th W. Yorks.—Wounded.
1/6/18	2/Lieut. W. G. Houghton, 5th K.O.Y.L.I.—Wounded.
2/6/18	2/Lieut. A. S. Champion, 2/4th K.O.Y.L.I.—Wounded.
4/6/18	Capt. A. R. Haigh, 5th W. Riding Regt.—Wounded.
5/6/18	2/Lieut. G. Mann, 62nd Bn. M.G.C.—Wounded.
,,	2/Lieut. G. A. Joslin, 312th Bde. R.F.A.—Wounded.
,,	Lieut. J. H. Banton, 8th W. Yorks. Regt.—Wounded.
7/6/18	Lieut. T. W. M. Wilkinson, 8th W. Yorks. Regt.—Wounded.
9/6/18	2/Lieut. G. H. Dodd, 5th W. Riding Regt.—Wounded.
11/6/18	2/Lieut. J. E. Knowles, 2/7th W. Yorks. Regt.—Wounded.
15/6/18	Lieut. L. J. Horne, 2/4th K.O.Y.L.I.—Killed.
21/6/18	Lieut. D. E. Cooper, Signal Coy.—Wounded.
23/6/18	2/Lieut. W. Donelly, 5th K.O.Y.L.I.—Wounded.
,,	2/Lieut. F. Bottomley, 5th K.O.Y.L.I.—Wounded.

IN OPERATIONS ON THE MARNE, 1918.

20/7/18	Lieut.-Col. H. V. Bastow, Cmdg. 1/5th Devon Regt.—Wounded.
,,	Capt. A. G. W. Church, 1/5th Devon Regt.—Killed.
,,	2/Lieut. J. Smith, 1/5th Devon Regt.—Killed.
,,	Capt. V. R. Winnicott, 1/5th Devon Regt.—Wounded.
,,	2/Lieut. C. D. Hall, 1/5th Devon Regt.—Wounded.
,,	2/Lieut. H. M. Patterson, 1/5th Devon Regt.—Wounded.
,,	2/Lieut. F. Stringfellow, 1/5th Devon Regt.—Wounded.
,,	2/Lieut. H. Mitchell, 1/5th Devon Regt.—Wounded.

Appendix

20/7/18	2/Lieut. J. G. Thomas, 1/5th Devon Regt.—Wounded.
,,	2/Lieut. R. J. Paton, 1/5th Devon Regt.—Wounded.
22/7/18	2/Lieut. R. W. Coleman, 1/5th Devon Regt.—Wounded.
27/7/18	2/Lieut. F. Huish, 1/5th Devon Regt.—Killed.
,,	2/Lieut. J. S. Loram, 1/5th Devon Regt.—Wounded.
28/7/18	2/Lieut. R. Hay, 1/5th Devon Regt.—Killed.
,,	Lieut. J. E. Skelton, 1/5th Devon Regt.—Wounded.
20/7/18	2/Lieut. T. R. Williams, 8th W. Yorks. Regt.—Killed.
,,	2/Lieut. S. H. Bray, 8th W. Yorks. Regt.—Killed.
,,	2/Lieut. W. H. Dawson, 8th W. Yorks. Regt.—Killed.
,,	Lieut. T. W. M. Wilkinson, 8th W. Yorks. Regt.—Killed.
,,	Capt. G. G. Kinder, 8th W. Yorks. Regt.—Killed.
,,	2/Lieut. E. H. Shuttleworth, 8th W. Yorks. Regt.—Killed.
,,	Capt. J. E. Appleyard, 8th W. Yorks. Regt.—Killed.
,,	2/Lieut. P. B. Wesley, 8th W. Yorks. Regt.—Wounded.
,,	Lieut. J. H. Banton, 8th W. Yorks. Regt.—Wounded.
,,	2/Lieut. W. Oliver, 8th W. Yorks. Regt.—Wounded.
23/7/18	2/Lieut. H. Horton, 8th W. Yorks. Regt.—Wounded.
,,	2/Lieut. W. Metcalfe, 8th W. Yorks. Regt.—Wounded.
,,	2/Lieut. F. Abe, 8th W. Yorks. Regt.—Killed.
28/7/18	Capt. N. Muller, 8th W. Yorks. Regt.—Killed.
,,	Lieut. P. H. Battishill, 8th W. Yorks. Regt.—Wounded.
,,	Lieut. A. F. James, 8th W. Yorks. Regt.—Wounded.
,,	2/Lieut. R. Pearson, 8th W. Yorks. Regt.—Wounded and Missing.
,,	2/Lieut. F. O. Lamb, 8th W. Yorks. Regt.—Missing.
,,	2/Lieut. W. A. Cliffe, 8th W. Yorks. Regt.—Wounded.
29/7/18	2/Lieut. P. Firth, 8th W. Yorks. Regt.—Wounded and Missing.
20/7/18	Capt. K. W. Grigson, 2/5th W. Yorks. Regt.—Killed.
,,	2/Lieut. C. A. de Ville, 2/5th W. Yorks. Regt.—Killed.
,,	Capt. R. F. White, 2/5th W. Yorks. Regt.—Wounded.
,,	Lieut. A. Dickes, 2/5th W. Yorks. Regt.—Wounded.
,,	Lieut. E. R. Waugh, 2/5th W. Yorks. Regt.—Wounded.
,,	2/Lieut. P. de Lacy, 2/5th W. Yorks. Regt.—Wounded.
,,	2/Lieut. L. T. Sawney, 2/5th W. Yorks. Regt.—Wounded.
,,	2/Lieut. R. Donkersley, 2/5th W. Yorks. Regt.—Missing, believed Killed.
,,	2/Lieut. E. H. Bardsley, 2/5th W. Yorks. Regt.—Wounded.
,,	2/Lieut. J. H. Simpson, 2/5th W. Yorks. Regt.—Wounded.

20/7/18	2/Lieut. R. B. Walker, 2/5th W. Yorks. Regt.—Wounded.
,,	2/Lieut. W. B. Schindler, 2/5th W. Yorks. Regt.—Missing.
22/7/18	Lieut. B. M. Riley, 2/5th W. Yorks. Regt.—Wounded.
26/7/18	2/Lieut. E. M. Kermode, 2/5th W. Yorks. Regt.—Died of Wounds.
29/7/18	2/Lieut. W. T. Cole, 2/5th W. Yorks. Regt.—Killed.
,,	2/Lieut. W. Jennings, 2/5th W. Yorks. Regt.—Missing.
20/7/18	Lieut. F. H. White, 5th W. Riding Regt.—Wounded.
,,	Capt. E. A. Sykes, 5th W. Riding Regt.—Wounded.
,,	2/Lieut. D. A. S. Haigh, 5th W. Riding Regt.—Wounded.
,,	Lieut. E. Tanner, 5th W. Riding Regt.—Wounded.
,,	2/Lieut. J. C. D. Moore, 5th W. Riding Regt.—Died of Wounds.
21/7/18	2/Lieut. R. J. Machin, 5th W. Riding Regt.—Wounded.
22/7/18	2/Lieut. H. Greenwood, 5th W. Riding Regt.—Wounded.
,,	2/Lieut. P. R. Barnes, 5th W. Riding Regt.—Wounded.
,,	2/Lieut. L. F. Walker, 5th W. Riding Regt.—Wounded.
,,	Capt. C. V. Bernays, 5th W. Riding Regt.—Wounded.
,,	2/Lieut. E. R. Storey, 5th W. Riding Regt.—Missing.
,,	Capt. J. B. Cockhill, 5th W. Riding Regt.—Missing.
24/7/18	2/Lieut. F. R. W. L. Thorpe, 5th W. Riding Regt.—Wounded (gas).
20/7/18	2/Lieut. J. I. Christmas, 2/4th W. Riding Regt.—Wounded.
,,	Capt. A. B. Keillar, 2/4th W. Riding Regt.—Wounded.
,,	Capt. H. E. Hinchcliffe, 2/4th W. Riding Regt.—Wounded.
,,	Lieut. G. McG. Fletcher, 2/4th W. Riding Regt.—Wounded.
,,	Lieut. H. H. Peet, 2/4th W. Riding Regt.—Wounded.
,,	Lieut. P. G. Conacher, 2/4th W. Riding Regt.—Wounded.
,,	2/Lieut. W. F. Moore, 2/4th W. Riding Regt.—Wounded.
,,	2/Lieut. H. O. Sykes, 2/4th W. Riding Regt.—Wounded.
,,	Lieut. W. H. Massie, 2/4th W. Riding Regt.—Wounded.
,,	2/Lieut. J. Maude, 2/4th W. Riding Regt.—Missing.
,,	2/Lieut. H. R. Stent, 2/4th W. Riding Regt.—Missing.
22/7/18	Capt. W. Smithson, 2/4th W. Riding Regt.—Wounded.
28/7/18	2/Lieut. F. K. Marsden, 2/4th W. Riding Regt.—Wounded.
20/7/18	Major G. M. J. Molyneux, 2/4th Hants. Regt.—Wounded.
,,	2/Lieut. H. L. Willsher, 2/4th Hants. Regt.—Wounded.

Appendix

20/7/18	2/Lieut. N. E. Smith, 2/4th Hants. Regt.—Killed.
,,	Lieut. A. Scott, 2/4th Hants. Regt.—Wounded.
,,	2/Lieut. R. O. Clapcott, 2/4th Hants. Regt.—Wounded.
,,	2/Lieut. H. L. Thurgood, 2/4th Hants. Regt.—Wounded.
,,	2/Lieut. S. W. O. Dixon, 2/4th Hants. Regt.—Wounded.
21/7/18	2/Lieut. F. C. Holbrook, 2/4th Hants. Regt.—Wounded.
22/7/18	Lieut. C. F. Wilson, 2/4th Hants. Regt.—Wounded, died of wounds, 27/7/18.
,,	Capt. W. H. Leggard, 2/4th Hants. Regt.—Wounded.
25/7/18	Capt. W. H. Ledgard, 2/4th Hants. Regt.—Wounded.
26/7/18	2/Lieut. T. R. Johnson, 2/4th Hants. Regt.—Wounded.
20/7/18	Lieut. M. E. Bornemann, 186th T.M.B.—Wounded.
22/7/18	Lieut. M. Howarth, 186th T.M.B.—Wounded.
20/7/18	Capt. W. Short, 5th K.O.Y.L.I.—Killed.
,,	2/Lieut. C. H. Crofts, 5th K.O.Y.L.I.—Killed.
,,	Lieut. A. Burnell, 5th K O.Y.L.I.—Killed.
,,	2/Lieut. A. Marr, 5th K.O.Y.L.I.—Wounded.
,,	2/Lieut. F. R. Corson, 5th K.O.Y.L.I.—Wounded.
,,	2/Lieut. J. Wagstaffe, 5th K.O.Y.L.I.—Wounded.
,,	2/Lieut. G. R. Maskell, 5th K.O.Y.L.I.—Wounded.
21/7/18	2/Lieut. W. G. Pretsell, 5th K.O.Y.L.I.—Killed.
22/7/18	Lieut. J. Ingle, 5th K.O.Y.L.I.—Wounded.
20/7/18	2/Lieut. R. N. Milburn, 2/4th K.O.Y.L.I.—Killed.
,,	Capt. J. J. Wellington, 2/4th K.O.Y.L.I.—Wounded.
,,	Lieut. A. Woodger, 2/4th K.O.Y.L.I.—Wounded.
,,	2/Lieut. P. G. Russell, 2/4th K.O.Y.L.I.—Wounded.
,,	2/Lieut. F. Cocker, 2/4th K.O.Y.L.I.—Wounded.
,,	2/Lieut. J. Blackstock, 2/4th K.O.Y.L.I.—Wounded.
,,	2/Lieut. R. Macbeth, 2/4th K.O.Y.L.I.—Wounded.
,,	2/Lieut. C. V. Smith, 2/4th K.O.Y.L.I.—Wounded.
,,	2/Lieut. J. W. Baldock, 2/4th K.O.Y.L.I.—Wounded.
,,	2/Lieut. C. E. Inchliffe, 2/4th K.O.Y.L.I.—Wounded and missing.
23/7/18	2/Lieut. E. Nicholson, 2/4th K.O.Y.L.I.—Wounded.
27/7/18	2/Lieut. C. Hirst, 2/4th K.O.Y.L.I.—Wounded.
,,	2/Lieut. T. C. Hunter, 2/4th K.O.Y.L.I.—Wounded.
28/7/18	2/Lieut. J. McCormick, 2/4th K.O.Y.L.I.—Killed.
20/7/18	Capt. C. G. Kirk, 2/4th Y. and L. Regt.—Killed.
,,	2/Lieut. J. Robson, 2/4th Y. and L. Regt.—Killed.
,,	Capt. J. Ellse, 2/4th Y. and L. Regt.—Wounded.

Appendix

20/7/18	2/Lieut. H. V. Ward, 2/4th Y. and L. Regt.—Wounded.
,,	2/Lieut. E. A. Thackeray, 2/4th Y. and L. Regt.—Wounded.
,,	2/Lieut. F. Proudfoot, 2/4th Y. and L. Regt.—Wounded.
21/7/18	2/Lieut. G. Longdon, 2/4th Y. and L. Regt.—Wounded.
,,	Lieut. H. Strachan, 9th Durham L.I.—Wounded.
,,	Lieut. H. V. Chisholm, 9th Durham L.I.—Wounded.
,,	Capt. T. Harker, 9th Durham L.I.—Wounded.
,,	2/Lieut. J. Dawson, 9th Durham L.I.—Wounded.
,,	Lieut. T. B. Renton, 9th Durham L.I.—Wounded.
,,	2/Lieut. A. Gibson, 9th Durham L.I.—Wounded.
,,	Lieut. W. J. Tesseyman, 9th Durham L.I.—Wounded.
23/7/18	2/Lieut. B. Sanderson, 9th Durham L.I.—Wounded.
28/7/18	Capt. J. A. C. Scott, R.A.M.C., att. 9th D.L.I.—Wounded.
20/7/18	Lieut. B. C. Orme, 62nd Bn. M.G.C.—Wounded.
,,	2/Lieut. H. H. Stirling, 62nd Bn. M.G.C.—Wounded.
,,	2/Lieut. E. T. Webster, 62nd Bn. M. G. C.—Wounded.
23/7/18	2/Lieut. W. Morgan, 62nd Bn. M.G.C.—Wounded.
28/7/18	Major F. Lismore, 62nd Bn. M.G.C.—Wounded.
,,	2/Lieut. G. W. Wardle, 62nd Bn. M.G.C.—Wounded.
,,	2/Lieut. A. L. Pentelow, 62nd Bn. M.G.C.—Wounded.
30/7/18	2/Lieut. A. F. L. Webster, 62nd Bn. M.G.C.—Wounded (gas).
20/7/18	Lieut. P. K. B. Reynolds, 310th Bde. R.F.A.—Wounded.
22/7/18	2/Lieut. H. E. Stephens, 310th Bde. R.F.A.—Wounded.
20/7/18	2/Lieut. J. N. Whitworth, 312th Bde. R.F.A.—Wounded.
,,	2/Lieut. W. Burt, 312th Bde. R.F.A.—Wounded.
22/7/18	2/Lieut. V. A. A. H. Draper, 312th Bde. R.F.A.—Wounded.
24/7/18	Major G. Stiell, R.A.M.C., 2/2nd W.R. Field Amb.—Wounded.

DURING THE ADVANCE IN PICARDY, 21ST AUGUST-3RD SEPTEMBER.

23/8/18	Lieut. Massey-Beresford, 310th Bde. R.F.A.—Killed.
24/8/18	2/Lieut. J. B. Cranston, 8th W. Yorks. Regt.—Wounded (gas).
25/8/18	2/Lieut. P. Moore, 5th K.O.Y.L.I.—Wounded.
,,	2/Lieut. H. E. Butterfield, 5th K.O.Y.L.I.—Wounded.
,,	2/Lieut. J. T. Porter, 2/4th K.O.Y.L.I.—Killed.

Appendix

25/8/18	2/Lieut. G. Hall, 2/4th K.O.Y.L.I.—Wounded.
,,	2/Lieut. A. Maylor, 2/4th K.O.Y.L.I.—Wounded.
,,	2/Lieut. S. Wiggins, 2/4th K.O.Y.L.I.—Wounded.
,,	2/Lieut. R. T. Fox, 2/4th K.O.Y.L.I.—Killed.
,,	2/Lieut. J. A. Longmire, 2/4th Y. and L. Regt.—Wounded.
,,	2/Lieut. W. M. Winfield, 2/4th Y. and L. Regt.—Wounded.
,,	2/Lieut. H. Partington, 2/4th Y. and L. Regt.—Died of wounds.
,,	2/Lieut. W. Lowe, 2/4th Y. and L. Regt.—Wounded.
,,	2/Lieut. J. R. Draper, 2/4th Y. and L. Regt.—Wounded.
,,	Capt. L. A. Wilkins, 2/4th Y. and L. Regt.—Killed.
,,	Lieut. A. Norman, 2/4th Y. and L. Regt.—Wounded.
,,	2/Lieut. H. Seddons, 2/4th Y. and L. Regt.—Wounded and missing.
,,	2/Lieut. W. Walker, 5th W. Riding Regt.—Died of wounds.
,,	2/Lieut. Mellalieu, 5th W. Riding Regt.—Wounded.
,,	2/Lieut. F. Chapman, 5th W. Riding Regt.—Wounded.
,,	2/Lieut. E. W. Flatow, 2/4th W. Riding Regt.—Wounded.
,,	Lieut. H. L. Hollard, 2/4th K.O.Y.L.I.—Wounded.
26/8/18	2/Lieut. C. B. Richmond, 2/4th Hants. Regt.—Wounded.
,,	Capt. J. F. Bennett, 2/4th Hants. Regt.—Killed.
,,	2/Lieut. F. G. Pendergast, 2/4th W. Riding Regt.—Wounded.
27/8/18	2/Lieut. E. Callear, 5th K.O.Y.L.I.—Wounded.
,,	2/Lieut. R. F. Tee, 5th K.O.Y.L.I.—Wounded.
,,	Capt. G. Skirrow, 2/4th K.O.Y.L.I.—Killed.
,,	Capt. G. Beaumont, 5th W. Riding Regt.—Wounded.
,,	2/Lieut. J. L. Rodger, 2/4th K.O.Y.L.I.—Wounded.
,,	2/Lieut. G. Cooper, 2/4th K.O.Y.L.I.—Wounded.
,,	2/Lieut. S. T. Swady, 2/4th K.O.Y.L.I.—Wounded.
,,	2/Lieut. R. B. Johnston, 2/4th K.O.Y.L.I.—Wounded.
28/8/18	2/Lieut. F. C. Holbrook, 2/4th Hants. Regt.—Wounded.
29/8/18	2/Lieut. P. F. Gumm, 1/5th Devon Regt.—Wounded.
,,	2/Lieut. J. T. Boardman, 5th W. Riding Regt.—Wounded.
,,	2/Lieut. H. Drabble, 5th W. Riding Regt.—Wounded.
,,	2/Lieut. G. F. Clay, 5th W. Riding Regt.—Wounded.
,,	2/Lieut. A. G. Saunders, 5th Devon Regt.—Wounded.
30/8/18	2/Lieut. F. Wallwork, 5th Devon Regt.—Wounded.

Appendix

30/8/18	Capt. R. G. Jones, 2/20th London Regt.—Killed.
,,	Capt. A. Reynolds, 2/20th London Regt.—Wounded.
,,	2/Lieut. W. L. Bright, 2/20th London Regt.—Wounded.
,,	2/Lieut. P. L. Smout, 2/20th London Regt.—Wounded.
,,	2/Lieut. A. F. Dyball, 2/20th London Regt.—Wounded.
,,	2/Lieut. R. Morrison, 5th Devon Regt.—Killed.
,,	H. B. Dunn, 5th Devon Regt.—Killed.
,,	2/Lieut. J. L. Look, 5th Devon Regt.—Wounded.
,,	2/Lieut. F. E. Read, 2/20th London Regt.—Wounded.
,,	Lieut. J. Copeland, 2/4th W. Riding Regt.—Wounded.
,,	2/Lieut. C. E. Adkinson, 5th W. Riding Regt.—Wounded.
,,	2/Lieut. J. E. Ward, 5th W. Riding Regt.—Wounded.
,,	Capt. E. G. Watkinson, 5th West Riding Regt.—Wounded.
31/8/18	2/Lieut. F. Barnes, 2/20th London Regt.—Wounded.
,,	Capt. A. F. I. Pickford, 525th Coy. A.S.C.—Injured.
,,	Major E. G. L. Whiteway, 5th Devon Regt.—Wounded.
,,	Capt. N. Geldhard, 2/4th W. Riding Regt.—Wounded.
,,	2/Lieut. R. L. Grant, 2/4th W. Riding Regt.—Wounded
1/9/18	2/Lieut. F. R. Stuart, 312th Bde. R.F.A.—Wounded.
,,	2/Lieut. W. J. Green, 312th Bde. R.F.A.—Wounded.
,,	2/Lieut. W. M. Bryson, 8th W. Yorks. Regt.—Killed.
,,	2/Lieut. H. Clidero, 8th W. Yorks. Regt.—Killed.
,,	2/Lieut. A. G. McCulloch, 8th W. Yorks. Regt.—Wounded.
,,	2/Lieut. J. Glennie, 8th W. Yorks. Regt.—Wounded.
,,	2/Lieut. H. R. Wright, 8th W. Yorks. Regt.—Wounded.
2/9/18	Capt. H. R. Burrows, 8th W. Yorks. Regt.—Wounded.
,,	Capt. S. R. Cooper, 8th W. Yorks. Regt.—Wounded.
,,	2/Lieut. R. M. Crabtree, 8th W. Yorks. Regt.—Wounded.
,,	Capt. C. E. Morier, 5th W. Riding Regt.—Wounded.
,,	Capt. F. T. Vasey, 9th Durham L.I.—Wounded.
,,	Lieut. H. C. B. Plummer, 9th Durham L.I.—Wounded.
,,	Lieut. J. F. Johnson, 9th Durham L.I.—Wounded.
,,	2/Lieut. F. J. Boyd, 62nd Bn. M.G.C.—Wounded.
,,	2/Lieut. J. Billing, 5th K.O.Y.L.I.—Killed.
,,	2/Lieut. W. C. Neilson, 5th K.O.Y.L.I.—Killed.
,,	2/Lieut. F. Bottomley, 5th K.O.Y.L.I.—Killed.
,,	Capt. A. C. Lynn, 5th K.O.Y.L.I.—Wounded.
,,	Lieut. R. A. Houghton, 5th K.O.Y.L.I.—Wounded.
,,	2/Lieut. J. S. Bowden 5th K.O.Y.L.I.—Wounded.

Appendix

2/9/18	2/Lieut. C. P. Howells, 5th K.O.Y.L.I.—Wounded.
,,	2/Lieut. A. E. Martin, 2/4th K.O.Y.L.I.—Killed.
,,	Capt. R. Townend, 2/4th K.O.Y.L.I.—Wounded.
,,	Lieut. J. F. Sutherland, 2/4th K.O.Y.L.I.—Wounded.
,,	2/Lieut. J. H. Fisher, 2/4th K.O.Y.L.I.—Wounded.
,,	2/Lieut. G. E. W. Pollard, 2/4th K.O.Y.L.I.—Wounded.
,,	Capt. J. Rodjers, 2/4th Y. and L. Regt.—Killed.
,,	2/Lieut. P. H. Hallmark, 2/4th Y. and L. Regt.—Killed.
,,	2/Lieut. A. L. Simpkin, 2/4th Y. and L. Regt.—Wounded.
,,	2/Lieut. W. B. May, 2/4th Y. and L. Regt.—Wounded.
,,	2/Lieut. G. A. Bryden, 2/4th Y. and L. Regt.—Wounded.
,,	2/Lieut. J. D. Johnson, 2/4th Y. and L. Regt.—Wounded.
,,	2/Lieut. L. Owen, 2/4th Y. and L. Regt.—Wounded.
,,	2/Lieut. L. W. Johnson, 2/4th K.O.Y.L.I.—Wounded.
7/9/18	2/Lieut. K. R. Steer, 2/4th Y. and L. Regt.—Injured (acc.)

AT HAVRINCOURT, 1918.

11/9/18	Lieut. A. Girvan, 62nd Bn. M.G.C.—Wounded.
12/9/18	Capt. A. C. Noon, 5th Devon Regt.—Wounded.
,,	Capt. J. Stocks, 2/4th W. Riding Regt.—Wounded.
,,	2/Lieut. J. H. Dunnett, 2/4th W. Riding Regt.—Wounded
,,	2/Lieut. A. C. Potter, 2/4th W. Riding Regt.—Wounded.
,,	Capt. B. C. Lupton, 2/4th W. Riding Regt.—Wounded.
,,	2/Lieut. W. Stott, 2/4th W. Riding Regt.—Wounded.
,,	2/Lieut. J. B. C. Hewitt, 312th Bde. R.F.A.—Wounded.
,,	2/Lieut. H. Bentham, 5th W. Riding Regt.—Wounded.
,,	2/Lieut. H. Bryant, 2/4th Hants. Regt.—Killed.
,,	2/Lieut. H. S. Weeks, 2/4th Hants. Regt.—Wounded.
,,	2/Lieut. C. A. Gadsby, 2/4th Hants. Regt.—Wounded.
,,	2/Lieut. W. J. Wilson, 2/4th Hants. Regt.—Wounded.
,,	2/Lieut. F. C. Isaacs, 2/4th Hants. Regt.—Wounded.
,,	2/Lieut. G. O. B. Viscount Uffington, 2/4th Hants. Regt.—Wounded.
,,	Lieut. F. S. French, 5th K.O.Y.L.I.—Killed.
,,	2/Lieut. A. Kilner, 2/4th K.O.Y.L.I.—Wounded.
,,	2/Lieut. T. D. Fisher, 2/4th Y. and L. Regt.—Wounded.
,,	2/Lieut. C. F. Caird, 2/4th Y. and L. Regt.—Wounded.
,,	2/Lieut. W. R. Forrest, 9th Durham L.I.—Killed.
,,	2/Lieut. S. Aberdeen, 9th Durham L.I.—Wounded.
,,	2/Lieut. F. J. F. Clarke, 5th K.O.Y.L.I.—Wounded.

Appendix

12/9/18	2/Lieut. J. S. Fernie, 5th K.O.Y.L.I.—Wounded.
,,	2/Lieut. E. B. Pratt, 2/4th Hants. Regt.—Wounded.
,,	2/Lieut. E. Morton, 5th K.O.Y.L.I.—Wounded.
,,	2/Lieut. A. J. Pitman, 2/4th K.O.Y.L.I.—Wounded.
,,	2/Lieut. F. Wilkinson, 2/4th K.O.Y.L.I.—Wounded.
,,	2/Lieut. F. Sagar, 2/4th Y. and L. Regt.—Wounded.
,,	2/Lieut. E. M. Hart, 5th Devon Regt.—Wounded.
13/9/18	2/Lieut. J. Porritt, 5th W. Riding Regt.—Wounded.
,,	2/Lieut. A. Rossington, 5th W. Riding Regt.—Killed.
,,	Capt. C. P. Bulley, 2/4th Hants. Regt.—Wounded.
,,	2/Lieut. J. C. L. Bradbury, 2/4th Y. and L. Regt.—Wounded.
,,	2/Lieut. J. P. Knox, 2/4th Y. and L. Regt.—Wounded.
,,	2/Lieut. J. W. Baty, 2/4th K.O.Y.L.I.—Wounded.
,,	2/Lieut. J. J. Gregory, 2/4th Y. and L. Regt.—Wounded.
,,	Lieut. T. Ridley, 9th Durham L.I.—Wounded.
,,	2/Lieut. R. Bedford, 5th Devon Regt.—Wounded.
,,	2/Lieut. P. G. Butcher, 5th Devon Regt.—Wounded.
14/9/18	2/Lieut. W. Herdman, 9th Durham L. I.—Wounded.
,,	2/Lieut. G. D. Hall, 5th Devon Regt.—Wounded.
,,	2/Lieut. A. E. Stock, 5th Devon Regt.—Wounded.
,,	2/Lieut. D. C. W. Sutton, 2/20th London Regt.—Killed.
,,	2/Lieut. H. J. Ellen, 2/20th London Regt.—Killed.
,,	2/Lieut. G. J. P. Holton, 2/20th London Regt.—Wounded.
,,	2/Lieut. J. Hirst, 2/20th London Regt.—Killed.
15/9/18	Rev. A. B. Wright, C.F.—Wounded.
25/9/18	Lieut. K. B. Nicholson, 312th Bde. R.F.A.—Wounded.

IN THE BATTLE OF THE CANAL DU NORD,
27TH SEPTEMBER—1ST OCTOBER.

27/9/18	Capt. C. B. Stead, 8th W. Yorks. Regt.—Wounded.
,,	Capt. G. M. Hirst, 8th W. Yorks. Regt.—Wounded.
,,	2/Lieut. H. E. Shenton, 8th W. Yorks. Regt.—Wounded.
,,	2/Lieut. F. J. Turner, 8th W. Yorks. Regt.—Killed.
,,	2/Lieut. H. J. Graves, 8th W. Yorks. Regt.—Wounded.
,,	2/Lieut. A E. Oddy, 8th W. Yorks. Regt.—Killed.
27/9/18	2/Lieut. F. Axe, 8th W. Yorks. Regt.—Missing.
,,	2/Lieut. W. J. Whittall, 8th W. Yorks. Regt.—Missing.
,,	2/Lieut. F. L. A. Tingle, 8th W. Yorks. Regt.—Missing.
,,	2/Lieut. C. E. Croft, 8th W. Yorks. Regt.—Missing.

Appendix

27/9/18	2/Lieut. A. E. Palmer, 8th W. Yorks. Regt.—Killed.
,,	Lieut. C. W. Eales, 1/5th Devon Regt.—Killed.
,,	2/Lieut. J. E. Evans, 1/5th Devon Regt.—Killed.
,,	2/Lieut. J. A. O'Neill, 1/5th Devon Regt.—Wounded.
,,	2/Lieut. A. E. Knight, 1/5th Devon Regt.—Wounded.
,,	2/Lieut. S. M. Bargetson, 1/5th Devon Regt.—Wounded.
,,	2/Lieut. T. N. R. Lowe, 1/5th Devon Regt.—Wounded.
,,	2/Lieut. W. A. V. Hoskins, 1/5th Devon Regt.—Wounded.
,,	2/Lieut. F. Jackson, 2/20th London Regt.—Killed.
,,	Lieut. V. Slaughter, 2/20th London Regt.—Killed.
,,	2/Lieut. S. Herbert, 2/20th London Regt.—Wounded.
,,	2/Lieut. G. F. Spence, 5th K.O.Y.L.I.—Wounded.
,,	2/Lieut. W. C. H. Stott, 5th K.O.Y.L.I.—Killed.
,,	Capt. C. Hirst, 2/4th K.O.Y.L.I.—Wounded.
,,	2/Lieut. J. Eckersley, 2/4th Y. and L. Regt.—Wounded.
,,	2/Lieut. H. C. F. Smith, 2/4th Y. and L. Regt.—Wounded.
,,	Capt. R. F. S. Oxley-Boyle, 62nd Bn. M.G.C.—Wounded.
28/9/18	2/Lieut. A. C. Matthews, 2/4th Hants. Regt.—Wounded.
,,	2/Lieut. W. Powrie, 2/4th Y. and L. Regt.—Killed.
,,	Major C. W. Lundgren, 2/4th Y. and L. Regt.—Wounded.
,,	2/Lieut. E. R. Murrell-Talbot, 2/4th Y. and L. Regt.—Wounded.
,,	Capt. B. C. Pennington, 2/4th Y. and L. Regt.—Wounded.
,,	2/Lieut. G. M. Hill, 2/4th Y. and L. Regt.—Wounded.
,,	2/Lieut. G. V. Charlesworth, 6th W. Riding Regt.—Killed.
,,	2/Lieut. G. M. Barnett, 6th W. Riding Regt.—Killed.
,,	2/Lieut. S. E. Briggs, 6th W. Riding Regt.—Wounded.
,,	2/Lieut. T. E. Morton, 6th W. Riding Regt.—Wounded.
,,	Capt. C. H. Lockwood, 6th W. Riding Regt.—Wounded.
,,	Lieut. E. Wilson, 185th T.M.B.—Wounded.
,,	2/Lieut. S. E. Pilbrow, 62nd Bn. M.G.C.—Injured (acc.).
29/9/18	2/Lieut. R. A. Young, 2/4th Y. and L. Regt.—Wounded.
,,	Capt. J. W. Frew, 2/3rd W. R. Field Amb.—Wounded.
,,	Capt. G. M. Hill, 2/4th W. Riding Regt.—Wounded.
,,	2/Lieut. A. E. Crookson, 2/4th W. Riding Regt.—Wounded.
,,	2/Lieut. R. D. Dodsworth, 62nd Bn. M.G.C.—Wounded.
,,	2/Lieut. G. W. Barraclough, 2/4th W. Riding Regt.—Killed.

Appendix

29/9/18	2/Lieut. A. Wood, 5th K.O.Y.L.I.—Killed.
,,	Lieut. C. H. Wilson, 5th K.O.Y.L.I.—Died of Wounds.
30/9/18	2/Lieut. W. J. Cottis, 2/20th London Regt.—Wounded.
,,	Capt. A. W. Simpkin, 8th W. Yorks. Regt.—Killed.
,,	2/Lieut. J. L. Percival, 8th W. Yorks. Regt.—Killed.
,,	2/Lieut. F. Ferguson, 8th W. Yorks. Regt.—Wounded.
,,	2/Lieut. F. Hall, 8th W. Yorks. Regt.—Wounded.
,,	2/Lieut. J. E. Gram, 2/4th W. Riding Regt.—Killed.
,,	2/Lieut. B. W. Bilton, 62nd Bn. M.G.C.—Wounded.
,,	Lieut.-Col. N. A. England, Cmdg. 8th W. Yorks. Regt.—Wounded.
,,	Lieut. F. Willis, 1/5th Devon Regt.—Killed.
,,	Capt. J. H. Edgar, 1/5th Devon Regt.—Wounded.
,,	2/Lieut. J. H. Stanley, 1/5th Devon Regt.—Wounded.
,,	2/Lieut. T. L. Osborne, 1/5th Devon Regt.—Wounded.
,,	Capt. H. C. B. Cottam, 2/4th Hants. Regt.—Killed.
,,	2/Lieut. T. Turner, 2/4th Hants. Regt.—Wounded.
,,	2/Lieut. C. P. Howells, 5th K.O.Y.L.I.—Killed.
,,	Capt. G. E. Spencer, 2/4th K.O.Y.L.I.—Wounded.
,,	Major W. Froggatt, 461st Field Coy. R.E.—Wounded.
1/10/18	2/Lieut. C. J. Stephens, 62nd Bn. M.G.C.—Wounded.
3/10/18	Lt. and Qmr. C. G. Gadsby, 2/6th K.O.Y.L.I.—Wounded.
4/10/18	Lieut. G. A. Murray, 62nd Div. Signal Coy.—Killed.
8/10/18	Lieut. A. C. Alexander, 9th Durham L.I.—Wounded.

IN THE BATTLE OF THE SELLE.

18/10/18	2/Lieut. T. Briggs, 5th W. Riding Regt.—Killed.
20/10/18	2/Lieut. S. J. Reading, 2/6th W. Riding Regt.—Wounded.
,,	2/Lieut. A. C. Matthew, 2/4th Hants. Regt.—Wounded.
,,	2/Lieut. J. McMillan, 62nd Bn. M.G.S.—Wounded.
20/10/18	2/Lieut. T. C. Dugdale, 2/4th Y. and L. Regt.—Wounded.
,,	Capt. J. Pyman, 8th W. Yorks. Regt.—Wounded.
,,	2/Lieut. C. Sharpe, 8th W. Yorks. Regt.—Wounded.
,,	2/Lieut. F. W. Cowling, 9th Durham L.I.—Wounded.
21/10/18	2/Lieut. H. J. Skardon, 5th Devon Regt.—Wounded.
22/10/18	2/Lieut. A. Clarkson, 8th W. Yorks. Regt.—Wounded.
,,	2/Lieut. H. J. Crane, 9th Durham L.I.—Wounded.
23/10/18	Lieut. Col. N. A. England, Cmdg. 8th W. Yorks. Regt.—Wounded.

DURING THE BATTLE OF THE SAMBRE, NOVEMBER 1918.

N.B.—No dates are given in the A. and Q. Diary opposite these casualties.

2/Lieut. C. P. Mollison, 62nd Bn. M.G.C.—Wounded.
2/Lieut. W. J. Phillips, 62nd Bn. M.G.C.—Wounded.
Lieut. F. D. Roberts, 186th T.M.B.—Wounded.
2/Lieut. W. Campbell, 2/4th K.O.Y.L.I.—Killed.
Capt. C. B. Dixon, 2/4th Y and L Regt.—Wounded.
2/Lieut. C. Revitt, 2/4th Y. and L. Regt.—Wounded.
Capt. H. Brown, 5th K.O.Y.L.I.—Wounded.
Lieut. C. Evers, 5th K.O.Y.L I.—Wounded.
Lieut. S. C. Bywater, 5th K.O.Y.L.I.—Wounded.
2/Lieut. T. R. Allott, 5th K.O.Y.L.I.—Wounded.
Major E. M. Body, 40th Bde. R.F.A. attached—Killed.
Lieut. J. A. Brown, 312th Bde. R.F.A.—Wounded.
2/Lieut. W. R. Ashplant, 1/5th Devon Regt.—Wounded.
2/Lieut. G. B. Yonge, 1/5th Devon Regt.—Wounded.
Lieut. E. Clapham, 5th W. Riding Regt.—Wounded.
2/Lieut. W. Saunders, 5th W. Riding Regt.—Wounded.
2/Lieut. E. Ellis, 5th W. Riding Regt.—Wounded.
2/Lieut. J. A. Ward, 5th W. Riding Regt.—Wounded.
2/Lieut. L. Martin, 5th W. Riding Regt.—Wounded.
2/Lieut. J. H. Vanstone, 5th W. Riding Regt.—Wounded.
Lieut. W. C. R. Rowland, 2/4th W. Riding Regt.—Killed.
2/Lieut. H. R. Harper, 2/4th W. Riding Regt.—Killed.
Lieut. S. L. Roch-Austin, 2/4th W. Riding Regt.—Died of Wounds.
Lieut. R. H. Porter, 2/4th W. Riding Regt.—Wounded.
2/Lieut. H. M. Slack, 2/4th W. Riding Regt.—Wounded.
Capt. W. Brierley, 2/4th Hants. Regt.—Wounded.
2/Lieut. C. A. Geer, 2/4th Hants. Regt.—Wounded.
2/Lieut. A. L. King, 2/4th Hants. Regt.—Injured.
2/Lieut. H. S. Phillips, 5th K.O.Y.L.I.—Wounded.
2/Lieut. W. H. Bosworthick, 5th Devon Regt.—Killed.
Capt. P. D. Rooke, 2/4th K.O.Y.L.I.—Wounded.
2/Lieut. F. Cotterill, 2/4th K.O.Y.L.I.—Wounded.
Lieut. W. P. Holt, 310th Bde. R.F.A.—Wounded.
Lieut. K. A. Latter, 310th Bde. R.F.A.—Wounded.
2/Lieut. G. Carruthers, 5th W. Riding Regt.—Wounded.
Lieut. H. C. H. Broadwood, 5th W. Riding Regt.—Wounded.
2/Lieut. F. N. Chapman, 2/4th W. Riding Regt.—Wounded.

"OTHER RANK" CASUALTIES, 1917—1918.

1917	K.	W.	M.	1918	K.	W.	M.
January	2	11	—	January	22	70	1
February	88	232	13	February	13	46	1
March	98	386	17	March	225	1289	570
April	156	540	19	April	83	456	10
May	254	1710	1220	May	62	392	14
June	7	63	—	June	54	353	12
July	45	189	4	July	521	3063	406
August	27	150	—	August	213	1231	111
September	75	296	8	September	551	2760	623
October	9	74	3	October	67	451	22
November	435	2330	469	November	123	702	61
December	2	8	—				
	1098	5989	1753		1934	10813	1813

Total Casualties, 23,418 :—

1917—Killed	1098	Wounded	5989	Missing	1753
1918 ,,	1934	,,	10813	,,	1831
,,	3032	,,	16802	,,	3584

INDEX

	PAGE
Amiens	19
Ancre, The	5
Anderson, Brig.-Genl. A. T.	30, 47, 123, 134, 141
Angre	138
Angreau	138
Armistice, The, Scenes on the Old Mons Battlefield	149
Artillery, Splendid work of the Divisional	33-37
Audigny	108
Australian Troops at Peronne	19
Banbury Hill	50
Bancourt	19
Banks Trench, 1, 3, 5, 6, 8,	13
Bapaume	1, 5, 9, 19, 20
Bastow, Lt.-Col. H. V., 11, 14,	100, 121, 135
Battles Nomenclature Committee, The (*footnote*)	21
Beaucamp taken	74
Beaulencourt	19
Beaumetz-lez-Cambrai	23
Beugnatre	1, 2, 5, 6
Beugny	6, 18, 20, 23, 26
Boggart's Hole	49, 55
Bois d'Hautmont	148
Bradford, V.C., Brig.-Genl. R. B. (*footnote*)	29
Braithwaite, Maj.-Genl. Sir W. P.	5, 6, 104, 152
Brigades, Infantry:—	
185th : 1, 3, 4, 6, 8, 9, 10, 13, 16, 17, 23, 30, 31, 63, 71 *et seq.*, 109, 127, 135,	137
186th : 1, 2, 3, 4, 6, 8, 9, 12, 14, 17, 23, 31, 43 *et seq.*, 71 *et seq.*, 109, 121, 127,	130
187th : 1, 3, 4, 23, 24, 27, 28, 29, 30, 31, 43, 46 *et seq.*, 71 *et seq.*, 91, 110, 127, 130,	137
British Line on Sept. 27th, 1918	69
Brook, Lt.-Col. F., 1, 46, 89, 90, 100, 103,	128
Bucquoy	5
Bullecourt	5, 19
Byng, Genl. Sir Julian	63
Calvert, V.C., Sergt. L.	49

	PAGE
Cambrai	5, 74
Canal du Nord, Battle of the, 67 *et seq.*; battle scheme, 70-73; eve of the battle, 73-74; bombardment, 74; Ribecourt captured, 78; Flesquières captured, 78; Enemy Treachery, 79 ; capture of Marcoing, 85–86 ; Masnières captured, 99 ; a difficult advance, 102 ; gallantry at the canal, 103 ; new line consolidated, 103 ; withdrawal of Division on relief...	104
Casualties and Captures from August 24th to November 11th, 1918	174
Charleroi	151
Chaytor, Lt.-Col. C. B., 25, 46,	85
Clarges Avenue	54, 55, 58, 78
Clayton, Lt.-Col. C. A.	129
Clery-sur-Somme	19
Cockburn, Maj. G. E. C.	112
Cogneaux	139
Combles	19
Courcelles	104
Coutant	140
Craddock, Maj. W. M.	121
Daykins, V.C., Sergt. John,	117-18
Delville Wood	19
Devonshire Regt., 1/5th Bn., 4, 5, 6, 7, 14, 15, 16, 17, 59, 62, 72, 101,	140
Drocourt-Quéant line, Battle of the, 23 *et seq.*; results of	31
Duke of Wellington's Regt., 2/4th Bn., 9, 10, 11, 14, 15, 16, 43, 59, 81, 82, 96,	113
5th Bn., 7, 9, 10, 14, 43, 46, 48, 52, 58, 60, 63, 81, 82, 89, 90, 92, 93, 94, 96, 99, 110, 111, 112, 113, 114, 115, 128, 132, 134, 140,	148
Durham Light Infantry (Pioneers), 9th Bn., 23, 25, 29, 30, 43, 44, 59, 60, 71,	127
Ecoust	2, 9, 14
Eden, Lt.-Col. A. G.	37

Index

Eeles, Maj. C. A. ... 47
Engineers Royal, Fine work of the ... 104
England, Lt.-Col. N. A. ... 121
Epehy, Fall of ... 64
Estourmel ... 108
Favreuil ... 1, 2
Flers ... 19
Forster, Maj. F. A. Arnold- ... 47
Fort Grevaux captured ... 147
Frasnoy ... 131, 132, 135
Fremicourt ... 19
Germany's fear in Sept. 1918... 65
Germany's " black day " ... 68
Grand Ravine, The 53, 61, 88
Grateful French Peasants ... 137
Haig, Sir Douglas (Tribute to the 62nd Division) ... 153
Hampden, Brig.-Genl. Viscount 8, 71, 100, 121, 129, 135, 149
Hampshire Regt., 2/4th Bn., 1, 2, 5, 6, 9, 43, 44, 103, 111, 138, 139
Hardecourt ... 19
Hargnies ... 140
Hart, Lt.-Col. L. H. P., 25, 46, 86, 112, 129, 147
Hautmont seized ... 145
Havrincourt, Battle of, 39 *et seq.*; Plan of attack, 41-42; Artillery barrage, 44; capture of chateau, 51; Havrincourt village cleared, 55; supply tanks, 55; counter attacks, 56-57, 59; General Byng's congratulations ... 63
Haynes, Private T. L. M. ... 79
Hendecourt ... 19
Hindenburg Line, attack on, 39 *et seq.*; effect of its breaking ... 105
Hitonsart ... 138
Hubert Avenue ... 50
Kaiser, Abdication of the ... 148
Kangaroo Avenue ... 48, 58
Keating's Lane ... 61
Kin Lane ... 48, 60
Kitten Trench ... 47
Knat Avenue ... 48, 51
Knuckle Trench ... 48, 58
K.O.Y.L.I. Regt. :—
2/4th Bn., 1, 2, 3, 4, 24, 25, 26, 28, 29, 43, 44, 73, 75, 77, 85, 86, 87, 88, 89, 97-99, 127 *et seq.*, 145 *et seq.*

K.O.Y.L.I. Regt. :— contd.
5th Bn., 1, 2, 3, 4, 24, 25, 26, 27-30, 43-4, 46, 48-52, 54-8, 71, 77, 87-8, 97-9, 127, 130, 136, 140, 146
Lagnicourt ... 18, 23
La Longueville ... 139
La Tomblain ... 138
Leignon ... 152
Lesbœufs ... 19
L'Homme Mort ... 3
London Regiment, 2/20th Bn., 4, 9-11, 13, 16, 61, 78, 79, 121, 138
Longatte ... 9, 19
Longueval ... 19
Loup-la-Chausse ... 148
Louvroil ... 147-8, 151
Ludendorff, General, 20, 63-4, 107
Luignon ... 152
Machine Gun Bn., Divisional 31, 44, 60, 72, 81, 104, 111, 127, 145
March into Germany, The, 151-3
Marcoing, The advance on, 85 *et seq.*; the village cleaned up 92
Maricourt Wood ... 26, 28
Marne, The ... 5
Maroilles ... 138
Marrières Wood ... 20
Masnières captured ... 99
Maubeuge, Plan of attack, 126-7; outskirts reached, 147; town entered ... 148
Meaurain ... 138
Mecquignies ... 138
Meuse, The ... 151
Mile-end Road ... 48, 49
Mont St. Quentin ... 19
Morchies ... 9, 18, 23, 30
Mormal Forest ... 138
Morval ... 19
Mory Copse ... 1
Mory quarry ... 13
Naval Division's Gallantry ... 74
Noreuil Valley ... 17
Nurlu ... 20
Obies ... 138, 139, 143
Oxfordshire Hussars ... 83, 135
" Pelicans," The, in a cinema theatre ... 124
Peronne ... 19, 31
Peter, Lt.-Col. F. H., 25, 46, 48, 52, 86, 128
Prisches ... 138

Index

	PAGE
Putney Avenue	48
Queer Street	47
Quene au Loup	139
Quievy	121, 124
Railway Trench	49
Reddie, Brig.-Genl. A. J., 3, 23, 30, 46, 56, 74, 85, 128, 129,	145
Recquigny	149
Rhine Bridge-heads	151
Rhonelle, The	131, 138
Ribecourt	70, 75, 77, 78
Riencourt-lez-Cagnicourt	19
Rocquigny	20
Roisin	138
Rousies	149
Ruesnes, A ruined chateau in	134
Rumilly	89, 91
Sailly-Saillisel	19, 36
St. Lazare	147, 148, 149
St. Leger Ravine	101
St. Python, occupied	113
St. Quentin, canal of, 86, 92, *et seq.*	
Sambre, The, crossed	146-7
Scarpe, Battle of the	18
Schlieden area, The	152
Sherlock, Lt -Col. D. J. C.	37
Shropshire Spur Road	53
Solesmes, Capture of, 108, 109,	112, 119, 121
Solre, The	149
Somme, The	19
Sous-le-Bois entered	147, 148
Sugar Factory, The, 3, 5, 7, 11,	12, 13, 16
Sunken Road, The, 4, 16, 18,	25, 53, 78

	PAGE
Swing Trench	48, 61
Tandey, V.C., D.C.M., M.M., Private Henry	93
" Tipperary " again in Nov., 1918	149
Tortille River	20
Triangle Wood	61, 62
Trônes Wood	19
Vaulx-Vraucourt, 2-3, 6, 7-8, 11, 12, 14-19, 23, 25, 27	
Villereau	132, 133
Vraucourt, 5, 8, 9, 11, 12, 13-14, 25	
Walker, Lt.-Col. J., 71, 89, 92, 95, 112,	128
Warde-Aldam, Lt.-Col. W. St. A.	61, 100
Watson, Major W.	135
West Yorkshire Regt., 8th Bn., 4, 8, 9, 11, 13, 17, 18, 80, 122, 138,	140
Whigham, Maj.-Genl. Sir R., 96, 103, 104, 108, 110, 125, 135, 148, 151,	153
Wilson, President	107
Wilson, Lt.-Col. P. P., 46, 89, 99, 112,	128
York and Lancaster Regt., 2/4th Bn. ("Hallamshires"), 1, 4 (*footnote*), 24, 25, 27, 28-30, 43, 46, 50-1, 52-3, 56-8, 72-3, 75-7, 82, 85-9, 91-2, 97, 99, 101, 111-12, 115-19, 124, 127, 129, 132, 134, 144-5, 147-8	
Yvoir	152

www.ingramcontent.com/pod-product-compliance
Lightning Source LLC
Chambersburg PA
CBHW061935220426
43662CB00012B/1921